THE CIRCLE GAME

BOOK 1

LIAM FARRELL

blaw
wearie
books

Published in 2016 by Blaw Wearie Books

ISBN Paperback: 978-0-9954905-0-5
Ebook: 978-0-9954905-1-2

Published with the help of Indie Authors World

ACKNOWLEDGEMENTS

My special thanks goes to Kim and Sinclair MacLeod at Indie Authors World, without whom this book would most likely never have seen the light of day.

Also a great gratitude is given to the Ordnance Survey open data for the maps, without which the book wouldn't be the same.

CONTENTS

A most warm welcome to this, my first book, based around the cycle runs that I do from my home in Glenburn, South Paisley. These are trips that I do to anywhere I can reach and return from in a single day, without the need for assistance or overnight stops. The trips that I cover in the book are mostly old acquaintances of mine, and most have been done many, many times over the past 14 or 15 years, since I started my passion for road cycling.

Let me make one thing clear right from the start. I am no natural athlete. Nor one lucky enough to be born with the genes of a champion cyclist, or a champion anything for that matter. I have never won a damn thing in any sporting event in my life, nor am I of a competitive nature; far from it. I should have said I have never won a damn thing in my life. I am just a guy, that's how I regard myself, just a guy. I enjoy the outdoors, mostly on my own, and I only undertook the challenge of doing fairly long cycle runs for the sheer pleasure and personal feeling of achievement.

I came to the world of biking in adulthood by what is often regarded as chance, or more accurately adverse circumstances, when on a raw spring day in 1997 I was climbing a couple of remote Munros that lie to the west of the Linn of Dee, just south of the Cairngorms. At this point I had been climbing Munros for a good eight years, all on foot and without the assistance of pedal power. On that particular day the weather turned very nasty indeed and I was a long way from the car. For once I was slightly under-equipped and the trudge back to my vehicle was a very long one, of extreme cold and wet misery.

When I say misery, I mean bloody misery. In fact, I still rank it as about the worst day's walking in the mountains that I have ever had in 20 years, and that is bloody saying something. The vast majority of the approach to those two hills was along Land Rover tracks that I knew would be greatly shortened by the aid of a mountain bike. And, vowing never to suffer like that again, I went straight out the same week and invested in a nice wee GT Talera,

which was at bargain price as it was painted in the previous year's colours.

That was the start of it. I soon found that the remote hills in the Cairngorms and Grampians were now a pleasure rather than a drudge to approach, and I was hooked. Soon not only was I riding rough but also hitting the tarmac and regularly covering the Clyde Coast run, where the extra enjoyable exercise made a total difference to my weight and fitness level. Being a naturally wee stocky guy – 5' 7 inches tall – weight loss does not come easily to me. And having the bike meant that there was no need to do a long drive north to get a big dose of weekly exercise, now I could simply open the door and away I went.

For the first time in my adult life my fitness went up to a good standard and the remaining Munros and the following nine years of climbing the Corbetts were a damn sight easier than the first seven years of hillwalking. During that period I was a heavy smoker, easily doing in 40 cigarettes a day; this would rise to around the 50 mark if I was having a small carry-out (bevvy) in the evening after finishing work. This was occurring far too often, and I was getting close to slipping into addiction. So on a drunken night in October 1996, I decided that it would have to stop, as my lifestyle was not sustainable. I have been smoke-free and completely teetotal since that night.

The point I am trying to make is a very simple but important one to anyone reading this book and wondering if the cycle runs here are beyond them. If I can do these runs then anyone can, including you. A lot of guys who you meet on the road were introduced to the sport by their father or uncle or older brother, but if you have no-one to mentor you, don't worry. I didn't either. My old man's passions in life were Celtic and drink, but not in that order. I abandoned being a football supporter when I left school and became a passionate trout fly fisherman, which was enjoyable but very sedentary. When I finally took to the hills in January '89, I was only 24 and as unfit as a young man that age could be.

I struggled – and I do mean struggled – on for about seven years, before that fateful day west of the Linn o' Dee, which was when it all turned around. Often in life I have learned that the real blessings can come in disguise; the great energy of the Universe lends its guiding hand to steer you in the right direction. But only when you are ready, of course, there's no point in try to rush it.

Let me tell you something else I discovered: a lot of what you do or don't do is all in the mind. The law of attraction plays a major role in all our lives and the early conditioning we get can be very limiting and difficult to overcome, but it can be overcome.

"If you think you can or you think you can't, you're probably right." Henry Ford said that, and he knew what the hell he was talking about. If you have a negative mindset, or you don't value your self-worth, or lack confidence, or have any other negative program running your subconscious, including that major adversity of fear, then it can be difficult to accept challenges and embrace and get the best from life.

However, the early negative programing, with all its ills, can be overcome by installing a new program into your subconscious mind, much the same as you would do a computer. Computers and brains both work the same way at certain levels, and by using proven techniques like positive self-talk or confidence-building CDs, a lot of unwanted baggage can be gotten rid of. Constant, constant, constant repetition of the positive is the key.

Add to that the motorcar that just about every one of us now owns or aspires to own, and which a lot of us use for even the shortest of journeys, and it's easy to see why a lot of people would regard it as being nigh impossible to cover 100 mile runs or more on a bike. I can assure you that if the bike turns out to be your thing, it will be damn near impossible to stop yourself doing them, not the other way round. And this will take place in a fairly short period of time, which is good news if you are a human, as we are not a very patient species.

Bonnie Scotland is a most stunningly rugged, beautiful country. I rarely holiday abroad unless it's a cycle tour of the battlefields of France, but that's a different story. However, whenever I meet people in the remote highlands and islands, over 90% of them are from south of the border; very few people I meet are actually Scots. I don't have a problem with that per se, as there are so many of us heading south looking for work while they come north looking to escape the rat race, so it's a fair swap in my book. But what is disappointing is the fact that so many of us stay in the central lowlands and holiday abroad chasing the sun, so have no idea just how beautiful our country really is. That is a real crime, and one I'd like to redress.

I recently climbed Tinto Hill with a big mate of mine who had travelled the world as a chef on board numerous sea-going vessels, including the QE2. But that day was the first time he had ever visited the top of the Clyde Valley, and he was struck by the serene greenness and beauty of the place. He'd no idea it was like that, and this was a man in his sixties.

I am in my late forties now and still going strong on both hill and bike. As I was taking a break on my last trip round the tough Arran run, one bike rider who flew by me turned out to be 72 years old and he was still in great shape. The health benefits of cycling are awesome.

I had to ask myself just who am I aiming this book at, as most established riders will know and most likely have done most, if not all, the runs in this book. They are, for the most part, either well-worn training runs or classic standards of long standing. So really I'm hoping to reach as many people who have either recently bought a machine and are looking for runs to do, or others who are thinking about getting fitter and don't fancy gyms or crunching their knees on concrete.

If the statistics are correct, then I might awaken the sleeping giant. For they say that there are as many bike owners in Britain as there are car owners, with the vast majority buying them with good intentions and using them once or twice before relegating the new machines to the back of the garage or garden shed, where they lie gathering dust.

So maybe if some clean up their hidden gems and get active again, it might help in some way towards us losing the unenviable tag of the sick man of Europe. This is despite the fact we are an undoubted rugged and hardy breed who, along with the Irish and Norwegians, have always had the toughest job in all of Western Europe in trying to eke out a living. Mind you, the weather doesn't help and I admit that it's easier to get motivated and look forward to a cycle in warm sunshine than it is in the rain and damp. But as Irish hardman Shaun Kelly once said, "You don't know how cold and wet it is til you're out there", as it often looks worse than it is.

Take it from me, the good days will come. And when they do, then boy, oh boy. Fancy it? Then just read on

Liam Boy.

If you are completely new to the game, here is some advice on what you need to get you started before we dive out the door for our first run together. Starting with clothing and starting at the top, a helmet is a very good idea. It's personal choice as to whether you wear one or not, and I know some guys who are very experienced road men who never wear one. Personally, I don't get out of bed without mine, and recommend you do the same.

Only once in a blue moon, if I am on a really quiet road round the back of an island, for example, will I take it off – and only then if it's a scorcher. In its place I will put on a cycling cotton cap, one of which I always carry to keep the sun off my head. The cotton cap's peak is also good under a helmet for stopping both hail and rain from battering into your eyes when it's so wet you have to remove your glasses to see where you're going.

The glasses themselves are also essential, and the ones with interchangeable lenses can be changed to suit the conditions. Some of these can cost the earth, but you don't need to pay top dollar for a good set. About £40 will get you a good quality pair.

Now although you don't actually need a cycling specific top, if you look the part, you'll act the part (or so they say). Cycling team jerseys do have the advantage of having three rear pockets, which are good for keeping essentials in. They come in short or long sleeves, and although most of us buy too many, probably two of each will be more than sufficient. For the short version, it's a good idea to buy a pair of arm warmers that go with them. I also have a couple of short-sleeved performance t-shirts that I wear under my cycling top on all but the warmest days.

You will also find most serious riders have more than one waterproof jacket – a heavyweight one for winter riding, and a lighter one for summer. The summer one can be rolled up and stuffed into one of the rear pockets, along with the cotton cap. Both rain jackets I have are yellow in colour to maximise visibility, which is a good safety idea. My helmets are always yellow for the same reason.

Having a pair or two of track mitts (padded fingerless gloves) stops hands becoming sore when pressed against handlebars for long periods. On top of this they protect the ulnar nerve, which runs from your palm to your arm and becomes painful if pressured and damaged.

Next comes probably the most important item of clothing – the shorts. Don't skimp on price here. The one thing that can really put you off cycling early doors is saddle soreness. Get a pair that retails for around the £40 mark to start with; anything cheaper I have found doesn't quite do the job. I like the Campagnolo brand, but any reputable brand will do. You don't have to go more expensive than that at first, but if you start doing really long endurance then a really well padded top-end pair is recommended. A pair of leg warmers is also a good addition, particularly for spring and autumn; they're not required on summer runs, and for winter ones more substantial leggings are worn.

Cycling socks are basically just short cotton socks; some do claim to have beneficial properties like improving ventilation, but most just sport team logos or the like. They help you look the part, so it's good to have them, even if only to match your track mitts and jerseys. Cycling specific shoes are now mostly a must, with the cleat and clipless pedal system now in use, and some models go up to about the £200 mark. These are only needed by the top end racers, however, both professional and amateur. The level entry shoe that all manufacturers make will be more than adequate to get you going. Correct fitting and alignment of the cleats is real important, so I will give you the technique for that at the back of the book. If you get that wrong, your knees will hurt like hell, so it's important to get that one spot on from the word go.

So too is saddle height and handlebar stem length; again, I will give you an accurate and easy to perform technique at the back of the book to leave you millimetre perfect. Remember, it's very easy to spend every penny you earn on equipment, so at first just buy what you need and take it from there.

Next the bike itself, which is of course the main piece of equipment and the biggest outlay. Now you can cover a lot of distance on tarmac riding a hybrid or even mountain bike, but life will be easier and more pleasant if you're on a racing machine. Thinner tyres, less weight, the right tool for the job, will make it a lot easier and faster. What bike, or rather standard of bike, you use doesn't really matter on most of these runs, with the possible exception of the five ferries.

I started off back in 99 with a Lemond Reno. It was steel-framed, a Greg Lemond-made bike, which was the bottom of Greg's range. The Reno's group set (gruppo), was also bottom range, being Shimanos SRX. Nowadays they call it Sora (Japanese for sky). Despite being bottom range, Greg made a good bike and I did just about every run in the book with it, including Edinburgh and back in a day. On that occasion they actually refused to let me into the castle with a bike and even refunded my money. I vowed never to go back there again and, true to my word, haven't done that run since.

So to get you going, any half decent road bike will do. It can be a difficult decision as to how much you want to spend, as you don't know how far you want to take things. To be sensible about it, don't break the bank early on.

You can get a lot of bike for your money nowadays, with a road bike in the £500 range being more than adequate for the job. The Government Cycle to Work Scheme is ongoing, which is a good idea in itself and you can get a machine to your liking for almost half price. You will have to source that one out for yourself to see if your employers do it, and if so, the guys in your local bike store will be happy to help on all matters, including sizing, and bargains.

Don't forget about Gumtree and eBay, where there are great deals to be had once you know what you're doing. But it has to be said that riding a real top-end machine is a pleasure and can make a lot of difference on a long run and also when hitting the climbs. It can even make the difference as to whether you can catch a ferry or not when doing the famous five.

The frame of the bike is the most important and costly item, and determines how a bike handles and performs. Next in line of importance are the wheels, then the gruppo itself. You'll soon learn that most serious riders have a good machine that they don't ride in the wet. For that, they have their training bike, armed with mudguards and a lower-end gruppo.

It's not always that easy to tell the standard of a bike by its frame; obviously the price is a giveaway, but so too will be the gruppo. They usually team up a top-end frame with a top-end group set. Shimano and Campagnolo are the two big name component providers, with Sram also now coming onto the market with a range.

Campag make some lovely gear, and a lot of guys like to ride with it. It tends to be more expensive than Shimano for two reasons. First, you pay for the Italian styling, and secondly, Shimano produce more so can do it cheaper. It's the same with a lot of Italian produce in general, including their bike frames.

I don't believe you get the same value for money from a Pinarello frame, than you would for say an Eddy Merckx or a Trek. If you start off by buying a lower-end machine and decide to further invest in a high spec model, that's great. Just put mudguards on your original and use it as your wet weather bike. My training bike is a Terry Dolan carbon fibre, with the Shimano gruppo comprising a mixture of 105 and Ultegra components. My top machine nowadays is an Eddy Merckx Cima with a Shimano Dura Ace gruppo. To ride the Merckx is a pleasure, despite the fact it's 11 years old and has a 9-speed set-up. The more modern have at least 10. It's all about justification here.

If you graft hard and want to splash out and treat yourself, why not? Some guys change their bikes every couple of years or so, but not me. I buy real good and keep it a lifetime if I can, that way I get quality and value for money.

Living in the west of Scotland will mean a lot of rain, of course, and a lot of wet weather riding. So having a good standard of training bike will be very beneficial as the majority of the miles you do, even in the summer, will be done on it. I then recommend having a bike with at least a mid-range group set. As for a real top-end machine? Well, only you can justify spending the money. Very few can justify Campagnolo top-end set, with some guys saying Shimano's Ultegra is the thinking man's gruppo, compared to the higher priced Dura Ace. You'll have to figure that one out for yourself.

Other on-bike essentials are a pump, saddle bag for carrying a spare tube, puncture repair kit, tyre levers, a multi tool, some dough, and your house keys. A more substantial track pump for blowing up tyres in-house will also shortly be required, as will some specialised cycle tools as you become more proficient in the art of cycle maintenance, along with your cleaning and lubeing kits.

The techniques required for correct saddle height (very important), correct stem length (nearly as important), and correct cleat positioning (helluva important), will all be given at the back of the book.

Don't let that lot jumble your brain. It will all come quite naturally to you in time. And with that, we are about ready to go. So it's on with the show.

The whole point of the book is to get people fired up enough to make them want to go out and ride the routes and enjoy the challenge that they present. So I hope that you will read the whole run through, and get in the mood to give it a real good go. I have, therefore, described the runs in great detail, much more so than most other guide books do. I also hope that the photos of our beautiful country and the history included will act as a spur to get you going and to keep you going.

To keep you on track to a certain extent when doing a route, I hope you will find the accompanying map and the route place names summary enough to guide you, for the most part. However some runs can become a little bit tricky in places, particularly when using country back roads for a few miles. Before you start out on any particular run, it might be worth checking with the relevant O/S map (if you have one) or even a large road atlas to give you a better idea of which roads to take, but that's only if you want to follow my way blow-for-blow, of course.

Remember that my route description may be only one way of many, and you might find a different approach road much more suitable for your needs. I am aware that everyone will be starting from a different location, bearing in mind that most people will begin the majority of the runs from their front door. Please don't forget that you are setting out on an adventure here, so a bit of trial and error on the road is more than acceptable and must be expected. If you don't get a route right first time round, that's fine, just check the map and correct your mistake the next time out.

Some cycling guide books give a brief description of a route and then provide a fairly long, though very accurate, set of instructions on how to follow the route. You know the sort of thing: turn left here, it's signposted such and such. However, I didn't want to do that, as it would mean constantly stopping to check you are on the right road, and that is the last thing you want to do on a bike ride. For me, flowing movement is the key to fun. Just having

the knowledge of your intended destination and some of the place names in between should get you there.

Bear in mind at all times that I personally just made tracks for any given place and made the route up as I went along, although I did use the O/S maps for guidance before I set out on most of them. So remember it can be done ad hoc and it all adds to the fun. Good luck to you all.

NOTE

Please note that when the idea for The Circle Game cycling book was first thought up and planned, it was my intention to produce only one book. It was not until it was just about finished that I realised just how big it was, and that it would therefore have to split into three books. Despite this, I have for the most part kept the original text for authenticity. Therefore, if for example you are reading about a run in book three and it mentions something that I have previously talked about and you have not come across it in book three, then it means that it is contained in an earlier book.

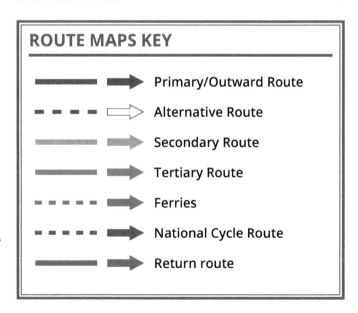

ROUTE MAPS KEY

⟶	Primary/Outward Route
- - - ⟹	Alternative Route
⟶	Secondary Route
⟶	Tertiary Route
- - - ⟶	Ferries
- - - ⟶	National Cycle Route
⟶	Return route

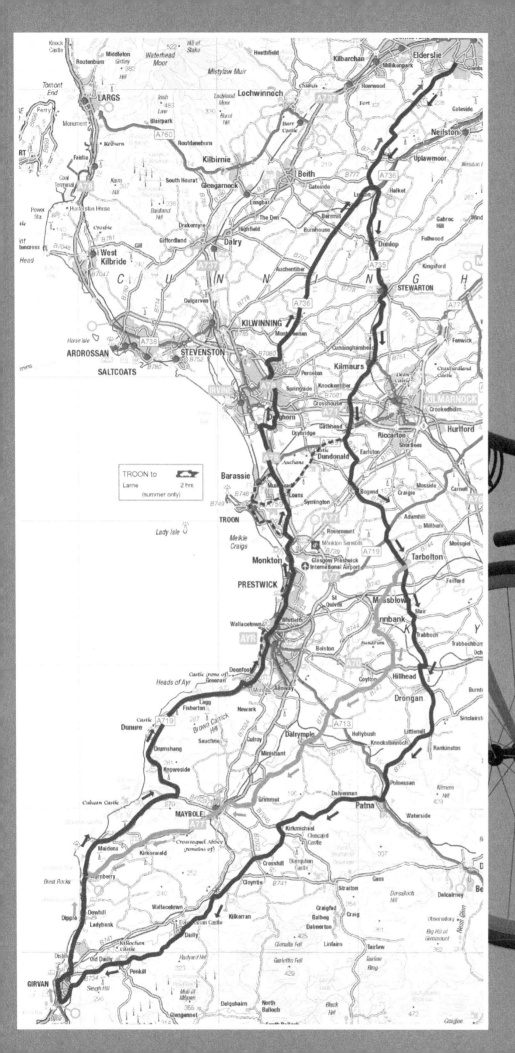

TURNBERRY & GIRVAN

TURNBERRY

100.6 Miles
6.33 Hours
Ascent 4100 Feet
3393 Calories burned

OS Landranger Maps
64, 70.

GIRVAN

114 Miles
7.20 Hours
4700 Feet/ascent
3780 Calories/burned

OS Landranger Maps
64, 70, 76.

ROUTE SUMMARY

BOTH ROUTES OUTWARD

Gleniffer Braes B-775
Lugton
Dunlop
Stewarton
Kilmaurs
Crosshouse
Gatehead
Tarbolton

SHORTER ROUTE

Gatehead
Dundonald
Loans/Troon

TURNBERRY

Coylton
Dalrymple
Maybole
Kirkoswald
Turnberry

GIRVAN

Stair
Coalhall
Drongan
Patna
Kirkmicheal
Crosshill
Dailly
Old Dailly
Girvan
Turnberry

BOTH ROUTES RETURN

Turnberry
Maidens
Fisherton
Ayr
Prestwick
Troon Or Loans
Girdle Toll
Lugton
Paisley

TURNBERRY & GIRVAN

THE SUMMER SHIRE

Long hot summer days can, some years, be very few and far between in this part of the world. But as I mentioned in the intro, they do come, perhaps only one day at a time, making them all the more special when they do. And when they arrive, accompanied by a soft south westerly breeze, then I'm off out towards the Ayrshire coastline, down through Burns country towards either Girvan or Turnberry.

Heading for either of these two Clyde coast gems is a day-and-a-half to remember, with both never failing to delight. You follow many quiet country roads with tranquil scenery on your way down inland, followed by the magnificent splendour of the Firth of Clyde as you return by the coastal route. They measure around or just over the 100 mile mark, and if you have half a mind to attempt such runs yourself, or are simply wondering what it's like to do one, then by all means come along for the ride. Let me assure you again, that it will be in the scope of most people to be able to complete the runs

and distances that I cover in the book, with a half decent machine, the right mindset, and some training.

I live in the Glenburn area of Paisley, which is a sprawling housing estate nestling at the bottom of the Glennifer Braes. This area of high ground rises above the southern end of the town and climbs to between 150 to 200 metres in places. It shows a uniform steep north front for most of its length, sweeping away toward the west, and is typical of a lot of our higher ground in the central belt. It contains reservoirs, golf courses, conifer plantations, and general rough sheep grazing ground, mixed in with bracken and heather.

The braes afford quite wonderful views over Glasgow and a lot of the lower Clyde Valley; views that would seem befitting much higher ground. Its northern sloping face is breached by Glennifer Road (the B-775), slanting diagonally upward from left to right, and which starts to climb from the Shieling filling station, which is situated at the very bottom of the street where I live. The filling station takes its name from an old store that once graced the site and was a real treasure trove of sweets and treats, which I and my mates would visit from our school across the road at lunch time. It was a solid stone white building and was ably manned by two old dears. One had an extremely high pitched voice, which I'm sure could, if she'd put her mind to it, have broken a wine glass from 30 paces. I remember back then the halfpence was still in circulation. Both the school and the store are long gone, but the name still lives on I'm glad to say.

If I am heading out anywhere south, then when I hit the bottom of my street and turn left, I'm immediately climbing. This will continue to the top of the braes which is somewhere in the region of 1.8 miles above, and I can normally reach there in under 15 minutes. It is a tough start to any run, but does have the advantage of getting you warmed up and well-oiled early on. That's a major plus, for as any athlete will tell you, the first strenuous session in any workout is the hardest and after that the rest get easier, with both body and mind then better prepared to cope with the forthcoming exertions.

So there is little flat to ride before I hit the Glennifer Road and turn left. Now heading south and gaining height, passing the two high flats on the left and leaving the urban sprawl behind, then I pass the national speed limit signs and onto the braes road proper. It's here it starts to get tough, as the gradient is much steeper than it looks and soon your heart rate monitor is up to about 160 beats per minute (BPM), as the effort starts to get your temperature up and lungs working harder.

Don't let that discourage you, if you're a new guy, because there is a very high chance that when you begin to take your riding a bit more seriously, you will relish the climbs and start to really enjoy them. It's what some riders get most satisfaction from.

The Gleniffer Road has an almost flat section after the initial right hand bend, before it rears up straight at its steepest section, passing the ramp-like start of the Sergeantlaw Road on the left. It continues to snake up past the now dry Bonnie Wee Well, before rounding the steepening left hander, to continue rising to the crest of the braes themselves. Now is probably the best time to give you your first cycling tip, and it involves the best technique to use on a climb.

You are more efficient when seated, as opposed to standing, because when you stand on the pedals, you bring your upper body into play and this requires more oxygen to service your top half. So staying seated, and spinning as low a gear as you've got, will keep your heart rate as low as possible, and the low gear will minimise muscle fatigue. Admittedly, some guys like to stand, as that is their preferred style; you soon find what suits you best. But staying seated is the more efficient of the two styles. Positive self-talk, when the going gets tough, also pays dividends, especially in the long run.

Relief, and what a feeling, as you top out and glide slightly downhill, going up the gears and getting your heart rate back down to normal. You will find it easier to supplely turn the cranks, heading south and straight, fairly flat and with all the trimmings of higher ground for company. This includes quite a few electricity pylons thrown in, adding to the bleakness. However, on a pleasant May or June day, a chorus of parachuting skylarks never fails to brighten up even the most barren of terrains.

So onward and still on the same road (the B-775), where there is a long straight two miles or so, through rough pastures first, before the big left hand sweeping bend which then climbs gradually up to its opposite number. This is a big sweeping right hander that abuts with the far end of the Sergeantlaw.

A long undulating descent past Hall Farm follows, bumpy and bouncy at times, which flattens out as it approaches the T-junction with the B-777. A left turn takes you to Lugton. A large, solid, sandstone, two-storey public house — for many years the Paraffin Lamp; now the Canny Man — is the mainstay of this small settlement. There's now a tricky left/right turn on the Irvine Road to be negotiated, before you start on the road to Dunlop and into rural Ayrshire proper.

Ten minutes through open fields and a bit of a pull-up later, you're in Dunlop, with the early part of the road (the A-735) full of great views away to the right of the Arran hills. When you enter the village, you don't actually ride through Dunlop; you meander. Meander through the curving, turning Main Street and accompanying buildings of this quintessential ferm toon. You can only guess at the age of the old stone cottages, some with red barn doors attached.

When you leave, by dipping and climbing out under the arched rail bridge, you're immediately back into the open fields. A pattern is now starting to form. It's recurrent, it's pleasant, and it's uplifting.

It's the sea-like patchwork of fields, undulating and ubiquitous, broken only by the isolated islands of small rural towns that you'll pass through one after the other. Each of these becomes a marker as you head ever deeper into the shire, towards the prize of the Clyde coast.

Stewarton is reached next and fairly quickly, too, with a dive down and under its rail bridge, before meeting its solid old crossroads. After turning right at the crossroads, it's under the magnificent rail viaduct, where Kilmaurs is only a short hop away. All this is done whilst still on the A-735, with hedgerows and dairy herds for company. Any cobwebs will be well blown away by now, along with any stresses that you have been harbouring, for they all melt away as you glide through the blanket green.

After a great fire down into the village, with barns on one side and houses the other, you must break off the main road in Kilmaurs or you'll end up in Kilmarnock. So a right/left shimmy takes you onto the deceptively stringy B-751, the road to Knockentiber. This is done at the second mini roundabout, which sits just behind the very old brown kirk spire which literally owns the middle of the road.

Only a few dairy fields separates Kilmaurs from Knockentiber, linked by a road that undulates and climbs in similar fashion to what has gone before. Then over the arch bridge spanning the long-gone rail line at Barry Devlin's Garage, and that's you in Knockentiber. Keep an eye open for a great old antique road sign, painted black and white, on the right.

Now it's only a few more fields to Crosshouse, where another shimmy, in reverse order this time, left/right (still the B-751), takes you away from the Crosshouse crossroads and quickly out of this village and onto the road to Gatehead. This finds you on a somewhat rollercoaster piece of road, as you rise and dip repeatedly several times, bridging the A-71, to run down to the junction with the A-759.

Gatehead itself is seen across the fields on the approach, and is typical of a lot of these small farm settlements, in that barns — in this case, a very large blue one — sit right in beside the houses. This one

may belong to a motor engineers instead of a farmer, though. A right turn onto the A-759 runs you straight into Gatehead, entered by a classic curving left hand bend, passing over a level crossing, then over the River Irvine, and straight out the other side. That was Gatehead. Well, not quite.

The leaf-covered Cochrane Inn is very pretty and a famous rail viaduct is signposted close by, but it is a field's walk away from the road so you can't get close enough to appreciate it. Sticking to the front road, you're straight out the other side before you know it, but not staying on it too long, for that would take you down towards Troon and Barassie. We don't touch there till later.

So first left can be taken, or second if you prefer, to keep you heading in the general direction of Tarbolton. First is slightly more direct and finds the 751 again, which is followed to its meeting with the A-77. This more direct route is slightly taxing at first before it goes under a great old arched bridge at Templeton Farm, where you can find yourself in among impressively large dairy herds. You turn right at the next farm, sign posted Symington/ Dundonald (still the B-751), to take you to the A-77 at the top end of Symington. This includes a deceptively tough wee hill that may find you out of the saddle for the first time since Gleniffer.

The Bachelors' Club in Tarbolton. I always stop and marvel at the fact that the great man himself was actually in this very building. In fact, the ale house he used to drink in was The Plough Inn, which also still stands today, right around the corner

To avoid this tough wee climb, take the second left after leaving Gatehead. Although a slightly longer route, I mention it because it runs into the village of Dundonald, which contains a most wonderfully sited castle that seems to have a real special quality. When you see it from fairly close up, as it stands on its impressive earth mound, its stone flanks seem to pull you back in time. It somehow feels as old as it looks. The castle is well worth a visit, particularly the dungeons, and I recommend the slight detour that it takes to see it, standing dark and high as it does, looking fit for a king — Robert II, to be exact.

Leaving Dundonald village by its quaint Main Street, you first pass a small B-road on the right, which will climb and take you over spectacularly to Loans and Troon. This is a great option if you want a shorter day on the coast from here, and is a run I have done many times in the past. But if sticking to the original route, you're going south east (on the B-730), shortly meeting up the old 751 for the last time, and then it's life in your hands stuff as you now must cross the precarious A-77. This can be easier said than done, although since they introduced average speed cameras there, it isn't the chicken run it once was[1].

Once safely over, it's a rollercoaster ride toward Tarbolton. At this stage of the run, you have been riding in fairly undulating terrain, which can sap the strength out of your legs, and experience tells you not to go flat out and to save some energy for all the long miles to come. It's very open country, still a pleasant green blanket of hedgerows and dairy , and at this point you may catch a bit more of the sea breeze as you're about level with Prestwick and not too far inland. On a really good day you will also be getting the sun about you, and when I start to sing to myself I know then I'm enjoying it. If you're reasonably fit, you should still have plenty left in the tank and not be suffering too badly.

The second cycling tip I want to give you is all to do with your pedalling style. If you think it's just a matter of sitting on the saddle and turning the cranks, and that's what you've been doing up til now, then try this and notice the difference. It will make you more efficient and is what is known as riding supply. That is using both legs equally and simultaneously; without it, the dominant leg will do most of the work and you end up to a certain extent almost riding one-legged and therefore nearly using only half your power potential.

Firstly, relax your toes, that's all, and feel yourself on the balls of your feet. Then second, and most importantly, at the bottom of each pedal stroke pretend to wipe mud off the bottom of your shoe as you bring the pedal up (this trick was dreamed up by the great Greg Lemond, no less). Third, at the top of the pedal stroke, pretend to roll away a barrel with your foot as it starts the down stroke. What this will do is give you a very efficient circular pedal stroke, which uses both legs equally and no dead spots in your motion.

You know when you are doing it right, because the muscles in your weaker leg will start to hurt, and that is because they are being used properly for once. Stick with this style til it becomes habitual and automatic. Stay in as low a gear as necessary to enable the weaker leg to match the dominant one in workload. If you use big gears too soon, the stronger leg will be forced to take over, so back off the machismo and get smart. Make this the first thing you concentrate on when you start riding, and wait til you have mastered your pedal stroke before thinking about any other aspect.

So with song in my heart, I enter Tarbolton about 26 miles from starting out, and my spirits are lifted by entering Burns country. You know you're in Burns country, because Tarbolton is home to the famous Bachelors' Club. It's the very building frequented by the great man and his associates to debate matters of the day, and which is still standing. It can be visited by the public at certain times. Also still standing is the Plough Inn, situated right round the corner, and this was used by Robert and the boys before they made their way into the club. Rabbie started the club when he was only 21, along with five other local men and his brother, Gilbert. I always stop and marvel at the fact that he was actually here in person, and I do believe people come from far and wide to see it.

The house, in fact the whole corner, was owned by one John Richards, and he turned his upstairs room into a larger one to accommodate dancing, debating, and such like. You won't be disappointed if you stop in and get a guided tour by the local guide and gardener, Davie Rodgers. Fantastic! With spirits lifted to a new height, I'm soon off again and there is a parting of the ways to come.

Up until now, the route I take towards both Girvan and Turnberry is identical, but as I leave Tarbolton, it's at

---

1 - **The new bridge being built, and nearly completed in 2014, should negate the need to make this risky crossing.**

this point I follow different roads. For Turnberry, I take the first right as I leave and follow another quiet country road the B-774, gaining some rare Ayrshire height. In the distance, the sweep of Ayr bay comes into sight for the first time.

Not for long, though, as descending down and delightfully over the river, Ayr itself comes next, by swinging left on the B-742 just before Annbank. You find yourself now in the southern part of the shire, and this part does have a richness that is missing in its northern counterpart. It couldn't be more distant from the rough upland moors above Dalry and Kilbirnie. It's also one of the really rare parts of Scotland that will, on occasion, return a Tory MP. The north is staunch Labour.

Pull up from the river, which on a summer's day can become a real heat trap, and then it's on towards Coylton.

The road dips and twists and then rises again as you approach the village itself. This is more delightful road riding, but tough ,too, and bear in mind that you've been in the sun now for a lot of hot, hard miles, and dehydration is probably in play.

You only need to become dehydrated by as little as 3 to 5% for it to seriously affect you, if you're not careful. The two water bottles that I left home with will have been refilled by now, and the secret is to keep sooking away at that old baw-baw. Drink little and often and you won't go wrong.

As I reach Coylton, it's a right turn onto the main road the A-70 (Ayr to Cumnock road), but only for a few hundred yards, and then a left onto the B-742. On this stretch of road you enjoy some more rare height as you fly past Martnaham Loch and then cross the A-713 (Ayr to

Inside the Bachelors', in the upstairs room. This was the very room that Robert Burns attended when he came to learn to dance. No doubt this was to add another string to his considerable bow as a ladies' man.

Crossing the River Ayr on the B-742 en route to Coylton. A tough wee section is just about to follow.

To continue on your journey to the coast, you take the left side and over the River Doon by hump brig and willow. Now you're on the road to Maybole.

I don't make directly for it on the B-742, but rather stick to the back roads a bit longer by turning left at the next crossroads (quaintly signed), and then entering the town itself by a side road, and therefore staying off the busy A-77 for as long as I can. It makes for both a safer and more pleasant approach.

As you do enter the town, you pass another small village field on your left, just as charming as the Dalrymple one. It's these small touches that give settlements like these their timeless quality. From here on in, I'm on the fantastic but busy A-77 till I hit the coast.

Maybole is a slightly larger settlement than most of the others that Patna road), which begins an elegant glide down towards quaint Dalrymple, and under the magnificent railway viaduct. Soon you're into the village itself.

This, like a lot of the neighbouring villages, has many traditional buildings of real character and it also has some delightful geometry. The main road sweeps round a left hand bend, elegant enough alone, but made all the more delightful by bordering a small field in the heart of the village itself. Yes, truly delightful. Then there's further enchantment when you're confronted by a partial Y-shaped junction, which is filled by a row of whitewashed houses that nestle delightfully and perfectly in their location. It used to be the local village store that took pride of place first in line.

we've just recently passed through. This is no ferm toon, but rather a town built up by the influx of Protestant weavers and textile workers who came across from Ulster. Very strongly-built buildings of age and character give this town some distinction as you cycle up its tight old Main Street and then head out west.

Soon after leaving, you hit the excellent old relic of Crossraguel Abbey; it dates way back to 1244 and was first manned by monks from Paisley Abbey, before it was finally sacked in 1307 by Henry Percy, acting for good King Edward I (the Hammer of the Scots).

You're keen to push on now, as you know that your prize is nearing. You stay with a fair bit of height as you eagerly turn the cranks toward Kirkoswald and Souter Johnnie's Cottage; he of Tam O'Shanter fame. For with

Approaching Maybole by the last quaint and pretty back road. All that is just about to change when we at last join the busy A-77.

It's the one you've been waiting for with great anticipation, the descent on the A-77 down to Turnberry. With 50 miles on the clock, it's the highlight of the Turnberry run for me, because of the way the whole blue briny scene hits you all at once just before the turn for home is made. It never fails to lift my spirits, no matter how tired I feel.

Souter Johnnie at his elbow, "*tam did na mind the storm a whistle*". Through the toon so fast you go, passing low-lying, dark, wooden houses that look out of place among their strong stone counterparts.

Just ahead lies a descent to anticipate, as the 77 is slender and sweeping here, drawing you down to sea level, closer and closer, all tiredness forgotten. The desire — and it is a desire — to reach your target, brings you extra. It brings you energy, determination, stamina, but it brings more; it brings hope and happiness.

All thoughts of what's gone before disappear, and the fact you're a long way from home doesn't matter. You're totally single-minded, even if that's not your nature. Sometimes at this point you get a glimpse into the mindset of life's achievers, for to really get anywhere in this world you have to be single-minded, and most of us don't possess that mindset. On occasions like this you can

Looking back as Maybole's tight Main Street is ridden, which just for once looks quiet. This is rarely the case, as just as many trucks as cars make their way along it, heading for the Irish ferries.

go close to it, for a little while at least; it's an interesting insight. As driven as can be, you propel yourself forward and there's a fairly long, fairly gentle climb in the road ahead now. This is climbed with great expectation; experience tells you what's on the other side, although it never diminishes the thrill, the thrill of TURNBERRY!!!

The sheer majesty of the whole setting hits you as you crest the hill on the 77 and glide delightfully down toward the coastline. The old Chas and Dave line of "You can keep the Costa Brava and all that palaver", always comes to my mind at this point. Enjoy this descent, as it is a most magical moment, full of joy and pleasure. The sea view, the sudden burst of salt air, sometimes breezy, sometimes near still, can be tasted even this far back, as deeply breathing you recover from the climb and marvel at the sight before you. It's the main highlight of the run to glide down from the top of the brae to the right turn into Turnberry itself, with the roof of the famous hotel just visible on your right.

The knowledge that it's mission accomplished means all ills and ailments from tiredness to saddle sores seem to vanish magically from thought. I don't think that anyone could ever get tired of seeing the shapely lump of Ailsa Craig, sentinel of the Clyde, sitting amid the ever-changing blues and greens of its aquatic backdrop.

From Paisley, you'll have around 50 miles on the clock by now, and it's at the point where you turn into Turnberry from the 77 that you would come back, together with the Girvan route (if you decided to go there). Both routes follow the same way home from here.

GIRVAN

Now to get to Girvan, as opposed to Turnberry, you don't take the first right out of Tarbolton, but rather continue straight on, sticking to the B-730, where you curve and rise slightly past Strandhead Farm. At the give way on the Mauchline to auld Ayr road, look far into the distance. You will see a large foreboding ridge running left to right, the best part of 20 miles away. This ridge must be taken to reach your destination, and furthermore an equally long climb must be done even before you reach that. One word of comfort, however, and that is when you see objectives and targets on the road and they look a helluva long way off, they are often much closer and reached much quicker than imagined. So don't think too far ahead, for therein lies despair.

All's well in amongst the East Ayrshire dairy herds. Countless ones are passed as the long road down is ridden, and here we're at a point just before Stair, Girvan-bound.

To help you on your way, the next bit of riding is a real morale booster. For once across the Mauchline road, gleefully start descending down toward the river at Stair by curving and bending, steeply and swiftly, crossing the River Ayr by a single lane stone bridge that does the place justice. Surprisingly, you now cross from South to East Ayrshire District, as I thought it would be the other way round.

Anyway we're over the Ayr, and follow this by pulling up on the other bank, twisting and turning through mature woodland, then on towards Drongan. It's it's whilst on this stretch of road that it hits me just how far and serious the Girvan run is, because it will now show 30 miles on my computer and I know that it is as near as dammit 60 miles to the far end of Girvan (57.8 to be exact).

So despite all the time and effort so far, I'm still only halfway to my destination, not to mention the long road back home. Add to that, the scenery is still the same, the same blanket of seemingly endless green fields, and it feels as if you are getting nowhere fast.

Quite often, at a halfway point you can't remember the start and the end seems a long way off, so it's easy to get despondent> But there's no time for that now, as it's time to earn your spurs, dig in, and soldier on. It's fairly flat and straight on the approach to tiny Stair, which is nothing more than a building or two, and a working welding shop, I believe.

A blanket of branches provides welcome shelter from a blazing sun, before you hit a climb and then level out on the run-in to the T-junction with the A-70. The often thought-of flat terrain of Ayrshire is anything but. You will notice if you take a closer look at the fields left and right of you, that they are all individuals, containing their own slopes, curves, hollows, and bends. The uniform clipped green baize hides meandering mini glens of streams and burns, all of which throw up dips and rises which transfer onto the road and make the ride more interesting and taxing.

When you hit the A-70 this time at Coalhall, it's a right turn, then under the rail-bridge and left again, re-joining the B-730, where — flatly at first — through an avenue of trees you approach Drongan.

You don't actually enter the village; rather just skirt the edge, after passing the Toll Bar pub that looks like it belongs in an English village. The brand new estate on this road gives the place a fresh look, which was needed, as this small Ayrshire enclave has — like many — a tough appearance about it, and was a former mining village known as Taiglum. It has been starved of investment and prosperity since two big nearby collieries, the Barony and Killoch, closed in the late eighties.

After passing Drongan, it's here you notice a change in the terrain, as the road climbs and double bends continuously away from the village, and takes you over Kayshill at a height of 130 metres, up into the rough moorland.

A great bit of riding follows, through long sweeping hedgerows, before you get into a real rollercoaster ride of climbs and dips. On one, you hurtle down and over a broad dark bridge, whose sides are painted in black and white stripes; these early road marking attempts are always a quaint and comforting site. Followed by… jings!

On the great wee back road from Patna to Kirkmicheal. This is a major highlight on the Girvan run, and things are about to get seriously pretty.

By the same again. Only, at the bottom of this rather hairy descent, you must swing hard right to keep on the 730, as the road running uphill, bolt straight ahead, is a dead end leading to Rankinstein.

The sign across from the former white farmhouse says Patna 4,, and the next stretch of road is quite a long meandering and fairly arduous snaking climb, done in a rather barren, bleak landscape of rough grazing land (pleasant enough on a good day, mind).

Only a few old wind-battered trees, sparsely scattered along early field edges, guide you along the initial flat section, then it's up towards the large Sitka spruce plantation that contains the Dunston Hill open colliery. The coal heaps themselves can actually be seen as you make your way round the higher bends, before levelling out at Broomhill Farm and the entrance to the colliery, too. Shortly after, the welcome relief of a lengthy gentle descent begins, just as you pass a derelict-looking schoolhouse, positioned on top of the hill at Old Smithston.

You will enjoy this great curving descent, with its lovely views across the valley, taking you down to join the A-713 at Polnessan. This is nothing more than an isolated row of former miners' houses on the very busy A road, and it means that you have finally parted company with the B730, your guide and companion all the way from Symington to this point.

This is followed by another bleak-looking mile to Patna, which thankfully is downhill and very fast. It was named after Patna in India by William Fullerton, who more or less built the village to provide housing for workers on his estate's coal mines. His father had worked for the East India Company, hence the choice of place name.

The first road on the right is the one you want to take (signed Kirkmicheal 5 miles) and in doing so you cross the River Doon by a delightful stone bridge. The river itself, of course, was made famous by Burns in his ballad *Ye Banks and Braes*. The village does contain a row of shops not far inside, should you require to replenish food or fluid, and the trip in there will confirm that this village also has a look of need to match its former mining counterpart Drongan only a few miles back. Again, the demise of this once great industry did leave large areas of not only Scotland, but Britain as a whole, in a state of decline that has never halted, even after thirty odd years.

The road over to Kirkmicheal is one I enjoy; so will you, because it's a belter even though it does climb a fair bit at the start, pulling you up into the moorland and conifers. This was the ridge you saw as you left Tarbolton some 15 miles back.

Passing the Patna war memorial, you leave the village on this small road which does not even attain B class status. If you are new to bike riding, you'll soon get to know and love these hidden gems, despite the fact that they often contain steeper gradients than the major roads, and also the surfaces often leave a lot to be desired. This is the case with this one, but only early on, which is especially frustrating as the poorest stretch occurs at the part where it descends quite rapidly after gaining the initial height, and therefore prevents you from enjoying fully what would otherwise be a great bit of road riding.

So the five miles over to Kirkmicheal starts off wild and high, then drops steeply where the surface is so poor that caution must be exercised at first. But then you hit smooth new tarmac and it's a wonderful long deep descent through the trees at length and then out into the open into full-on farm land. Down and round long sweeping shapes of road, you pass regulation dilapidated farm buildings, such as those at Dalvennan, where the surrounding country starts to blend a lower softness with the harsh that's gone before. This is a herald of things to come, for as the village is approached, then magnificent is not too strong a word to describe the scene you enter and play lead role in. Everything around you simply becomes better and better.

Coming down the Telegraph Road on the final approach to Girvan. Girvan Glen has just been ridden and iconic Ailsa Craig, which has been showing for some time now, continues to act as an irresistible beacon, always drawing you further down.

The road stays high, just after you re-enter South Ayrshire District, on the north side of what quickly becomes the compact, elegant valley of the Dyrock Burn. It curves and descends enticingly down toward a most delightful finish in the pretty streets of this once covenanting stronghold.

You meet the village sign before you actually see the place, so dense is the foliage here. To add to the setting, in the distance another ridge is visible, but this one is most striking and fair. There's the comfort of knowing it not only doesn't need to be climbed, but as it runs the whole length of the Girvan Glen's south side, then it is also your guide rail to the whole run's furthest point.

As you go in, beware of a fierce right hand bend, before it's relax time among the prettiness. The contrast from the previous villages couldn't be more marked. You enter into a street of clean, cute cottages, slate-clad, windowed small, and whitewashed solid. No miners' rows here, these are weavers' dwellings, and this settlement — along with the next port of call, Crosshill — are both just inland of the aforementioned Maybole. Likewise, it was the same textile workers who settled here to ply their trade.

The Kirkmicheal town sign isn't slow to tell you that it was the resting place of one Covenanter Macadam, and this staunch Presbyterian tradition still, though not to quite the same extent, exists here today. The initial street of entry contains an equally quaint old kirk and also an old hump back bridge which, if crossed at the first left turn, will guide you on your route.

However, it would mean you miss out on a great wee store just ahead on the left and the best reason for a stop there is the homemade fruit scones. Tell them I sent you. No matter which way you go, leave the village by going south/south east on the B-7045, out past more white cottages, but not for long. Soon the sign for Crosshill comes into view, and it's a right turn which shortly takes you over the water of Girvan, followed by another fierce bend that leads into a long, flat, hedgy straight running alongside the Girvan Water for a while. This climbs up into open farm land and then begins the straight run in to Crosshill itself, which matches Kirkmicheal for attractiveness.

At first it's fairly modern bungalows you meet, but in the village centre, my, oh my, those old weaving whites steal the show big time, especially those running away to your left up Dalhowen Street. The rural prettiness is added to by the way you navigate the village centre, by a quaint right then left turn, as you follow the signs for Dailly down the B-741. The sign lets you know it's only 12 miles to Girvan now, and five to Dailly.

The road at first still bends and climbs a bit past Kileekie Farm, but then it enters a wooded stretch, which is one of my favourite stretches on the whole run. A long, gentle, meandering descent takes you down then over the hidden River Girvan and beyond, before it opens up, real broad and flat, at the top of the Girvan Glen.

Another re-crossing of the Girvan Water on a solid black and white striped stone bridge sets you up for what is a most glorious finish to this long and wonderful run.

Below the bridge, the water runs quiet and still, through long rich fields, as richness is now all around you. The valley starts to open up to a considerable width as the road takes a line on the south side of the glen for the remainder of the trip. The two places the road crosses the Girvan are outstandingly enjoyable, because these parts are not only particularly scenic, but also the road is descending down at a most delightful angle and making onward progress swift, easy, and pleasant. More pastoral and wooded road riding takes us down and along the side of Dailly, another village we just skirt the edge of.

A most fantastic view opens up of Ailsa Craig behind Girvan's church steeples, as the final back road over to the far side of town is taken. This scene is one that I personally cherish as much as I do the drop-down to Turnberry, and rate it as one of my favourites.

Just to prove how wrong you can be, when I was planning this run out for the first time, I had to use both a road atlas and ordnance survey map, as I'd never even driven this road let alone ridden it. Now I must be honest and say that I was a little disappointed to learn that the road down from Crosshill was not the continuous gentle descent that I'd hoped it would be, especially the road between Dailly and Old Dailly. I soon discovered that it would require some effort on my part to propel myself onward. I admit I had a vision of me on easy street, gliding down to a serenely calm Clyde coast, while soaking up the summer rays. And as good a feeling as it was to get to Girvan, it wasn't quite the plain sailing finish I'd envisaged.

The point I want to make here is that using maps to plan any long trip, especially for the first time, is crucial.

And the more detailed the better. O/S Land Rangers are excellent, but the larger scale standard road atlas also has a role to play. I started doing these runs before bike-fitting GPS's were popular, and to date I still don't have one for the bike. As far as I can tell, they are still the domain of the off road rider, and I know they have their uses on hillwalking trips. However I believe some guys do use them on longer jaunts, especially down south, where there is a more hectic road system.

Maps come into their own at the planning stage, and I want to point out that the routes I describe for some of the runs in the book are only one option.

For example, I once went to Girvan via Cumnock, Dalmellington, and Straiton, adding another 21 miles onto the trip. You can shorten or lengthen any run you wish; by all means, suit yourself. These runs are not set in stone and are only meant to provide the nucleus of ideas. There are options to shorten or lengthen any run, like I mentioned back at Dundonald, so adjust to suit yourself.

As I was saying, a bit more huff and puff is required down the Girvan Glen, as another old mining outpost in Dailly is passed. I read somewhere that a fire once started here in one of the mines and, believe it or not, it was still burning fifty years later. It was a most dangerous and unhealthy existence being a coal miner, and I admire them all.

So the trees are still with you and the South Ridge is still with you, as a long, long haul is required to pull you up on the way down the three miles to where you fly past the small hamlet of Old Dailly. It has a most impressive-looking, old, derelict church and graveyard attached. And with that, at last it's onto the home straight.

The height gained by the previous pull-up has the excellent advantage of allowing Ailsa Craig to come into view from a fair bit up the glen, and it is a most welcoming sight after all the hard-fought miles to get here. Unfortunately, so too does this big ugly factory that sits just on the outskirts of the town, but not even that can dampen the old Farrell spirits at this stage. In fact, nothing could.

However, we're not finished yet. We don't head straight down the B-734 to the front of the town, but take the minor road on the left, which starts halfway down the telegraph poles at the Brae Toll Cottage. This will fortunately rise slightly, as it carries us over to the south end of town and to the big roundabout that signals the furthest point from home. On the way over there is a most wonderful view between two grassy hills. Ailsa Craig can be seen beyond the town rooves and church steeples, and on the right day it's a most shimmering, awesome sight. So into the top end of Girvan you go

Was it worth all the effort? You bet. Time to relax for a little while and enjoy the view, as Girvan beach is finally reached. A well deserved pat on the back is justified as that stunning sentinel of the Clyde welcomes your arrival. Not for too long can you linger, however, as thoughts will soon have to turn to making the long road home again.

On this occasion it's Girvan's promenade, as opposed to the road, that starts the return journey home. Already distant Arran's outline is visible and will become more prominent the further up the coast you go.

(keeping an eye open for big Peter McCloy), by diving under the railway and running along the top of the town on the Coalpots Road. Its tree-lined on one side and a real mixed bag of housing all around, from quaint bungalows to the odd concrete block.

Soon the far end is reached and, although a roundabout on the busy 77 is hardly a fitting end to such a great run, it is accompanied by the striking high ground on the left and, of course, the breakers coming in from the sea ahead which are a fitting end. In the middle of the roundabout, a large brick structure reads "Whits yer hurry?" I like that I must say.

I've got all the way back to Paisley to go, which is my answer, of course, and I start by rolling gently into town on the A-77 til I reach a mini roundabout, and I usually dive into the wee store there and treat myself. It's called Doune Burn Stores. After this, I head down the narrow adjacent side street and onto the shore front on Bay Terrace.

I always cruise along the shore front, slowly meandering back, never tiring of seeing my beloved Clyde coast with its jewel in the crown, Ailsa Craig. This is especially so when I'm on Le Velo[2]. Driving along is also a pleasure, but when I've gotten down on two wheels, it makes it so very special, as now I'm feeling on top of the world.

The sight of both Ailsa and Arran from here, is one of the highlights of the whole cycling year, due partly to the fact that it was so hard fought to get here. I like to meander real slow along the water front til I'm back near

2 - The bike.

the town centre, before the serious business of getting home gets started.

The harbour has been tidied up into a small marina, but behind it there is still a bit of the old boatyard remaining. Girvan's churches and steeples are all around you now, and the backdrop of hills behind them makes the town centre a most pretty sight.

When the return journey does start, it's out past the rows of houses and under the bright red rail bridge, then onto the open A-77. That bloody big ugly factory you see coming down the Girvan Glen is now dead ahead, and dead horrible, but even the modern fast 77 here has an elegance about it, as it glides away in the distance between the wheat fields. Anyway, Ailsa is still glorious away to your left, don't forget.

The stretch between here and Turnberry was, for a long time, the only time I ever touched the old girl (the 77 that is). For it is one heavy load-carrying dude and not the ideal place to cycle. However, it is flat and short, say five miles, and it does for a good bit have a slight hard

Leaving Girvan on the snaking A-77 and heading firstly for Turnberry, as the long haul home begins. The unofficial cycle lane to the left of the white line is an absolute godsend on this busy stretch of trunk road.

shoulder beyond the white line, making for a very good unofficial cycle lane.

Once you get motoring on it, there is a great flat sweeping view of the Clyde, and Turnberry Bay in particular. Not even a big blue shed-clad factory at Dipple, which is passed halfway along, can take anything away from this glorious setting, a setting which is always a field's width away from the shore.

To the right, the ground rises quickly and dune-like in places, which doesn't leave the farmers a lot of room

Right in between Girvan and Turnberry,
and on the Ayrshire flat.

to play with. The magnificent Turnberry Lighthouse becomes more and more prominent the closer you get to it, and on reaching Turnberry it's time to turn left onto my beloved A719, which I know on a summer's day is the start of something special. Both the Turnberry and Girvan routes are now one and the same again, just as you are greeted by that bastion of opulence, the Turnberry Hotel, standing guard magnificently above. Surveying as it does, the whole scene below and beyond. And what a scene it is; one of the finest golf course settings in the world.

As you come in off the 77, you pass the former post office — now an art gallery-cum-café on the right hand side — which will serve you tea and snacks. With a coffee in hand, I often go down the adjacent sandy track for a few yards and sit on the bench on the par 3 fourth tee, (the holes called, Woe be tide). The golfers never seem to mind an uninvited audience. I'm no golfer myself[3], but who could forget the famous duel in the sun, the 77 Open Championship, when big Jack Nicklaus and Tom Watson went head-to-head for two whole days. Big Jack holed an enormous putt on the very last green to force wee Tam into making his putt to clinch the claret jug by a single stroke. It's no exaggeration to say that they are still talking about it.

Break over. It's back on the bike. I'm a long way from home as I start to trundle my way along the flat road of Turnberry, legs loosening up again. Still, I can't help but take a detour across the course itself on the single track road to the lighthouse.

3 - I've now since taken up the game.

There's something about lighthouses that seems to draw people, there's no doubt about that. For some, to "collect" lighthouses is a game in itself. The setting of this one, between the craggy Clyde coast and the classic course, is extra special. On the approach, just before reaching the white walls, look back over the fairway to the magnificent red-roofed hotel and another unforgettable sight looks back, greatly enhanced by the stunning green carpet of smoothed, clipped fairway that encompasses all around. Like the first site of Ailsa Craig, it stays with you for a long time after.

The lighthouse itself shone its first light in late August 1873, and was strategically placed there to warn sailors off the treacherous Bristo Rocks lying just offshore. It stands white and tall for 24 metres, and was designed by those engineering gurus, David and Thomas Stevenson. It was one of their many. Built at a cost of just over £6500, it was constructed by John Barr and Co., of Ardrossan, with Milne and Co. providing the lantern and all its workings. Money well spent, I dare say. The old keepers' houses are now in private ownership after automation came to Turnberry in 1986. Just try and ride away without looking back.

Returning to the main road, after filling the water bottles from the course drinking fountains, it's along the flat now to Maidens. Entered by gently dipping down into this shore-side village, with salt air and tail breeze for company, the scene is greatly enhanced by the sight of the sandy beach running away from you on your left side, before it merges into the woods of Culzean.

The approach to Turnberry is always heralded by the sight of its iconic lighthouse. It's not long now til the left turn is made onto my beloved A-719, at which point both the Turnberry and Girvan routes become one, and the same again after the parting of the ways in Tarbolton

A special moment for me is to make a point of crossing the famous course to reach the lighthouse on a warm summer's day. The gate to the road is seen shortly after passing the clubhouse on the left. This, at first, takes you across the Kintyre course, and then the prestigious Ailsa. Please note that water bottles can be filled from drinking fountains en route.

You pass a great wee store as you turn inland[4] and at that point the honeymoon's over. There's got to be a climb off the coast sometime and it starts here, on the Kirkoswald Road, going up past the caravan site, which once held the brilliantly named but unfortunately gone now Barley Bree pub, and on toward the majestic Culzean Castle.

More than ever, getting into a good climbing rhythm early, riding supplely, and using positive self-talk, can make a difference. They help take the sting out of even the longest and most sustained of climbs. This one is a climb I know well, real well. I often struggle early on, on its lower slopes, and it usually takes me until the entrance to Culzean to get fully going again. For, as always, I've lingered too long at the course and I've cooled down too much.

This is no brutal ascent, however, but rather a long snaking climb[5]. It goes up through open fields at first, and despite the openness of the terrain here, if the sea breeze is slight and it's warm, then it can be a stifling struggle up.

That is before the shade of the trees around the entrance to the castle are reached, which is greatly welcome on a scorcher. I would also recommend, if you feel you have the time or the energy, to take a quick dive down into Culzean itself. It is a most beautiful ornate castle and, sitting atop the cliffs as it does, it's perched in a most

4 - It serves good cheap grub, if you need it.

5 - You're heading up through the Penny Glen.

A fantastic view of Ailsa Craig and Culzean Castle is to be had as height is gained on the A-719, after the left turn beyond the entrance to Culzean is taken. The stretch of road to follow, after the famous Croy (The Electric) Brae is taken, ranks in the top three of my favourites, in all the runs that I do.

stunning location. You can gain free entry to the place if you go fast enough downhill through the gate (it's all part of the fun), and one of the finest sights I've ever seen was across the field above the castle on a late summer's day, as the hay bales waited patiently to be collected.[6]

Admittedly, I only consider visiting here or the lighthouse if I'm just doing Turnberry, because the Girvan run is long enough in itself without additional detours.

After a visit — or not — the passing of the castle entrance finds the road still meandering upwards, the going slightly easier now, as I find I'm back in the flow. The gradient slowly levels out and it's a relief when it does, because this particular climb is the best part of four miles long, which all the time turns inland as it goes. Shortly after it levels off, you turn left, though still stay on the 719, and it means you're making for the Heads of Ayr.

It starts off with a plunge down, then up, and the road swings back west and sits well up on the hillside above Croy beach. This is followed by another lengthy descent, with the ground sloping gently away to the shore on the left, and the ground on the right rising up into the Carrick Hills. Again, the road bends westward and, as it does, you ascend — at least, I think you do — Croy Brae; the famous Electric Brae. This is (for the few who don't know), the hill where you speed up as you climb and slow down as you descend. For years, the locals thought it was to do with electrical magnetic forces in the ground, hence

the name, but it's since been discovered that it's all to do with the lie of the land and is merely an optical illusion.

Once you clear the brae, it's only a couple of hundred yards til you swing round the hillside, and the whole Clyde coast opens up in front of you. On a clear day it is possible to see the Antrim coastline, as the height you're up affords an excellent all round vista, and one of Arran in particular. This jagged sentinel always gives a striking appearance from any viewpoint, and it's hard to take your eyes off it as you pedal along in this most perfect position. You're coasting along at this point, for now the summer breeze is behind you and the first thing you learn as a bike rider is that all's well with the world when you have a tail wind.

That, helped with some warm sun on your back, makes you feel wonderful, and nothing is more important than how you feel. The motor car is convenient, yes, but no matter how expensive or prestigious a model, it will never give the same pleasure or happiness you'll get from the bike.

So, purring along the old 719 soon finds you passing above the small village of Dunure. It has another great old castle, whose outline can be seen against the sea, and also contais a really pretty wee harbour, which is nice to visit. But be warned! The steep road down means a steep road back up, so make sure you've enough oomph in you before you go charging down.

The small village of Fisherton comes next (if you stick to the main road) and is passed in an eye blink.

Despite the fact that it's been a pleasure to ride this high ledge of tarmac with its beautiful blue view, there comes shortly after… well, what can I say? A descent-and-a-half that is payback time for all the ascending you've done since Maidens. You literally fly down towards the Heads of Ayr, gleefully and gratefully, and this is some real quality, effort-free riding. To add to the taste, the coastal resort of Ayr is getting closer, real fast: *"auld Ayr wham nere a toon surpasses, for honest men and bonny lassies."* But first there comes a taxing wee rise as you pass the holiday camp of Craig Tara, then it's across the Doon again as you enter the town itself. Stop in the town for a break, and you're sure to get some banter from the honest men themselves.

After the tranquillity of the green fields and coast, there is always a definite hustle and bustle about Ayr and Prestwick, particularly if you stay on the main road running continuously through them both, and which

6 - **I actually stopped the bike to admire this scene, and I never do that.**

leads directly to Prestwick Airport. The alternative is to go via the coast as much as possible, and this is done by taking the official cycle route which is a small insignificant left turn, made just before reaching Ayr itself. This allows the shore to be followed almost to the airport and, despite being slower than the direct road route, it will give a quieter and astonishingly pleasurable ride on a lovely summer's day.

There's fast food-a-plenty in this renowned old holiday haunt, and if it's a warm weekend jaunt you're doing, the crowds will let you know that the home front beaches are as popular as ever. With at least 80 miles under my belt, and another 20 to go, I often treat myself to a chippie (one of the rare times I do), not only because I need the energy or that there's no danger of weight gain, but because it puts me in the seaside day out mode, and suddenly I'm a kid again.

One thing a town's busy environment can do is give you an added buzz and a bit of a boost. This is most welcome at this stage, for it's a tough wee run home, and I start it by seamlessly entering Prestwick from Ayr, and shortly after pass the pure dead brilliant terminal of the airport itself.

Once clear of the terminal, you have a choice of two routes to help you negotiate Troon. One is by taking a cheeky wee left turn down the cycle path, and that will run you alongside the railway, then then into the town itself. This is followed on the other side by another great shore ride, after first cutting through Troon's small, solid town centre. The shore road will eventually turn in to guide you under the rail bridge and past Barassie station. There then follows a short trip round a housing estate and

The Heads of Ayr from the last high spot on the A-719. There now begins a fantastic screamer of a descent down to Auld Ayr itself, which can just be seen in the background.

back onto the main road via a path. Hardly a fitting route for a true road man, admittedly, but this is the official cycle way and, despite this rather ignominious ending, the earlier charm of the town and beach make it an option worth considering.

The faster alternative is to continue on the main road, after passing the airport terminal, and take the first left (B-749). Once on it, it's relief time. For soon you hear the cars on the busy dual carriageway you've just left behind become background, as quietly you slip back into the fields and woods, spinning ever closer to this wonderful old town. But before you get too close, the trick is to take the small side road which runs off to the right and quickly leads out to the top of the B-746. From the top of this road, it is literally a charge down and through the crossroad into Loans, with the rooftops of Troon now away to your left, glinting in the early evening sun. It starts to lower slightly over the Firth now, as it will be well into the afternoon and you are getting your last view of the Clyde on this particular run.

It's always a poignant moment when you reach this point, for you leave behind the coast, along with all its draw and magical memories, and thoughts now must turn to getting home. This for me is still an hour and a half's ride away.

After quickly slicing through the village of Loans, continue on to take first left at the Barassie roundabout, where you immediately meet the cycle route coming out of Barassie itself. From there, continue on past the quaint old former army camp of Dundonald, which still smacks of National Service days. Whilst you're still counting your blessings that that madness has ceased, Irvine rears its ugly head.

Yes, the Scottish New Town. Irvine was one of five. An idea dreamed up in the fifties, by God knows who, to create the ideal living and working environment for those lucky enough to stay there. I dare say it looked good on paper, but the reality appears, to me at least, to be countless concrete roundabouts, soulless streets, and hideous housing. As far as I can tell, the only good thing to come out of Irvine so far has been Eddie Reader[7], but that's just my opinion.

No prizes for guessing you soon hit a roundabout, which turning right on, leads onto the B-7080, and this is followed all the way to Girdle Toll, which entails going through no fewer than another nine roundabouts. You

7 - Graeme Obree goes without saying in a cycling book.

Crossing the River Ayr on New Bridge Street in the evening sunshine, with the bustle of the town an envigorating pick-me-up after all the solitude of rural Ayrshire, which has been the norm for the last few hours now.

enter this Irvine outlier by a roundabout; you gratefully leave by a roundabout, having suffered some unavoidable speed bumps and a roundabout. Time, though, to put my hands up and say I much prefer them to traffic lights any day[8].

When you reach the other side of Girdle, it's time to make the long haul back to Lugton. It's nine miles from here, which doesn't seem a lot, but it does feel that it goes on a lot longer.

You do gain a fair bit of height as you climb up past Torranyard and back up into the sheep country. No rich pastures in this part. After all the miles you have in your legs, it's a godsend to have a westerly breeze behind, as any climb you do now will take all the strength you have

left. Torranyard itself seems comprised of an isolated static caravan park and the former Torranyard Inn, now a tandoori restaurant. They both sit to the right of the A736, as you make your way inland. This is another favourite road of mine, but more for driving than cycling, if I'm honest.

A word of warning about fast single carriageway A-roads; they can be lethal. Pay particular attention to, and keep your wits about you for, cars that overtake coming toward you. Some drivers — both male and female, I've found — once committed to the manoeuvre, won't be giving a damn if you're on the road or not. And as they will be coming straight at you at breakneck speed, be prepared to take evasive action pronto.

But other than the occasional kamikaze driver, it's still a great cycle up and along this road. The 736 has long

8 - Roundabouts, that is.

straight sections and not too many hills left for you to tackle. As you purr along in the evening sunshine at 90rpm cadence, with the gentle westerly breeze at your back, you don't have a care in the world.

If you have built up well for this sort of distance, and have conserved your energy well, it's a real joy to be feeling good even at this late stage and the miles start to close in all too quickly. Seeing as we have a few spare moments together on the home run and as it's been our first outing together, let me just say thanks for the company and I hope you enjoyed the ride as much as I did.

I'd also like to explain why I choose such a long run to begin with, and one or two other things as well. No-one who has just bought a bike for the first time in a long time, would start off with such a lengthy outing.

Obviously, it would be like planning to run a marathon, which would entail a gradual build-up. For some people that would mean going out and jogging a mile, if they could. For others, even that would be beyond them initially. But take heart, because as I've said already, you'll be amazed at how quickly your fitness level will rise and just how many miles you can cover in a fairly short space of time. So that was the reason for starting off with such a lengthy ride to begin with. I want to get it known right from the start that a ride of this distance is well, and I do mean well, within the capabilities of most.

They say everyone has a comfort zone — a limited zone within which we feel a relative amount of comfort and security, due to a lack of threat and fear from the unknown. Well, I've got some news for you: you don't have a comfort zone, no. You actually have a familiar zone. That's a different thing. In your familiar zone, sure you might feel a relative amount of safety within its boundary, but you're not comfortable. All those fears and insecurities are just outside that boundary, and on your own, you don't really want to go out there and face them.

Firstly, like I said earlier, most people's idea nowadays of how far you could go on a bike would be very, very limited. Well, straight away, welcome to your new familiar zone; one which enlightens you to the fact that sooner than you think, great days of cycling distances of 100 miles or even more, will soon be doable. That's if you want to. The ball is in your court.

Secondly, when we are out on the road, I will give you some tips and point you in the right direction, on how to get to know yourself better and also how to rid yourself of a lot of the fears and insecurities that hold a lot of us back.

If electing not to go via Troon town on the return journey, then the great fly-down to Loans on the B-746 is the fabulous alternative. The Clyde can still be seen glinting above the town's rooftops, usually in the evening sunlight for me, and will be just about the last view of the coast you will get on the day

This isn't just a book about bike riding; this is also a book on personal development.

So stick around, you've nothing to lose. Cycling, unlike jogging, is non-weight bearing and even for someone in middle age or older, the damage to joints, tendons and ligaments will be minimal, if care and a steady build-up are applied.

Matters of cycling technique have been kept to only one or two thus far. The reason being that I wanted to concentrate solely on the run itself, and not allow anything to detract from the description and the pleasure of the outing. First and foremost the message is clear; it's well within the scope of the modern day, car-owning, fast-paced individual, who has, due to work and other commitments, found themselves out of shape and overweight before they could say road tax, to be able to turn things round, pronto!

Tempus fugit (time flies). It will seem it was only a blink of an eye ago that you were chasing a ball, or playing and running all day long, carefree and tireless. Do yourself a favour, get back on the bike and become a kid all over again. Could be that you'll find the simple things in life bring most pleasure, with big rewards for your efforts. With that, comes the feelgood factor, and again nothing is more important than how you feel.

If you've previously coveted material gains, then this could broaden your horizons, for all that glitters isn't gold. The ending of a long hot summer day's run can bring a personal satisfaction that money can't buy. Also, don't forget that once the bike and gear are bought, the rest

If you're still in one piece at this stage, there is one last treat left for you to enjoy. No! Make that two. The first will be the sight of the vast Clyde Valley opening up to meet you, as the crest of the braes is breached. Your eye is drawn into the length of flatness, then up into the Kilpatrick Hills away in the distance, and before you lies one of the rare flatlands in the whole of Scotland. This includes the mighty city of Glasgow, which hits you right in the face as you start the descent back down bonnie Gleniffer.

The contrast of all the solitude and empty fields that have gone before, make the impact of seeing

A fine view of the Arrochar hills is seen as the approach to the top of the Gleniffer Braes approaches. On this occasion, they are in brilliant late evening red as I've left it late this time.

practically comes free. Simply fill the water bottles, open your front door, off you go.

So, once I reach Lugton, I turn left and now head north towards Paisley. There is one final lengthy rise to negotiate, which starts as you pass through the Hall Farm crossroads. From there, you make your way grittily up to the start of the Sergeantlaw Rd. Now you make a sharp left turn and coast down to the right hand bend, where I start the long wind down back towards home.

It's a good couple of miles from here to the top of the braes, and all smart riders know that this is the point to ease up and take the lactic acid out the legs and cool down properly. Don't hammer it all the way to your front door; spin the last couple of miles out easily, it will do your legs the world of good.

On nearing the crest of the braes themselves, it's prudent to be extra careful here, as many drivers overtake recklessly after being frustrated on the road up. The pronto evasive action which I mentioned earlier has been used to good effect at this very point on more than one occasion.

such a mighty metropolis even greater, and it never ceases to amaze me how rural land can suddenly change into even the largest of settlements. The sometimes hairy, always thrilling, descent down the braes road is the second treat I promised you, and it's easy to hit more than 40 MPH on the steepest section, even if you're not a good descender.

It's a fitting end to any run, even the mighty Turnberry, and at the bottom after entering Glenburn, the Shieling is passed and home awaits.

With a great feeling of satisfaction and achievement, along with a fair amount of fatigue and dehydration, I arrive at my front gate. I must say, that was quite something. Quite something to savour, quite something to reflect on for a moment, before going through the front door where the recovery process will begin.

There will be either about 100 or 115 miles on the computer, depending on my destination. And just how do I celebrate my return home, you may wonder?   Well, just like Francie and Josie, I like to wachil hame and put the kettle on the boil.

Liam Boy.

THE ARRAN RUN

FROM PAISLEY
102.5 MILES
6.54 HOURS
ASCENT: 5580 FEET
3581 CALORIES BURNED

FROM ARDROSSAN
55.4 MILES
3.44 HOURS
ASCENT: 2940 FEET
2402 CALORIES BURNED

O'S LANDRANGER MAPS 64, 63, 69.

CAL-MAC ARDROSSAN TEL NO 01294-463470

ROUTE SUMMARY

Gleniffer Braes (B-775)
Mid Hartfield Cottage (Minor Rd)
Rowbank Reservoir (B-776)
Gateside
Dalry
Ardrossan Harbour

ISLE OF ARRAN (CLOCKWISE)

Ardrossan Harbour
Dalry
Gateside
Rowbank Reservoir (B-776)
Mid Hartfield Cottage
Hartfield Farm (Minor Rd)
Gleniffer Braes
Paisley

ARRAN SHORTER ROUTES

Ross Rd
String Rd

THE ARRAN RUN

THE KING OF RUNS

This one is waited for. This one is timed. The expectation is high; very high. When the right day is forecast with the breeze from the west, and the sun is doing what it was meant to and you're in good nick, then doing the Arran run feels like you've died and gone to heaven. Don't believe me? Then try it yourself. You won't have gone very far to realise that I'm in no way exaggerating. It has taken up until the last day of June some years until I get the perfect conditions to take on what I call 'the king of runs'. The island gives you a good run and day out in itself. The road round is 55 miles approximately, however due to the amount of climbing involved, it's the equivalent of an 80 to 90 mile flat run. This lay observation was conveyed to me by fellow Paisley rider and distance man, big Les Muir.

Many people drive to the ferry terminal at Ardrossan before unloading the bike and doing the island that way. Fair enough. Just for information, there is a car park right at the pier, and you can park there for only a couple of pounds. This can be your best bet, depending on where you live, and it is good to know that your day's work is all done when arriving back at the ferry after circling the isle.

For me personally, well, I must be honest and say that I don't feel I've done it right unless I do it door-to-door. Living in Paisley, it's a distance that is just about achievable and comes in at just over the one hundred mile mark. The ferry I aim for is the 9.45am sailing and, as it's roughly an hour and a half's riding from home to there, I leave just before 8am if I can get away quick enough.

There's only one thing more demanding than starting your run on the Gleniffer Braes, and that's starting your run on the braes first thing in the morning. I'm straight out the door and onto them, and it can be a difficult thing for your body to adjust to, especially if you consume a lot of fluid just before starting.

One part of the day that I don't normally see enough of is morning (I tend to work late in the evening), and I

The majestic Rowbank Reservoir, seen across the meadows from Windy Hill, is the finest reservoir in all Renfrewshire, in my opinion. By this point, I am warmed up and well on my way. If it's a very warm summer's morn, the pleasantness and airy freshness of this scene make a perfect balance.

must say that the cool freshness of the morn does have a unique quality to it that you don't get any other time of the day. The braes usually take less than 15 minutes to clear from my front door, and the coolness of the early air tends to stop you overheating, even on the steepest parts of the climb. It's always in the back of your mind that today, more than most, it's important not to take too much out of yourself early on, as there is a lot of tough, though excellent climbing ahead.

Despite your best efforts to be smooth, you're sure to find your heartbeat going up to around the 170 mark. Again, staying seated and regulating your breathing helps with the level of your beats per minute (bpm), though sometimes you feel it's desirable to get out of the saddle to keep the momentum going. After you ascend hills on a bike for a while and as your fitness starts to improve, it's then that you begin to notice the changes in steepness which most long hills possess. You tend not to notice this when you're in a car, or when you're so unfit that you're still working hard when a subtle change in a gradient takes place. When you do start to notice, it's a sure sign that you're definitely getting fitter.

As I top out onto the crest, I always allow myself a wry smile. I know then that, despite the fact I'm feeling puffed out, there are still 100 miles to go and it will be after 7 at night before I'm back at this spot again.

It's nice and rewarding now to get the breathing slowed down and to up the gears as you head south on the Gleniffer Road (the B-775) towards Lugton. But you don't go so far as that this time. Instead, it's time to head into real rural Renfrewshire, as the next part of the journey is

Much further down the road and only four miles shy of the ferry, this still morning finds Munnoch Reservoir's boats still sleeping quietly in their watery beds, so I slip past quietly so as not to wake them.

carried out on small back roads all the way to Dalry. After about two miles, it's a right turn up toward Mid Hartfield Cottage[1]. This is your first taste of single track roads today, and it isn't a good one.

It's a rough climb up and into the remote fields, but it's a great swerve past the cottage, and half a mile beyond it you take the first left onto another single track road, up and over Windy Hill. This is another rough barren climb, but from there the majestic Rowbank Reservoir comes into view.

The condition of the road here is so bad in places, I'm convinced that the tarmac was laid for the imminent arrival of Oliver Cromwell. When you reach the end of this road, you hit the Howwood Road (the B-776), and it's left up past the Greenacres ice rink and then take first right, diving down and heading west on more single track.

Now you meet and turn right onto the B-777, on which you fire fast down into the small village of Gateside. This is followed by more ducking and diving, then a left turn just past the Gateside Inn, then straight along to the end of this single track road till the T-junction with the Barrmill Road (the B-706). All the time, you will feel closed in by hedgerows and the like either side.

When you turn right, you're down a short steep hill, at the bottom of which you turn then left. This takes you past the ordnance place, where the road becomes single track again after crossing a hump bridge. This, likewise, is followed to the end, in a couple of miles' time, also ending in a T-junction and also tightly lined by hedges.

You're getting close to Dalry now, and soon it's into the town after two right turns then a left in quick succession. Entry to the town itself will be fairly fast, as

it's all downhill, finished off nicely by crossing over the flowing Garnock by hump brig. One way of getting to know the shortcuts and back roads for any rider, is to get an ordnance survey map of the area or areas where you intend to do most of your riding. Not only do they help you to plan routes, but they can make for an interesting read at the end of the day when you return home. Then you can see which roads you took, when perhaps you got

One of the finest moments on the whole of the Arran run is the descent down into Ardrossan town from high up on the B-780 Dalry Rd, which begins once the small Busbie Muir Reservoir is passed. All the hard work is over for now, and as your waiting red tub is clearly visible at this point, you know you've made it and the pressure is off.

a bit disorientated and rode blind for a section of your run and through terrain that you were none too familiar with.

When you get into Dalry, you'll find it has that reassuring old look about it. You climb up to the traffic lights and then turn left, right, and left again onto the well signposted road for Ardrossan, this is the B-780. It's a dip and then a long pull-up out of the town, as Dalry — like a lot of Ayrshire settlements — seems to sit in a hollow.

Once free of the town, the road is sweeping and open, dipping and climbing on long curves towards West Kilbride. After being hemmed in on the tight back roads, there is now a real feeling of space, and the warm sunlit

---

1 - This is unsigned, so check out the map before you go.

open fields unfold all around you and airily invite you westward. Soon the next left turn at Munnoch Reservoir tells you it's only four miles to the coast.

Despite taking a turn, you are still on the B-780 and, as you still can't see the sea yet, it's very easy to think you may not make the ferry at this point if you are cutting it fine. You simply don't realise that you're closer than you think.

Once you're clear of Munnoch, the last rise is met and it's a wee bit frustrating, as you are now getting anxious about time and want to see some coastline. On levelling out, you pass another smaller reservoir — the Busbie Muir — which is now overlooked by the ubiquitous wind turbines. Personally, if I go clockwise round the island, then the three starts are all tough, but the three finishes on each section of this run are simply sublime.

The descent into Ardrossan starts at the end of the reservoir, and is a real piece of tarmac to savour. It's a glide all the way down at a fair old speed, I hasten to add, whilst knowing that you will make the ferry and that all the work is over for an hour or so at least.

If you've been worrying in the back of your mind that

You know you're on your way when the battered old mini lighthouse guarding Ardrossan harbour gives you a wink as the boat passes on the way out.

you might miss the ferry and your day will be lost, you can now afford to sit up and enjoy the descent and view, as you will now be in very good spirits. The road down is still good, but it was even better in the past before the inclusion of those so-called traffic calming islands.

The new bypass is also crossed, via a large roundabout, and this can force you to check your run, which isn't what the doctor ordered. However, nothing can stop your enjoyment now and, as soon you hit the lights at the bottom, you turn left, before making your final right turn and going straight as a die down toward the ferry terminal itself on Glasgow Street. I usually get there in about 1 hour 25 or so for the 23.5 miles covered. Cyclists are usually allowed first on the car deck, and then it's time to head up for a coffee or two in the Cal-Mac cafeteria.

So here we are for the first time on one of the Scottish islands' life blood ferries. The first of many for you, I hope. There is always a real feeling of excitement when you board one as, just like a kid, you know that a bit of an adventure awaits across the water. I can't begin to tell you what the ferries and the islands mean to me, and I am

Just about to board at Ardrossan.

It's easy to see why the Vikings named this the Breidr vik (broad bay) as you approach Brodick.
High above, overseeing all, sits the mighty Goatfell.

always most grateful for the respite and comfort that they provide for this tired and hungry rider on occasions.

For the record, they started operating way back in 1851, though it was not until the 1870s that David MacBrayne became in charge. The company wasn't always called MacBraynes, in fact; for a long time it was known as the Caledonian Steam Packet Company.

The modern Cal-Mac company, as we know it today, came into being on New Year's Day 1973. I could be wrong here, but I think the Ardrossan-Brodick sailing is one of the few profitable ones it has. Most of the rest are heavily subsidised. Long may it continue.

The crossing time is an hour approximately, and after refreshments I usually have a stretch and then try and find a quiet spot to shut my eyes and relax. It can also

be very uplifting on a good day to go out on deck and admire the salt view, with the diving gannets providing spectacular entertainment. The one issue you will have at this point is to decide which way to go round the island.

I have done it both ways many times, but clockwise is my preference. And it's this way I will describe, though as with all runs, the wind direction and wind strength will have been taken into consideration.

As the ferry nears the isle, it is a rare treat to stand on deck and admire the rugged beauty of what is to come. Many first time visitors fall under Arran's magical spell, and soon there is talk of leaving the rat race and settling there. It's easy done.

The mountains will be dominating the view, with the bulk of Goatfell stealing the show. This magnificent hill was known to the Norsemen as Geit fiall (Goat

Although I've described the island section going clockwise, as that is the way I usually go, I have also gone anti-clockwise on many occasions. Despite this leaving the toughest stretch until last, it does mean you have a screamer of a finish down to the ferry as your finale. It also means you get a fantastic view of the eastern mountains — like the one above — from the road as you near the end of the run. This gives a great view of the so-called sleeping warrior, though I for one have never been able to fully suss that out.

Mountain), and the modern name is just an anglicised version of that.

The Vikings held all the islands for quite a considerable time, even after they conceded what they controlled of the mainland back to the Scots. As such, a lot of place names in all the islands are modern versions of the original Norse or Gaelic. The Norse for bay was vik. They called Arran's capital Breidr vik; it means broad bay, and from that we get Brodick. When you finally dock, it's cars off first then bike riders.

A gentle approach is best as you run the length of the pier and then amble out to the junction with the A-841, which will be your constant companion on the grand loop.

Now, a word of warning! For if you're going clockwise, the very second that you turn left onto the road, you immediately start climbing. Be ready for the fact that there is not so much as a foot of level ground as the long and at first steep pull-up starts straight away on the road to Lamlash. This climb is a fairly brutal start to the island, and goes on for over a mile, from sea level up to about 114 metres. However, the first section is steeper than the rest, and it soon starts to lie back and allows you to recover your breath for the bulk of the climb. Nonetheless, it's a good way to get warmed up for what's to come.

That brings me to my second word of warning! As majestic as the south of the island is, the first 19 miles will prove to be the hardest. It really is a stretch of road that has everything. It's as unforgettable as it is hard. Some of the climbing is long, rhythmical and enjoyable; some of it is short steep and brutal.

And now my third and final word of warning! The road surface. As great as Arran is, the one thing that really lets it down is the state of the roads. In places, they are bloody awful — truly awful, and dangerously so. There is some old bloke on YouTube who sings about them, but they are no laughing matter.

I once wrecked a good rim coming off the Boguillie one time, and seriously advise that you exercise caution when descending the fast unsighted bends on the island's southern half. With that last warning over, it's on with the show.

You'll find yourself hemmed in by the conifers at first, but as the climb starts to level out, the place opens up and you start to get a taste of what's to come. Remember, it's still fairly early at this point, around 11am, and with the salt breeze in the morning air it can be a refreshing start to this coastal jaunt. All this combined is a guaranteed spirit-lifter. No matter what you're facing in life, it will be all forgotten at this point.

No sooner are you up, then it's straight back down again into Lamlash Bay, with a sweeping, diving, entry on a right-hand bend that requires your attention. Then

Talking of screaming descents, this is the one that flies you fast and furious down to fairly forgotten Kildonan. Ahead can be seen Pladda Island, with the lighthouse just about visible. The descent itself is great, and so is the scene that awaits you at the bottom. However, and it is a big however, the bolt straight brutal rise back up to the main road is usually enough to put me off taking this dramatic scenic side-loop most of the time, and therefore I tend to stay on the high road which is tough enough in itself at this point.

The sight of Pladda lighthouse on its rocky island outcrop is one I always look forward to seeing every time I do the Arran run. On this occasion, it and the Ayrshire coastline behind are quite clear, which isn't always the case.

behold the picturesque bay with the perfectly set Holy Isle making it a true natural harbour. So much so that King Hakon anchored his fleet here before the Battle of Largs in 1263. It was only when his boats emerged from here that they got hit by a storm which knocked hell out of them.

You travel straight and level as you make your way along this shorefront, and on a beautiful morning it can be hard to see much of the town as the bay is so pleasing to the eye that you can't take your eyes of it.

It's very easy to ride by and not notice that in front of the houses there is a monument, placed here to commemorate the sailing of the Caledonia, a ship which took displaced islanders to Canada as part of the sheep clearances. A local minister, the Reverend Alexander

Another great view of the dynamic duo, and this is the one I usually spend most time at because it is not only the first view you get of the pair, but is also such a fantastic position. So much so, that a bench has been set at this spot in someone's memory for others to enjoy the view just as much.

The stunning Ailsa Craig, also seen from the main A-814 above Kildonan. It is a mesmerising site, I think you'll agree.

McKay, preached a sermon to the 86 poor souls who were forced out of their glen and onto the boat. They ended up in the Megantic area of Canada and were still in tents when the ferocious Canadian winter roared in. It is testament to their hardiness that they survived and flourished in the new world. Arran was no different from the rest of the Highlands in the way the crofters were treated during the clearances.

Lamlash shorefront is quickly covered, and you leave by the quaint Monamore stone brig over its namesake burn. Once over, it's a sharp left turn then an excellent long, meandering climb begins. This has the added bonus of allowing a look across to Holy Isle as you ascend the hillside on some real quality tarmac. Each of the three east side towns has climbs as you leave them, and each one is better than the one before. I relish this one more than the last, and like how the road ascends among the

A view of both Pladda and Ailsa together, and what a combination they make. Every time you view this scene is different, and for that reason I tend to linger a while and find it hard to pull myself away.

residences perched in the most idyllic of locations — some are old traditional stone-built cottages, and others are the more modern type. You can't help but think, "Oh, to have money." Then the road itself gets interesting as it turns and twists over the first of many burns. The initial one is crossed by a bonny stone bridge, just as you are about level with Dippen.

Dippen is derived from the old Gaelic da pheighinn, meaning two pence, and comes from a pre-Viking, Dalriadic system, where land rental was paid in pennies or fractions of a penny. Numerous place names around the island come from this ancient system.

native deciduous trees and bushes and not the planted sitka spruce. That makes a real difference and it's more open than the first climb, along with the advantage that you are warmed up now, so it feels easier and is also more scenic.

It doesn't climb quite as high either, so you top out without the same effort as the opening pull-up. The road here tends to hold a fairly straight line as you approach Kingscross, which has an old Viking fort to its credit. As you pass it, there's another fast descent into Whiting Bay and along another pleasant shorefront. This stretch of sea level road lasts longer than Lamlash and stretches south toward Largymore. For the experienced Arran rider, this is taken fairly slowly and enjoyed, because all too soon the honeymoon is over and the serious stuff starts again. Not that I'm complaining, because the next stretch of road for me is the highlight of the whole shooting match.

It starts off fairly straightforward enough as you steadily climb out of the village and away the hillside. But, unlike the climb out of Lamlash, you do not level out quickly this time; far from it. You climb, and you climb, and then climb some more. On the way up, you pass numerous

It just gets better and better as the road then starts to open up as you swing round the south east tip of the island, then it levels for a bit. In front of you now is the Firth of Clyde, and from this vantage point it's an awe-inspiring sight. Before you have a chance to recover your breath, you will soon meet a road going down left to the village of Kildonan, and you have the choice of either descending to it or staying up on the main road.

And just so you can't say I didn't warn you, despite the fact it's a great elongated descent down to this picturesque village with its old castle and beach, the almost straight road back up is truly brutal, even by Arran standards. The first time I made this detour, I rode along the shorefront and wondered what way the road ascended back up to the main road, because I could not see its route no matter how hard I looked. Then I discovered why. The road took a very tight right turn and, as it did, it reared up like an untrained stallion mounted for the first time. I can't begin to tell you how bloody relieved I was when I reached the main road at last, and I can't quite recall my exact thoughts at the time but it was probably "never again".

But soldier on we must. And after reluctantly pulling myself away and starting to head for Blackwaterfoot, I usually can't resist a final look back at my favourite Clyde coast scene, which as always looks great. Here it's seen beyond the South Arran sheep fields.

However, staying high on the main road and passing the road to Kildonan, the climb you're on is also very tough and deceptive. It's one I always find myself getting out the saddle for, and its descent is just as steep and can get a bit hairy in places. This comes before it crosses another wooded burn on a tight bend, and just after that, as it levels out, behold Pladda Lighthouse and Ailsa Craig! Let me just say that as a man who has walked the West Highlands' highest mountains for over 20 years, this view of the western seaboard is equal to the best.

For me, this is the finest sight on the whole run and I assure you that is bloody saying something. I always, and I do mean always, stop at this point and am mesmerised by the silver light of the sea and the vastness of the ocean, which does seem to have a profound effect on me, and on most people.

It can be such an overwhelming feeling of scale, where you get a real sense of your size and place in the whole arena, that it leaves you very much humbled but grateful to be witness to it all. I actually find it a real wrench to start riding again, such is the draw of the setting above Pladda. My feelings can quickly change, however, for some great road and the grand buttress of Bennan Head jutting into the sea lies ahead, always pulling you west.

The road is fairly level on this stretch and it is a welcome rest from all the hard climbing that's gone before. It's across a narrow arable belt that the road now takes you, as there are fields to your left, but high rough ground to the right, fit only for sheep and forestry.

Beyond Bennan, the ground opens out as the long descent down to Kilmory begins, and it suddenly feels like you've dropped into rich dairy farm country. You then plunge into the hollow of Lagg with its palm trees, and you then wonder if you're still in the right country. Lagg is the Gaelic for hollow and, with such a short steep entrance and exit either side of it, it's hard to imagine a

On the big long drop down, heading west on the A-814 towards Kilmory and Lagg. Although the southern half of the island is the more pastoral part, the road is much tougher than its northern, more mountainous counterpart. For the first time, the Mull of Kintyre has come into view

the First World War, then you look around the area and hardly see a house, you can only wonder: where did they all come from? And how did they ever recover from such a heavy loss?

Another historical link can be seen on this memorial, if you know what to look for. One lad who never returned was Lance Corporal Ronald Murchie; he had been with the Canadians. Murchie and McMurchie are surnames found on Arran and the Kintyre peninsula. It just so happened when Hakon left Arran in 1263, he gave the island to one of his men called Murchard. This was a rather unstable appointment, as he was already losing his grip on power. However, it is from Murchard that all these people derive their surname.

Continuing on, the route soon arrives in Sliddery and it is a tough climb out of there, but this one is done in the knowledge that it is the final pull-up on the south coast, after which it gets a lot easier. Your computer should be showing around 19 miles on the clock, and if you haven't tired by now then you are in very good nick indeed.

The road gets a little less challenging now, and if you thought the southern view from the isle was open and airy, then just wait till you swing round west. A full flow

more appropriately named settlement. When you emerge out the other side, huffing and puffing, it's back into a rhythm as you make your way round to the next point of interest, which is the junction with the Ross Road and its old kirk and war memorial.

If, for any reason, you wish to turn back to Brodick, then now is the time to do it, as the Ross — just like the String — offers a short cut back to the ferry.

The Ross is an interesting ride, to say the least, and is the only main road on the island that is still single track. But it can be a tough road too, as it climbs a fair bit before a white knuckle descent drops you back down like a stone into Lamlash. The war memorial that stands guard at its junction is a well-placed reminder that it wasn't just the clearances which depopulated the highlands and islands; Kaiser Bill did his bit as well.

When you see the amount of young men lost, particularly during

Shortly after leaving Lagg, you will soon arrive at a small abandoned kirk which signals the start of the Ross Road. This is a shortcut back to Lamlash, should you require it, and it just so happens to be the only bit of main road left on the island which is single track. It starts off very pretty and pastoral, as can be seen in the sheep fields above, and the single track helps with that feeling.

Another dramatic stretch of coastal road awaits when you start to swing up on the far side of the island. Ahead can be seen the last long gradual pull-up before the equally long gradual descent down into Blackwaterfoot begins. You're high above the water at this point; which adds some drama and also gives a great view across the Kilbrannan Sound to the Mull of Kintyre.

The Ross Road might start off gently pastoral, but it ends rather dramatically with a long, swooping, narrow, twisty fall from great height down into the village of Lamlash right at sea level. The white knuckle ride starts from just about where this picture was taken.

of salt and blue crystal clear water is what you'll find lapping well below you, with the long dark bar of the Mull sitting enticingly across the Kilbrannan Sound.

Make your way fairly speedily down towards the largest west coast settlement of Blackwaterfoot, where the western hills — and in particular, Beinn Bharrain — are prominent from this descent. It is here that the difference between them and the eastern hills is most noticeable. These ones are bulky and rounded, whereas their eastern counterparts are slender and jagged. The significant geological split in the centre of the isle is well highlighted from this point.

Also here, one branch of the String Road offers a way back to the ferry, if you so wish it, and it's a magnificent climb in its own right. However, if continuing on is the plan, then head into the village and be prepared to be

On easy street for a bit now, as it's all downhill into Blackwaterfoot. Plenty of provisions are available there, which is always good to know, and the backdrop of Arran's more rounded western hills adds another dimension to the scene.

charmed by the sight of the small Clauchan Water as it flows into Drumadoon Bay.

Stores are present here, so it's a chance to resupply if you want, and it's a delightful wee seaside bumble over the bridge and along the front. Then as you leave the village, you're soon on a climb that is a lot tougher than it looks and which also overstays its welcome a fair bit.

Away to the right, the flat and wild land that contains the Machrie Water and famous Machrie Moor Standing Stones, lies dense and still. People must have lived here and eked out a living for centuries; God knows how they managed it. The height afforded by this tough wee climb gives a good view of the harshness. The good news is that once you clear this hurdle, you then ride onto a stretch of road that is worth all the effort, for it's Arran's west coast and it's another true gem.

The pleasure starts as you descend to the Machrie Water and its assortment of old boat huts and the like. This place always strikes me as the place where time stood still, fittingly leading you onto the shore and to Machrie itself, with its none too threatening golf course and clubhouse.

I often stop for a bite to eat here, as this spot is as near as dammit the halfway point round the island. It makes sense, with regard to the ferry, to have at least

one break. For if you ride continuously, without stopping, then you arrive back in Brodick in about four hours' time, leaving you around a two hour wait for the next ferry. That's because they depart for Ardrossan roughly every three hours and, as it is well beyond the scope of most riders to do the island in less than three hours, there's no point in busting a gut to get round to Brodick, only to have to sit and twiddle your thumbs for an hour or two.

After the golf course, there is a road on your right that also joins the String Road, and this is the last chance saloon back to the ferry if you are running short of time or energy. Let me warn you, doing the road round the island is a pastime where time can run away very quickly indeed, and you may find yourself even struggling to make the second ferry at 4.40 pm if you dally too much.

The second and last chance to cut the run short comes in the shape of the String Road, which practically splits the island in two. It can be picked up from either Blackwaterfoot or further up at Machrie. It is not an easy option, however, requiring a considerable climb to gain the road's rather fine summit before an equally lengthy descent delivers you back down to Brodick. The photo above is from the high point on the String, just before the drop down to the island's capital begins.

Rowing boat beached at Machrie. And boy, do I really enjoy it here. It is one of my favourite stretches of road to ride, partly because at certain times of the year you can actually just walk onto the pebbly beach and find the gulls' nests without effort. Simply enchanting.

I arrived at the terminal just in time to see the gangplank being lifted. And what made it worse was it was by now a wet, windy, and miserable night. The best part of the next three hours was spent in a local restaurant (the only shelter available), making polite conversation with some old English bloke who came to Arran every year to do a bit of sightseeing and walking. Unfortunately, that year the walking was out of the question, as his legs had gone. All I can remember about him was that he was an Oldham Athletic supporter. (You have been warned. Again!)

As a result of this and other bad experiences, I always carry a certain amount of cash in my saddle bag and strongly recommend you do, too. There is always a chance you might miss the last ferry off an island and need a wee B&B for the night. Even on the mainland, an emergency might crop up — either a mechanical or physical problem — where the train, bus, or perhaps food or some other unexpected resource, is required pronto. So for that reason I've always got a fair wee stash tucked away to ensure that I'm not left totally snookered in the middle of nowhere by some unforeseen circumstance.

On one occasion I had to ride back from the coast totally unwell and starving, because I didn't have a bean to my name. That turned out to be one of those real hard

I speak from bitter experience here. On my first run round the isle, I ended up in Lochranza at 3.40pm, which left only an hour to catch the ferry. Now, on a flat road me and my Lemond Reno could cover that no problem, but I knew that there was a big climb between the two of us[2].

As it happened, despite an all-out lung-bursting effort,

2 - This is the Boguillie.

knock-learning days, you know the ones; the ones you don't forget ever, never mind in a hurry. So take this tip from your old china here, and always carry some dough.

Okay, enough of the warnings, dear rider. What comes next is a stretch of road that features easily in my top three. It's some flat calm tarmac, with usually a light breeze following behind that enables you to simply purr along the road at a tempo that's to your liking, with the sun on your back.

And if that's not enough, this place is so magical that at certain times of the year you can actually pull over and see the gulls' nests only a few yards away on the pebbly shore. It's mostly common gulls and the odd tern's nest that you'll find, with the camouflage pattern of the eggs a delight to witness.

Dropping down into Pirnmill after the vicious; short; sharp pull-up at Imachar point. From here up to Lochranza is none too taxing; and the setting along cliff sides with crashing waves below makes for some top drawer riding.

to Pirnmill. This small settlement was named after the wooden bobbins (pirns) that were once made here for holding thread and were sent mostly to the mills in Paisley.

I've no idea where the mill was, as I can find no remains of it. The modern village, however, does seem to be going fairly strong, as there is a shop/post office, small bistro, and primary school to be found here.

The going is still flat and gentle as you continue to purr along the coast out of the village, but after a mile or so, you encounter the road going up and down fairly violently like a roller coaster ride. Not for long, though. When you clear this rocky headland, you glide into the curvaceous Catacol Bay, with its stunning glen and strikingly steep heather-clad braes.

As a keen hill man, let me tell you that there are few places I have ever seen from the road whose setting entices me so much or so continuously as Catacol Bay.

Suddenly it becomes idyllic as the Kilbrannan Sound is met face-to-face again on the island's far side. The deceptively tough wee section coming out of Blackwaterfoot is behind us now, and it's onto the flat coast road we trundle. This photo was taken beside the odd-shaped boathouses and their launch jetties, seen above, at the mouth of the Lorsa Water.

To add to the tranquillity, the Kilbrannan Sound can, on occasion, be almost mirror-like, as it gently shimmers away into its great broadness, spreading all the way across towards the gentle height of Kintyre, semi-hidden in the far distance. This Shangri-La continues til you hit the abrupt ramp at Imachar Point, and then you're up like a rocket. Short and brutal are the only words to describe this rise, but you soon level out at a house full of roosters and other assorted fowl.

This rather unwelcome interruption to your nirvana is soon remedied, however, as you just as quickly dive down to the shore again. First, heading through the Norse-named Whitefarland, and then along the coast

Approaching Catacol Bay, with the Kilbrannan Sound looking like a mill pond. Calm hot conditions can make the far side of Arran a total Shangri La to ride.

Looking across Catacol Bay to the row of white cottages that are known as the 12 Apostles. The skirt round the bay itself is up there with the best of them for charm, as is the much anticipated run in to Lochranza which is just about to follow.

The geometry of the valley, with its rounded tops smartly dressed in their fern green and heather purple coats most perfectly complemented by the natural glen of the Catacol Burn, always strikes me as an avenue into this hidden prize that's secretly stashed away in this quiet corner of the island.

As you curve out of the bay itself, you meet the so-called 12 Apostles — the row of white cottages which were purpose-built to accommodate some of the displaced crofters from the glens. Needless to say, twelve houses were nowhere near enough to fill the demand, hence the need for the earlier mentioned emigration from Lamlash.

The lapping waves from the Kilbrannan Sound, which has been your constant companion the length of the west coast, will at all times show a uniform clearness as they pound the rocks and pebbles either below or beside you,

Finally, the top of the island is reached, and after passing the Lochranza to Claonaig ferry terminal, it's round the bend and into the stunning shelter of the loch itself.

Lochranza Castle looks stunning as always, set against the backdrop of grandly risen hills. It is very difficult not to fall in love with the village at first sight and to start planning your retirement here, literally. I usually linger a while due to the prettiness of the setting and also because I know what awaits the moment I leave the village — the long hard haul up the island's longest climb, the Boguillie.

This is the scene that greets you if you arrive into Lochranza from the other direction, after dropping straight off the Boguillie. It is equally as enchanting as coming the other way, of course.

Despite being long, though none too sustained, and with several false summits, the top of the Boguillie is eventually reached. You know when you are getting close because that unmistakable jagged gash high up in the mountains, the Ceum na Caillich (the witch's step), puts in an appearance.

and constantly throw you fresh salt air to power your lungs and boost the feelgood factor.

Then before you know it, the village of Lochranza is upon you. This means that you have reached the top of the isle, and the first thing you see is the ferry terminal which links the island with the Kintyre Peninsula. From here, you swing into the village itself, with its sheltering loch and stunning setting, enhanced by its prominently placed castle. Picturesque is a word that does not do Lochranza justice. It really is the sort of place that visitors can and do fall in love with at first sight. It only takes a glimpse of the village's cottages and its ambling shore road, running alongside then round the head of its small sea loch, for this to happen.

It is the sort of place where you could easily see yourself contentedly living out your retirement, without work or deadlines to care about. The castle has been restored to a pretty good standard in the last few years, and it certainly adds to the feeling off 'specialness' in this quiet delight.

The building itself dates back to the 13th century when the McSween family appear to have been the first owners. But it soon became royal property and was granted to Walter the Steward by Alexander III (he of the Battle of Largs fame). Robert II used it as a hunting lodge, but it was strictly business for James IV who used it as a base to tackle the Lords of the Isles. And it was put to similar use by the unstoppable Oliver Cromwell in the 1650s.

Initially it was an L-shaped tower house, but was added to extensively in the 16th century and that's what you see restored today. To sit at ease on the shore of Lochranza itself and watch the sunset, is a most enjoyable and memorable way to finish your day if you're staying in the vicinity.

There are two things that make you want to linger in the village — one is the aforementioned scenery, and the other is the Boguillie. This is the longest and most sustained climb on the whole island. It starts the second you leave Lochranza and takes about 15 minutes to clear.

Now, it does have a fairly steep and brutal beginning to it, but once you clear that, it takes a less serious route up and through Glen Chalmadale. In fact, it actually goes downhill slightly at one particular stretch. So just the thought of the bugger can make you linger a while longer down by the shore, but you know in your heart of hearts it needs to be tackled, so off you go.

As always, after lingering a while longer than is good for you, you have a struggle getting into the swing again, but it doesn't take too long to do that on the early steep section of the Boguillie. Then the downhill stretch is a

This is the view from the top of the Boguillie looking right down Glen Chalmadale towards Lochranza. Even if I am going the other way and am Brodick-bound; I always stop and have a look back; knowing that the last tough climb on the island is now behind me.

welcome relief, which allows you to get your breath back, before the bulk of the hill is tackled.

As it starts to re-ascend, it's simply a case of slogging your way up, getting a good rhythm and douring it out. Like a lot of good climbs, the gradient tends to increase as you near top-out. However, the real sting in the tail of this climb is not only the amount of miles that you have in your legs, but also that it has several false summits.

Two things will let you know when you're nearing the top. The first will be the magnificent Ceum na Caillich (the witch's step), which is the jagged mountain gash appearing high up to your right, which starts to appear only when you gain most of the height required. It is a most awe-inspiring sight, and reveals more and more of itself as you get higher.

The second marker, which does indicate the actual top, is less dramatic though just as handy, and that is the parking sign for the top layby. When it comes into view, you're almost over. Now comes a long, fast, and at times precarious descent down the other side.

A fairly close up view showing the grandeur and fearsome steepness of Arran's northern mountains, in particular the Cioch na h-Oighe (the maiden's breast) can be seen just before you drop down into Sannox.

After hitting the bottom, you then cross the burn coming out of North Glen Sannox, where another rise presents itself. But I can assure you that you will be so pumped up by now that you will simply fly over it, before enjoying the speed downhill, which brings you back into the woods and dry stane dykes of Sannox.

Your speed will be checked quite abruptly as a very sharp right turn over the Sannox Burn must be made, and then… what do you know? You're back on the coast. Congratulations are kind of in order here, for although it's still around 7 miles back to the ferry, all the climbing and hard riding is over and it's time to enjoy the flatness of the east coast road this time.

The small settlement of Sannox itself is quickly passed through, as you make your way back down the shore road and next you reach the very picturesque village of Corrie. It is such a pretty village that you may find yourself slowing down just to enjoy it that little bit more, especially the small harbour with its quaint touches. The road also pleases here, with a curve and twist that adds to the pleasure.

Some of the stone-built cottages really do look like they are the last word in cosy delightfulness, and I believe Corrie itself won some sort of award for being one of the country's most beautiful places to live. As you leave

Well, it used to be precarious, or at least a lot more precarious, because only recently did they resurface the road coming off the Boguillie, which has made a tremendous difference. On the descent it is possible to get up and over the 40 mile an hour mark, easily, with some real daredevils going a lot faster than that. Certainly, now that the worry of wrecked rims and dodgy surfaces has been taken out the equation, it's a lot faster, safer, and exhilarating to descend at speed.

The Holy Island likes to put in an appearance continuously as you fly down the island's wonderful waterside flat tar. This takes you for all of 7.7 miles through Sannox then pretty Corrie, all the way to the ferry while hardly rising a foot. As you go, keep your eye open for basking seals just offshore.

it, you do feel slightly uplifted by its prettiness and also because it is the last settlement you pass through before Brodick.

The east coast of the island can be a bit of a suntrap and also tends to be more sheltered and less breezy than the west. So if it has been a hot day, you may start to feel the effects here of all the heat and the hard riding that you have done. It helps to know that the end is drawing near, as you skirt the rocky coastline on hot, dry tarmac.

As you do, keep an eye out for seals basking on the boulders and skerries just to your left. Merkland Point is a favourite place for them to do their

A silent sleepy Brodick Bay is found on this occasion, but that isn't always the case. Far from it. Here it's pointed Beinn Nuis (hill of the fawns) that overlooks a solitary yacht lying berthed in the bay awaiting a sail on another day.

sunbathing and these guys always delight whether in or out of the water. It's about this time that you will start to draw level with Brodick Castle's grounds and the massive covering of rhododendrons.

You come off the coast slightly as you ride towards the bridge over the Rosa Water, going under lovely deciduous woodland as you do, and then it's back to the hustle and bustle, because the bridge is just on the edge of town and also meets up with the String Road right here.

One thing I have noticed about a lot of island main towns is that there is always a tremendous buzz and busyness about them, particularly with traffic, but the moment you are over the town boundary the vehicles all seem to vanish. Well, it's exactly the opposite in reverse. From a tranquil country road, you are now suddenly faced with autos a plenty, kids with cones, kids in prams, kids with mums (some very stressed), more people than bloody Sauchiehall Street, and for the first time in 55 miles, drivers with parking problems. Now where have they all been hiding, I hear you ask? Well don't ask me, I don't know either.

By now you are back at the ferry terminal and on a sunny summer's day, particularly if it's the weekend, the place will be let's just say a bit too busy for my liking. However, I will not let the crowds — or anything else for that matter — take away my feeling of contentment at once again having circled the island. It's a great but tiring achievement to do the round, and at this moment the fact that I still have to ride the lang Scots miles back to Paisley doesn't yet enter my mind.

The next period is one of rest and recuperation. What you do next is personal with regard to rest, and in particular nutrition. Some guys will head for the chippy and reload the carbohydrates, or visit the supermarket across the road and get something else to refill the fuel tank.

One rule of nutrition that is good to know if you are just starting out, is that after a hard run, any carbs you eat within 20 minutes of stopping will go into your liver and be stored as energy in the shape of glycogen. After the 20 minute mark, however, they will be stored by the body as fat. So only reload with the carbs for no more than the first 20 minutes.

After that, it is just a case of waiting for the ferry to arrive back, before embarking again. Rather than head for the coffee club straightaway this time, it can be quite memorable and poignant to sit on the deck and bid Arran farewell with a promise to return. As you do this, I assure you that all the suffering on the hot hard climbs will be long forgotten, and only the feeling of fatigued pleasure will remain.

You do often feel tired on the way back, but not always; it depends on how fit you are at any given time. The hour crossing back to Ardrossan will, of course, feel faster than the outward journey, as the thought of having to remount the trusted steed is none too appealing. But mount it you must, before you're off again into the evening sunshine, with the breeze hopefully behind.

It does take a bit of an amble up the harbour road for the old stiff limbs to get going again, but you at least have a flat stretch of road to do it on. The home route back to Glenburn is exactly the same as the outward route, but of course that great ride down to the ferry earlier in the day will now prove to be a real tough test as you climb out of Ardrossan back up the hill towards Dalry.

This pull-up is probably the hardest one of the whole day, if not physically then certainly mentally. But once you clear it, it's then flat and down among the green and the reservoirs. The sweeping curves and bends on the B-780 bring you quickly back to the North Ayrshire town, which you don't actually see till the last minute, as you dive very fast into the hill that leads toward the centre. I try and make the most of going through Dalry, because I know it's a fairly steep pull-up out of there, and at this stage of the day it isn't what you want, as muscles are feeling the effect of the effort.

The single track back roads are pleasant enough to follow, though, hemming you in and carrying you homeward through the rough pastures. And while not being too demanding, there is one exertion to negotiate, which is in fact the short steep climb on the B-706, which links the two long lesser back roads which carry you west to east, all the way back to Gateside. Then when Gateside is reached, it is for the most part a long meandering rising road back up to the Greenacres Hotel.

With the sun glistening on the majestic Rowbank Reservoir, turn right at Tower Cottage, where it's back onto the Cromwellian tarmac then up and over Windy Hill. As Windy is crested, you know the worst is over as you're at the highest point on the return.

Batter on down this great scruffy hill road until its junction, then head up right to the farm of Hartfield, again on an equally scruffy road. This time, instead of going straight on, turn left — this will be the only slight detour from the outward journey.

You find yourself on a quite sensational tree-lined road leading to the farm itself, which has, if you know where to look, a small memorial in the left hand field, situated between a gap in the trees. It was put there in memory of a young Yankee flyer called Herman Carey, who crashed his Mustang while out flying in December 1941. After passing that, it's onto the farm itself and the only drawback of coming this way is that sometimes the road can be covered in a lot of muck, though sometimes not. If not, you're sorted.

After the buildings, the road gets better as it double bends brilliantly away to the left at first, then hard right, opening up as it does a superb view away north, in which, more often than not, mighty Ben Lomond will be the star of the scene.

This is followed by a straight fast dive down, all done — with a bit of luck — in brilliant evening sunshine, while still on the tight scruffy back roads in which this area specialises. It really is a screamer, which should provide enough oomph to propel you on as far as the bridge over the Brandy Burn. From there it's an easy pull-up to the main road, my old mate the B-775.

A left turn leads towards Gleniffer and this is a spectacular way to finish as always, but more especially so when returning from such a mega day out. The Arrochar and Loch Lomond hills are easily seen away to the northwest, and as I crest the top of the Braes, it will be near as dammit 7pm — 11 hours from when I was here on the road out, and a good hundred miles on the clock.

More than at any other time, I am grateful for not having to turn the cranks til I reach my front door, for as buoyed up as I am, I am still glad to climb off and rest.

That, to my mind, is the King of Runs done once again, and I can't help but hold a special fondness for that most magical of places; to ride it door-to-door is a day that no other day can match for specialness.

I hope I have conveyed in some way the wonderful quality of day and enchantment that a ride round this Clyde coast gem can bring. I know the world over has wonders I have never experienced, but although no doubt they are equally as good, there will be none better than

And with the return to the ferry, it means that finally another great run round this most special island has come to an end. Some will be elated and happy with what has gone before, but others will be exhausted and glad it's all over. Magnificent it is, but easy it's not; 55.4 miles according to my computer. However, no matter what my state of mind, I always go out on deck as the boat leaves port and make a promise to return. I advise you to do the same.

our own western seaboard, sensational in the sunshine, but as magical in the mist.

Till we ride again…

N.B. CALMAC ADDITIONAL SUMMER SAILINGS.

From the summer of 2013, additional summer sailings were provided on the Ardrossan to Brodick route, with the inclusion of a second vessel, the *Isle of Arran*. This old stalwart is now the fleet's relief vessel, after years of plying between Kennacraig to Islay, though as her name suggests, she originally started off on the Arran run. The sailing times mentioned in the route description will still apply from autumn to spring, but from May to September a bit more scope for manoeuvrability is now possible.

As a general rough guide, the service in 2013/14 was practically doubled from Monday to Wednesday, with one ship leaving Ardrossan as the other leaves Brodick. From Thursday to Sunday, one or two sailings a day were missing, with regards to the relief boats sailings only.

This was because Cal-Mac are also using the *Isle of Arran* (the boat that is) to try out a new route between Ardrossan and Campbeltown, which in 2013/14 only took place in the latter part of the week. Therefore, the *Isle of Arran* had to be pulled off the Ardrossan to Brodick route to cover the Campbeltown runs between Thursday and Sunday.

The main boat, the *Caledonian Isles*, is unaffected by this and so the two main sailings I highlighted on my trip — the 9.45am from Ardrossan and the 4.40pm from Brodick — are always your reliable stalwarts.

The new boat did, however, provide one or two really good options on most days in 2014, though that may not be the case in subsequent summers. That is because the Campbeltown run does not appear to have a very good initial timetable and this may be subject to change. If so, this would have a knock-on effect and subsequently change the additional sailings from Ardrossan to Brodick.

These additional sailings across to Arran were first introduced in 2011, but not 2012, where they were used for freight only. Cal-Mac made no mention of these extra sailings in their 2013 timetables, and this prompted me to think that the additional sailings had been a pilot scheme which had been abandoned.

It was only when I was crossing on the 9.45am to Brodick, with cup of tea in hand and gazing out the window, that I spotted the other ferry going in the opposite direction and realised what was going on. When I enquired at Ardrossan why there was no mention of the additional sailings in the brochures, I was told that there had been some doubt early on as to the exact timetable and, as the printing is done well in advance, it was decided not to include them.

As it stands at the time of writing, there are one or two of the new sailing times which can be very handy for the bike rider. Most noticeably, the 11.05am sailing from Ardrossan allows you 4½ hours to go round the island and catch the 4.40pm sailing from Brodick, and means there is no slack time to kill. This is also the case with the 3.15pm sailing from Brodick (not Sunday, unfortunately), which means if you caught the 9.45am sailing from Ardrossan, then the island can be circumnavigated, but again with no slack time to kill. This pairing also allows you 4½ hours to do it in, and most competent riders can do it comfortably in 4.

At the moment, it will have to be a case of wait and see what the timetable will be when the summer season arrives, and make your best plans then. As far as I can gather there will be additional sailings running till 2016 at least, though this is unconfirmed. Although we are no worse off if they don't run, I must say they have been a very welcome addition to the show. That said, if I'm being honest, I would have to say that taking your time and aiming for the six hour time slot is a lot more leisurely and enjoyable. But as always, you suit yourself

Liam Boy.

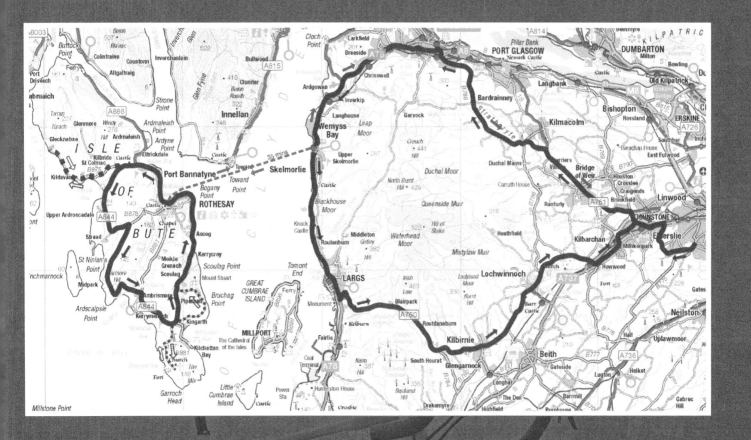

THE ISLE OF BUTE

RETURN VIA LARGS
94.8 MILES
6.11 HOURS
ASCENT : 4320 FEET
4071 CALS BURNED

RETURN VIA GREENOCK
92.5 MILES
6.04 HOURS
ASCENT: 4400 FEET
4072 CALS BURNED

FROM WEYMSS BAY
39.2 MILES
2.31 HOURS
ASCENT 1380 FEET
1710 CALS BURNED

O'S LANDRANGER MAPS 64, 63.

CAL MAC WEYMSS BAY TEL NO 01475 520521.

ROUTE SUMMARY

Elderslie
Johnstone
Kilbarchan
Quarriers
Auchmountain Rd
Greenock
Inverkip
Wemyss Bay

Isle Of Bute (Anti Clockwise)

RETURN VIA LARGS   RETURN VIA GREENOCK

Wemyss Bay   Outward Route In Reverse Order
Largs
Kilbirnie
Lochwinnoch
Howwood
Johnstone
Elderslie
Paisley

THE ROTHESAY RUN

I f the Arran run is the King of runs, then this next one seems to have an equally magical hold over me personally. And despite the fact people say you should not have them, I have to confess that this one is probably my favourite and the one I like to do most often. That is the tour round the Isle of Bute, or simply the Rothesay run.

I would like to point out that before I did any road riding, I had never put foot on the Isle of Bute as an adult or a kid. I have met numerous adults in my surrounding area that spent time there with their families when they were saucepan lids (kids), and as such have very fond, nae a rose-tinted specs view of the place.

Not so your old mate Liam boy, no siree. Up until I rolled the old Lemond Reno onto its hallowed tarmac some summer's day back in the early noughties, I had never so much as shoved a tiny plastic spade into its sands or stuffed a cone into my tiny gub. There was no expectation in my mind's eye or golden memories of bygone days to lull me into dewy-eyed romantic views of a place that has long since seen its heyday, and is now enjoying a retirement of tranquil gentle decay. For the record, my family spent those sorts of days in either Saltcoats, Largs, or Ayr.

Why do I mention this? Well, it's because I want you to realise that, just like all Scottish islands, the Rothesay girl is no less attractive than her other more vaunted cousins in the Inner or Outer Hebrides, and is also in no way taken from by the fact that she was once a tourist hotspot, albeit a long time back. Quite the opposite, in fact. She has a charm all of her own that is as unique as it is gentle, and in that lies her secret; her gentleness. Compared, that is, to a lot of her counterparts, in particular next door neighbour, the jagged Isle of Arran.

So that is what awaits at the end of the half hour ferry trip from Wemyss Bay. A delight that isn't appreciated from the shore of the Clyde coast as you wait the Cal-Mac ferry's arrival. What is appreciated, however, is the finely built Victorian railway station which is adjacent to the pier itself. This was built by James Miller back in

61

Hay bales waiting for collection at East Green Farm on the B-788 Kilmacolm to Greenock road. This is my normal approach road, though I usually join it slightly further up at Gateside. It is very soft and pastoral in its early stages, but becomes much rougher and more moor-like when it becomes the Auchenfoil Road up ahead.

1903 and, despite it being erected in the Victorian era, the outside and clock tower has a sort of Queen Anne, mock Tudor front, which does lend it a certain antiquated charm.

Inside, you are met by a most impressive piece of architecture, as the ticket office is housed in a semi-circular central pillar, from which sprouts the most magnificent array of curving iron girders and intertwined glass panels, radiating skyward in such a way as to shame any ornate church interior. This, when photographed using a wide angle or even fish eye lens, produces the most stunning of shots.

To gain your ticket for the crossing, you have two choices. For expediency, you have a small cabin at the top of the car park, or you can make your way into the station, then down the enclosed wooden pier to the main office. I read somewhere that the pier was enclosed to protect the ladies' hats from the wind as they made their way from steam train to paddle steamer. I don't know if that is true or not, but if so, it certainly strikes of no expense spared and would be in keeping with the times of the Clyde's Victorian holiday heyday. Even now, Rothesay still gets over one million visitors a year and that is quite incredible in a country of less than 5 million people.

To get to Wemyss Bay for me is also quite a run in itself and is around the 26 mile mark from Paisley. It can have a few variations at the start, but once Greenock is reached, it tends to be a fairly straightforward route. I will more often than not leave around 10 o'clock[1] to give ample time to make the noon ferry, which for years left at 12:15pm,

1 - I am no early bird, being a night-time worker.

but recently was brought forward to midday exactly, to coincide with the trains or some reason like that. This has made catching it a little bit more stressful on occasion.

Bearing in mind the type of road that will be taken near the start of today's run, I want to give you another important riding tip; this one is on cornering and how to take a bend safely and quickly. When approaching a corner or coming into a tight swift bend, get down low and spread your weight evenly. If it is a long, fast descent, get low in the hooks and bend your elbows as your arms will now become your shock absorbers in such instances. Lean the bike into the bend but keep your body as upright as possible to maintain your centre of gravity.

Put your weight onto the outside foot, where the leg should be more or less straight, and you can either have your inside knee (the one on the side you are leaning into) either tight up against the top tube, or swung out pointing into the corner. I use both methods, and recommend you try both ways to see which works best for you.

If you have to use the brakes, only feather them slightly so that you don't lock up the back brake. On top of that, look where you want to go, because simply where you look you will go. This technique will allow you to corner quicker and better than any other I know, but be smart and start off on gentle slow bends until you get the hang of it.

So armed with that, off we go on today's jaunt, and Wemyss Bay here we come. The most pleasant and traffic-free road route I take is to leave Glenburn by Foxbar Road, after which we continue on down into the fast-bending and little known Mackie's Mill Road, leading onto the fast-bending, very well known Glenpatrick (Brandy Burn) Road. This runs us into pretty Elderslie, where the first left turn takes you on the Abbey (cemetery) Road, running the row of white houses, and shortly leading by leafy bend to the Thorn Brae at the start of Johnstone.

The route continues by following the Beith Road as far as either Quarrelton or Milliken Park Road, where a right turn on either will lead you down toward the village of Kilbarchan. If you know where to look on some of the houses as you enter the place, you will see them marked as being built around the 1770s. This old textile village seems crammed full of fantastic old buildings of that period, and makes the fairly tough climb ahead a lot more bearable as you hit it. Then, after making your way up the lengthy gradient, passing the old solid white houses of the Wheatlands estate, it's out into open country for just a short time, before entering into the top end of Bridge of Weir.

It's a short, pretty stretch of road you cover between the two, and — being quite high — you can enjoy the view across the fields for some distance, which includes far Ben Lomond. Unfortunately, the height is lost rapidly, as a steep descent is made into the village itself. You only need to stay on the busy main road for a short time before taking the first left under the old rail bridge, then you are out on the road towards Quarriers Village. The rail bridge now houses the Glasgow to Greenock cycle track and can be used to access the coast or surrounding area, if so wished.

I often use it myself as far as here or beyond, though I prefer to stay roadside a lot of the time, otherwise I find I have to constantly slow down to avoid seemingly deaf dog walkers and their mutts, prams and their pushers, and

A fantastic view of Greenock and the Clyde is accompanied by the full-on rush of speed as the early top steep bends on the Auchmountain Road are negotiated. This comes when the high point on the B-788 has just been ridden and the fall down into Inverclyde begins. All in all, it is a sensational situationand one to look forward to with great anticipation every time. It will never disappoint.

carry-out swigging young teams on a Friday and Saturday night. So the road is my preference, and it's certainly true of this one.

There is a great delight in riding out of town on the Torr Road with the pretty River Gryfe for company, meandering gently down to your right. This continues til the approaching Y-junction is reached, and the right hand fork takes you through the incredible Quarriers village.

This is not a village as such, but rather a collection of large sandstone houses, built here in 1876 to house orphaned children. And it was all the brainchild of

Glasgow shoe maker and philanthropist, William Quarrier. It has to be said that it is a most stunning array of individual buildings and quite an achievement by this remarkable man. All the buildings are different, and each one is as splendid as the next, with the Mount Zion Church probably just stealing the show. I just hope that the accommodation and the beautiful surroundings were a comfort to, and had a positive effect on, the quality of life for the unfortunate souls who found themselves orphaned in harsh Victorian Britain.

It's a straight road through, so you leave as fast as you enter, and it's then into the pretty dairy fields as you approach the Lochwinnoch to Kilmacolm road (the B-786). It's there you turn right and then immediately left, up alongside the Mill Burn, past Glenmill and South Newton Farms, twisting and turning on the single track road for a mile or two, eventually leading out onto the Kilmacolm to Greenock back road (the B-788) just at Gateside Farm. At first it's still enjoyable rural road riding, but passing Cairncurran Farm you find yourself on a steep but short, fairly brutal wee climb, which when topped out opens up the road and fields ahead of you.

The road brings you down and then along, straight as a die, to a difficult and meandering pull-up, which means you're onto the Auchenfoil Road.

This leads from green pastures to rough moorland and a highly-perched electricity substation which, when passed, means you're over 200 metres above the Clyde and perfectly positioned and privileged to witness a panorama of hills and sea lochs that open up to almost take your breath away. It is a sight that is both as fast moving as it stunning, because after passing the small Knockensnair's Hill Reservoir, the top of the Auchmountain Road is reached at a diving left hand bend. This will then allow the full panorama of Inverclyde to open up as you pick up speed very quickly, hitting some inviting early bends. At the same time, the dramatic sweep of the Arrochar Hills, the Clyde along with the Gare Loch and the entrance to Loch Long, all hit you simultaneously. So, too, do the old shipyard towns of Greenock and Port Glasgow, as you curve and accelerate wonderfully through the top bends of this magnificent descent.

The speed you can reach coming down the Auchmountain can take you up to the high 30s or so very easily, so a lot of focus is required to keep you safe on the descent. Therefore, not too much time — or anything else for that matter — is left to fully take in the sensational setting that you are diving into. But it is such a striking seaboard, that even this fast-moving glimpse will be etched on your memory.

Coming out of the early high bends, the road straightens as it enters the top end of Greenock itself, and you're into a different world entirely. No more dairy fields and moorland vistas, not now, for this is the home of James Watt and the steam age, ship building, and sugar refineries; or rather, it was.

Like the rest of the heavy industry that once supported this part of the world for well over a hundred years and then some, it's now no longer. Once the massive crane of the Scott Lithgow shipbuilding yard dominated the skyline, but I believe it was sold off to some South Korean yard.

Just to give you some idea of the tradition of this great industrial town, when Scott Lithgow closed its doors in 1988, it was the oldest shipyard in the world. It also once boasted 14 sugar refineries, and that was partly because the town was ideally situated to provide a main ingredient for the refining job — fresh, fast flowing water. This comes from the hills above the town in the shape of numerous burns, and Greenock's reputation for high rainfall is well justified.

Also, but probably more importantly, the sugar cane was imported directly to Greenock from the Caribbean, and deposited in the James Watt Dock, where the volume constituted around 400 ships a year. So that is the contrast that greets you at the bottom of this magnificent descent of two miles or so, which is finished off with a near ramp-like drop and turn under the rail bridge and onto bonny Belville Street.

Go left down to the lights, still descending, then that all stops rather too abruptly when you turn left again, this time onto Baker Street, where you hit the opposite number of the ramp you came down a minute or so ago. The road rears up steeply, forcefully and grittily; the grittiness added to by the close proximity of old and red-bricked buildings, til it turns the bend, and only then does its gradient relent.

Just to test your stamina, it climbs long and relentlessly up through the Broomhill estate, climbing most of the length of the Drumfrocher Road and Cornhaddock Street. No disrespect to the residents of this area, but although I would say that it still appears a really poor-looking, run-down and dank road, especially in the rain, it has been greatly enhanced by the removal of the old

Tate and Lyle sugar refinery which once graced both sides of the street. To further add to the gloomy appearance, there was a part of the factory which crossed above the road in the shape of a dark blue iron corridor, and gave the whole place a really oppressive look.

The Tate and Lyle plant was the last sugar refinery to close (in 1997), and so ended 150 years of that industry in Greenock. It's fair to say that the company is the best known sugar supplier in the country and came together when local refiner Abraham Lyle (also a cooper and shipbuilder), joined forces with his Liverpool counterpart, the equally successful Henry Tate. The rest, as they say, is history.

As the crest of the Drumfrochar Road is reached, the turn for the Old Largs Road (scenic route) is passed on the left, then it's over the top with a speedy dive down Dunlop Street. This, believe me, is greatly welcome, before you then you hit the busy A-78 Inverkip Road and, after turning left, it's a straight road all the way to Wemyss Bay.

There is, however, a fair bit of upping and downing between here and the ferry, and it starts right away with the pull-up to Branchton station. But it's followed by a great drop that carries you out of Greenock and into the Spango Valley, passing the impressive-looking former IBM Plant. Now there's a place! I say former plant, because it's now only partly-owned by the American corporate giant, but back in the eighties it was one of the few big employers in the area. They, along with one or two others, were offered sweeteners by the Government of the day to come to the town to take the sting out of losing our heavy industry.

These modern hi-tech companies were supposed to be the future in investment and employment. Suffice to say, they were a spent force after only twenty years, while the heavy industry supported the area for nearer two hundred.

As you pass the factory, there is a long inviting pull-up ahead and one I always relish the challenge of, because no matter what gear I'm in, I only allow myself one gear drop on the entire climb. Then I get my breath back on the equally long and elegant descent that follows back down to sea level, ending at the large roundabout which can take you back into Gourock, if you so wish.

Straight ahead is our choice here, though, and it takes us almost immediately into Inverkip, with its large marina and dazzling display of yachts, along with its overpriced quayside development.

The superb central pillar of Wemyss Bay station is as fine an example of Victorian architecture as you will find anywhere. I always go in and admire it every time I'm down there. The old Victorian toiletsare also more than fit for purpose, whether to answer a call of nature or — just as important — to fill the old water bottles.

If you live too far away to ride to Wemyss Bay, then coming down by train for a jaunt round the island, especially with the kids, is a most scenic and enjoyable way to get there. This will be the classic Clyde scene that greets you when you arrive at the station.

This view of the station shows the grandest of enclosed walkways down to the ferry and ticket office. You don't have to ride all the way down there to get your ticket, however, as there is a conveniently placed cabin out in the car park that does the same job. I believe the enclosed walkway was constructed to prevent the wind blowing away ladies' hats when they were boarding the steam ships of old.

The road here feels tight and busy with traffic, as the A-78 trunk road is down to single carriageway, which wasn't the case as you passed IBM. There it was roomy dual carriage and the traffic felt a lot further away. It's a flat road right through Inverkip, though, as you're right down at sea level with the Clyde close by on your right. So it takes no time to fly through it, and next stop is your destination. But there is still one more climb left and it is a bit of a pecker. At times you will be hard pressed to make your ferry, and a time-consuming pull-up is the last thing that you need.

However, it must be done and it is best tackled with a moderate rhythm rather than a lung-bursting attack. It is a hill that goes on for longer than anticipated and, as there has been a fair bit of climbing done since leaving home, it would be all too easy to blow up a bit at least. The good news is that once over it, there is a straight, flat section of road, followed by a great descent down and under the rail bridge, then along to the ferry and rail station itself. So, just over 26 miles from leaving home and around the 1 hour 40 mark, I find myself outside the Sea View Café and opposite the pier, with the new electronic sign displaying when the next sailing is due to depart.

If I have time, I grab a coffee and treat from the café, then like to go into the station and marvel time and again at the magnificent Victorian glass and iron construction of yesteryear. The other thing of note at the terminal is the war memorial to the fallen of Wemyss Bay and Skelmorlie and, like all our war memorials, the First World War part

Right across the road from the ferry sits my favourite café, and I do like to go in and get a wee sweet treat and a coffee before boarding. You will be spoiled for choice with regards to cakes and scones. Don't worry, you won't gain any weight after all the fairly tough riding down, as any carbs consumed will only replenish the glycogen stores.

has many more names than the second. One particularly sad note about this one is that there appears to be three brothers called Dixon (Alexander, Neil and William; all Privates), who fell and never returned — a devastating blow for any family. Neil, incidentally, won the Military Medal.

Most ferries leave approximately one hour apart, though not always on the hour. So it's best to know your times and the one you are aiming for, to help you get your timing right. Soon the ferry arrives and on you go, with a hey and a ho, and a hey nanny no.

It's break time for half an hour or so and that is a real nice length of time to sail; not too long to get bored, yet enough time to replenish the food and fuel stores. The crossing is pleasant, though not spectacular, and the one

The author killing some time and messing around on the sail over to Rothesay. On this occasion, I'm wearing one of my favourite tops once worn by the Spanish Banesto team.

main point of interest is the gleaming white structure of Toward Point Lighthouse, which is passed roughly halfway on the starboard side. Then, before you know it, Rothesay Bay is reached, turning and swirling all around, as the ferry manoeuvres itself stern first into position to allow disembarkation to Scotland's Madeira.

Similar to Arran, you have a dilemma as to whether to go round the isle clockwise or widdershins, and as before, the wind will be a major factor in that decision. However, here it's not as serious as Arran, and the shortcut roads and distances are less daunting so a more relaxed approach is definitely recommended.

It is my belief that to fully appreciate either Bute or Arran, it is best to do both islands in both directions and preferably several times each. Just for fairness, as Arran was done clockwise, I shall take you round Rothesay anti.

A lone yacht out enjoying the sunshine just as much as me, as we pass Toward Lighthouse. It is a fine structure and sight, and one of the highlights on the way over.

Just before the swirl into Rothesay Bay is made, there is a tremendous view up the Clyde towards the mouth of Loch Striven. The broad blue of the Clyde, with the first real view of the day of its mountain backdrop, is a mesmerising sight which is guaranteed to hold your gaze.

So, like its big neighbour Arran, the first taste of Bute is the main town Rothesay, which is identical to Brodick in its hustle and bustle. Cars, kids, taxis, ferry traffic, coming and going all in the one small space and a bit of a seafront atmosphere, all make for a noisy and exciting entry to this well-worn gem.

Take a right turn and glide along the seafront and, in only a couple of hundred yards or so, it soon all goes quiet again and feels like the land time forgot. The buildings on your left stare out into the bay, with most of them looking as old as the island itself, and as you curve flatly round, the salt air, along with the whole setting, blows away any cobwebs that you may have gathered sitting on the boat, leaving you raring to go.

But one thing that will break your stare of the Clyde and the Striven will be Rothesay itself. It has a warm welcoming none-too-threatening persona about it, as does the whole island, to be honest. The soft gentle decay that encompasses most of its buildings makes you feel like you are stepping into a pair of your comfiest old slippers. That said, I think the jagged peaks of Arran sitting behind, give it some edge.

The buildings themselves are a real mixed bag, with not more than two in a trot being identical, so it comes across as a real hotchpotch of individual properties, and this also adds to the uniqueness and charm of the place. As you head north towards Port Bannatyne (formerly known as Kamesburgh), you pass the Skeoch Wood and it's this bit of greenery that sort of separates the two places. At the same time you are looking into the mighty Loch Striven, along with the Cowal Hills, and that, along with the gulps of more fresh salt air, puts you in real true up-time. You're on a natural high at this point.

Just for the record, the Second World War came to Rothesay big time, and there was a specialist midget submarine flotilla that was based here. It did a lot of its training in the Striven. These men had the audacity to attack the Tirpitz, and also launched attacks in enemy ports such as Palermo and La Spezia. For such a small unit, they were awarded an outstanding three VCs.

Now you have a choice to make, for you will soon reach a fork in the road and it is either right to hug the coast, or left to go along the Ardbeg to Port Bannatyne main drag. The coast may appear the more scenic option, and therefore the best choice, but as good as it is, the main drag is just as good in an entirely different way.

Like Rothesay Town itself, it's crammed full of the most individual and delightful buildings along the way, with as many nooks and crannies as one small place could hold. Go either way and enjoy, because at any rate they both re-join about a mile ahead, and that is you at the start of Kames Bay. This short stretch of shoreline is even more in keeping with Bute's gentle backwater image, and the shorefront of Port Bannatyne has always been a quieter alternative to Rothesay, for those who seek such a thing.

Heading up to Ardbeg, after skirting the west side of Rothesay Bay, and already you will have settled in and be looking forward to plenty more fairly easy, fun-filled riding that's sure to come.

Abandoned and forgotten is how I'd best sum up Port Bannatyne, which I always whirl through with great delight. Even in its heyday it was seen as a quieter alternative to Rothesay for those who required such a thing.

Despite the fact it's had a bit of a makeover, with a new look marina opened in 2009, the shops and shorefront still retain the semi-rickety old look that gives this place so much charm.

The pubs and hotels, in particular, add a splash of colour to the proceedings, and the old pier for yesteryear's paddle steamers still holds its own. All in all, it has the appearance of what you want and expect from an island seafront. The other thing to note is that on a hot summer's afternoon, the bay is a real sun trap, and you feel the heat as you drop down from the breezier west side (if you decide to do the run clockwise). So enjoy the warm, picturesque amble round the port, with the yachts' masts at times sitting still and stifling in the bay.

Next, turn left and gently rise out of Kames, still staying on the A-844, and straight ahead will take you up the north east side of the island to the Rhubodach/Colintraive ferry, more of which later.

There is a natural, low-lying fault line which runs through the island here, so it's no great effort to go from east to west, and as the small rise is climbed, the sight of Kames Castle comes into view on the right. This is one of the oldest inhabited dwellings in the country. Amongst its numerous former residents were the early powerful Bannatyne family, and it was they who changed Kamesburgh to Port Bannatyne. How's that for blowing your own trumpet?

No matter how quaint and delightful the dwellings of Rothesay have been, the moment you climb out of Kames Bay and into the fields and hills of the island, the delight factor goes off the scale, such is the charm and prettiness of the rural part of this beautiful place. Very soon you have a choice as to whether you go left, or straight ahead to the north west of the island, towards the top end of Ettrick Bay. At Ettrick there is a busy and popular café, but beyond that it's a quiet corner, which you can ride for a mile or two in near solitude up to the tarmacked road end. This does finish rather disappointingly and is also ridden mostly on what could be a better surface, but the quiet setting may find you coming back here once in a while.

You can, of course, drop into the café on your return, which you must make as this stretch of road is a dead end; obviously, you must also return to the road junction and turn right just beyond the roofless St Colmac's Church. This takes you along to the south side of Ettrick Bay, then on down along the west side of the island. Unlike Arran, a number of dead end roads do shoot off from time to time, and it is a personal matter as to whether you want to explore them on any particular occasion. There are four of them on the west coast and they do provide a slightly

However, no other road on the island can match the northwest one that runs single track up to its dead end near Kilmicheal. I do like to take it every now and then, even though it leads nowhere, for the sheer tranquillity it provides.

Pulling up and away from Ettrick Bay, and starting to head down the west side. This is the view you'd get if you looked over your shoulder. There is a bit of climbing to come, though not too much, and the reward you get of the views over the Sound of Bute make it a big payback.

This once busy herring smoking station is only a quiet hamlet now, but does afford a slightly closer and different view of both Arran and also Inchmarnock Island, which lies close offshore. This small uninhabited isle was named after St Marnock — as was the Ayrshire town of Kilmarnock — and close by is a bay named after St Ninian, which to this day signifies the important role that Rothesay played in early Christianity. The Commandoes incidentally used Inchmarnock for training during the war. Straad is the proud owner of a now fairly rare, red phone box.

So you must go back on up to the main road and then it's fast and flighty down to another of Rothesay's gems, its quaint junctions and signposts. Straight ahead for the town, but a delightful right turn and curving climb for more of the same. I deliberately used the name Rothesay for the whole island there; as it was formerly known as that, and appeared thus on very old maps. The road ahead now shows Bute at its best. It's one of dips and glides, on a road bordered by dry stane dykes covered in fern, flanked by fields of dairy or crops. Behind them sit stunning sea views, and with all that comes an overwhelming feeling of joy and contentment.

The road eventually turns then climbs up to the glorious viewpoint of Ardscalpsie, which sits above Scalpsie Bay,

different view of the Clyde and surrounding islands, so on a good day it can be very satisfying to head down one or two now and again and enjoy the vista.

If you just stick to the main road with no diversions, the total mileage is around the 22 mile mark. So, having turned at St Colmac's, it's now a pleasant, sometimes breezy riding to the south end of Ettrick, with the sweep of the bay, the hills behind, and the West Kyle of Bute, making it a real rich canvas of blue and green.

The waterline will be patrolled by curlew and oyster catcher, as you take your leave of sea level for a short time and start to climb up into farmland that holds a straight road of gentle ascent for not quite two miles. This only stops when you reach a left hand bend of such severity that it would probably not be allowed on the mainland nowadays. It is also at this very bend that the second detour can be taken by turning right and meandering gently down to the small settlement of Straad.

A slight detour can be taken if you want to break right of the main road and head down to the old herring smoking hamlet of Straad. It can offer great, different views of Arran, which can make it a worthwhile visit. On this occasion the clouds are covering Arran's high peaks.

and there the jagged outline of Arran dominates the view down the Clyde. You're at the highest you'll get on the island here so the view is one you'd expect, and it is worth stopping for at least a moment to appreciate the surroundings. Even though I know it's something a lot of serious road riders don't like to do[2], at least linger a moment on the road. When the sun is shimmering on the Clyde, it is an unforgettable moment.

The height is quickly lost, however, as the road swings left, level at first, but then goes right and down a fairly hairy tight bend by Scalpsie Farm itself. The straight section ahead takes the sting out of your speed and safely draws you down toward the T-junction, as you cruise over the island's flat central belt with Bute's two lowland lochs lying to the left.

On reaching the junction, again it's left for the main town and right for the rest of the west side. So right we go, and continue with more of the same real top drawer riding, on past numerous fantastically named farms, such as Kerrymeanoch and Langalbuinoch[3], and then gently descend til we reach the road beside the cemetery. This takes you out west toward the wonderful relic that is St Blane's Chapel.

This road is without doubt the most interesting of all four branch roads, and not just because of where it leads. The first point of interest just after you turn right is a grass airfield. I never knew the bloody thing existed until I was on the road out there and a small aircraft was taxiing to take off. "Well, blow me down!" I thought (or words to that affect).

There is a tough wee climb on this single track gem which takes you up past Largizean Farm[4] and then you double back and level out as you pass Lubas Farm. Another sensational single track mile, on what is known as the Plan Road, takes you under Dunagoil Crag and to the road end car park.

Like a lot of roadies, I don't often get off my bike and hike over fields to see old relics or anything else for that matter, but for this one I did make an exception and would recommend to anyone to do likewise. It is a very short walk up the field and track to the pristine remains

This sign-posted junction is probably Bute at its most endearing, and just goes to show that the island retains so much of its yesteryear charm. For the record, we turn up sharp right here to keep us going down the west side on the great A-844.

---

2 - There is now a great information platform in place here.

3 - These incidentally are Norse-named places

4 - It means the daisy field.

of St Blane's, and if the chapel isn't enough, then the view across the Sound of Bute to the mighty Arran is the icing on the cake. The chapel itself and the surrounds are delightful and so beautifully kept, they make you feel uplifted as you make your way back down the farm track to your concealed machine — only if you've bothered to conceal it, that is.

The road back up gives different views across the Sound, and lets you see a rugged part of this isle which is still little visited. This slightly different view across to the jagged outline of its neighbour, highlights another difference between these two distinct islands, in that Rothesay is an island of subtleties with each branch road giving a variation of what you've been seeing, whereas Arran periodically has dramatically changing seascapes and landscapes.

Inchmarnock island shows its full length on the continuation down the west side. Here, its southern tip is semi-shrouded in sea haar, as is North Arran.

On arriving back at the main road, turn right again, and almost immediately you come to a straggly crossroads, guarded by the Kingarth Hotel, and a choice has to be made as to the next route to take.

Although a dead end, the pleasant trip down to Kingarth itself will again give another slightly different and closer view of the Isle of Great Cumbrae (Millport), along with its wee brother, and an extended look up the Clyde. The buildings are no more uniform here than they are anywhere else on the island, and another quaint stone pier gives a hint to a bygone age of steamer traffic to Kilchattan Bay. When you retrace the road back to the crossroads, it's now that the last decision has to be taken as to which road you want to take back to the east side of the island.

If it's the main road, that's fine. I really like the main road, and especially the way that it climbs steadily up to a high point, giving a unique feeling of moorland, which you don't get on the rest of the isle. It's here you find a small war memorial to the men of this district who never returned from Flanders and all. The reason I mention this memorial in particular is because it contains the details of Lord Ninian Stuart, the second son of the 3rd Marquis of Bute, who fell in October 1915 leading a night attack near La Basse. It shows just how intense the fighting was when even former Members of Parliament were in the front line.

The road passes the monument and cuts through Torr Wood, passing a side road to the right, then begins an excellent long and meandering descent, down through the high beech hedges that border the gardens of Mount Stuart, and drops most perfectly to the shore at Kerrycroy

with its mock Tudor houses. The other route from the Kingarth crossroads to this point is to take the minor road to the right of the main road and follow the south coast. By taking this road, the danger on a damp or wet day is that you have a very high chance of being covered in cows' muck, leaving both you and machine needing a hose-down when you reach home.

However, it is slightly more scenic than the main road, and in about two miles time will lead to a red brick house that wouldn't look out of place in rural Surrey. Take the right fork at this house, and for the first few yards it is akin to a track, but tarmac will soon materialise and then lead you into the grounds of the magnificent Mount Stuart House. If you don't, for whatever reason, elect to take the right fork here, the road will climb — and I do mean climb — back up to the main road, which it joins just inside the Torr Wood (this is the aforementioned side road).

I have only pulled up on this road once, and it was the time when the route into Mount Stuart was blocked off because, unbeknown to me, Stella McCartney was having her wedding reception there. I'd been in the saddle all day at this point, when the unexpected and difficult diversion was thrust upon me, and after the climb up to the main road I vowed there and then never to buy a single item of Stella's ever again. True to my word, I haven't; though, to be honest, I'd never bought bugger all from her before, so she's no worse off.

The going could not be more pleasant as you meander along, curving down through all the farmsteads, while heading south on the A-844. Some of these farm names go way back to Viking times when the early Norsemen decided to stay and settle here. Very shortly Arran will start to dominate the view west, especially as the long, gradual pull-up towards Ardscalpsie Point is taken.

Take my advice and go right at the house, despite the poor road surface, for it will soon improve and then you're into the grounds of Mount Stuart House, the former court of the 3rd Marquis of Bute, John Patrick Crichton Stuart. I will not go into any great detail about the house or the man himself, as it would take a book on its own, I dare say, to describe the place and him. But what I will say is this, it is a most spectacular building which was built in the 1880s, and was not only the first house in the country to be lit by electricity, but also had its own heated swimming pool. To give you some idea of the money involved, it was said that the Marquis was a man who had "no occasion to consider the question of expense", as he was the richest man in Britain.

Looking just a little further south, also from high above Scalpsie Bay, gives great views of the Holy Isle and St Blane's Hill this time. This is you at the highest point you will reach on the island. Although it requires a long steady rise if coming down from the top, will in contrast require a short, sharp, shocking, swerving, ramp-like rise right through Scalpsie Farm, if coming from the south.

Arran, her highest peak in mist and her lower flank shrouded in haar, makes for a very show-stopping scene from above Scalpsie Bay. It is the height gained here that allows the Dark Isle to look her best, and it is rare that I don't stop for a few moments at least.

The 300 acre estate is landscaped and open to the public, and it is the grounds and interior roads which constantly attract me in, with a wonderful selection of trees from the Americas and beyond, which are as rare here as they are stunning. It does take just a little bit of weaving and bobbing to navigate round the estate and find your way to the gate which takes you out to Kerrycroy and another stone jetty.

So, either route from the Kingarth crossroads will delight you as the short trip back to the east side is made. In case you are wondering at this point about the English style of the Kerrycroy buildings, the reason is that this is an estate village, belonging to Mount Stuart, and was so designed to make the English wife of the 2nd Marquis feel less homesick.

We're now on the home straight back into Rothesay and the ferry home. And one thing that always strikes me about this particular stretch is the tremendous feeling of openness and space you ride into on your glide back. This may be due to the width of the Clyde at this point and the effect of the Cowal Hills, giving a lot of impact to the big blue.

The run up now has lost the green fields but the blue aquamarine and the charm of this dear old place make it a very special run in. It's been all special from the word go and this part is no different, as the run nears its end. How you tackle this stretch will depend a lot on the timing,

This time Arran's flank is in clear view after the fantastic fly-down through Scalpsie Farm has just been done, and you're on the bolt straight section that leads to the next major T-junction. We want to go right again, to keep us west side.

I'm breaking all the roadie rules here, because this is a photo of St Blane's Church which can only be reached by walking up a track, it's only for a short distance. The church is reached by taking the Plan Rd, which begins at the cemetery and is well signposted. Even if you don't dismount and visit the place, it is worth the ride along in itself just for the views it gives of Arran. I know most roadies wouldn't normally leave the bike to visit a relic, and I wouldn't usually do so either, but in this instance I thoroughly recommend it, especially on a glorious summer's day.

Walking back down to the road after visiting St Blane's. The parked cars indicate the end of the Plan Road where my bike is stashed, though there was probably no real need to conceal it. The Sound of Bute and Arran make a sensational silent backdrop on a rare glorious day that particular year (2011).

Looking right into Arran's corries from near the end of the Plan Road, and what a scene it makes. The big payback you get if you decide to make the effort to ride any or all of Bute's dead end side roads, is the stunning and different viewpoints they provide at just about every turn.

but well run museum has old photos of Bute, representing the past well, as do some of the exhibits which were found on the island. It's well worth a visit, I am told, though I've never been in myself. I keep promising myself I'll go in next time.

But you must leave at some point, and when I do I like to sit outside on the uppermost deck of the ferry. It always causes a real heat haze on a hot summer's day, when those big Cal-Mac diesels start to pump out smoke as the boat slowly leaves port. Then it's time for some quiet contemplation about what you're leaving behind and what you've just done, along with the feeling of contented satisfaction. There is still the rest of the bay to clear before thoughts turn to refreshments and then the long haul back to Paisley.

One of the hardest parts of any island run is when you return to the mainland and have to motivate tired and stiff legs into action again for another 20 odd miles. And the reality of facing busy roads after the tranquillity of an island, is a daunting task; especially if it's a weekday and the home-bound rush hour traffic is in full flow.

Arriving back at Wemyss Bay, a decision has to be made whether to return by the outbound route, or go home via Largs. Although the Largs route is slightly longer, it is usually my preferred option and makes for a great round trip.

The advantage of taking the coast road to Largs is that it is nice and flat all the way there, and gives both body

Looking across to Arran from St Blane's Church. For years I wondered what it was like, having seen the signs for it many times as I rode by. I had never visited it until curiosity finally got the better of me one fine June day.

and you may find yourself putting on a spurt to catch a particular ferry, if you think you can make it.

I never really bother about which one I'll get back until I get close to the pier again and then I see how it's looking. All the early afternoon ferries leave on the hour, after which the times become a bit more erratic. It's a lot more relaxing and pleasurable, however, to just glide up the seafront, curve round Bogany Point, and arrive in the town, ready to deal any hunger you have a lethal blow by visiting one of the cafes. Enjoying your grub on the seafront does make it feel like a real seaside day out, and you start to feel like a kid again. The town itself has one or two other attractions which are worth a visit if you are filling in time waiting for the ferry.

The castle is an absolute cracker and especially the dungeons, which are always my favourite. And it is interesting to note that the castle itself was once right on the seafront, which gives you some idea of how much land has been reclaimed over the years. Also, the small

Another quaint and important crossroads for us is the one at the Kingarth Hotel. From there you can go down and visit the village of Kilchattan which, although a dead end in itself, does afford great views over to Little Cumbrae. But it's more likely the route to take you towards Rothesay Town which will be of most interest to you from here. You can stick to the main road and climb up past the war memorial, or you can take the more circuitous minor road to the right which leads you through the grounds of Mount Stuart House.

Taking the minor road back to the inside of the island allows a fine early view back across Kilchattan Bay to its namesake village. There then follows a most fascinating quiet purr through the specimen trees of the gardens of Mount Stuart House. Just watch out for copious amounts of cows' muck on the road as you pass the farms en route. The cows' muck is the main drawback of going this way.

and legs a gentle warm-up of about six miles and gets the old engine back into flow. This is further aided by the very close proximity of the Clyde, which means that the energizing salt air is a constant companion on the ride into this great seaside town.

And if it's a hot day, it will be busy and bustle when you hit its shore and centre. The Largs traffic is always at its slowest on the bend near the ferry terminal, and once past this, the road starts to rise gently at first, as the bottom of the famous Haylie Brae is approached.

When you start the climb out of the town on the Haylie (the A-760), the beginning is steep and arduous, for it gets up to about 10% early on as it passes the cemetery. But then rounding the first left hand bend, the road straightens out and eases a bit, and then it's get-into-rhythm time. Dig in and make your way up as best you can, as heart rate will steady itself after the initial shock, and the lengthy straight rearing up ahead gives some time

Passing the great old gatehouse at one of the entrances to Mount Stuart on the main road back to the east side and Rothesay. Note the numerous coats of arms on the outside. Regardless of which road you take from Kingarth, they both converge again at Kerrycroy at the far side of Mount Stuart's grounds.

It's not only the houses attached to Mount Stuart that display a coat of arms; so, too, do all the lamp posts in Rothesay Town. As such, they make a most splendid touch, and add colour, splash, and charm in equal amounts.

for recovery before the sweeping right hander is reached. Then the road doubles back and climbs up to the last part of the brae which, like all good, hard climbs, steepens a little just before topping out.

The hardest part of the Haylie only lasts for about six minutes or so, but when you clear the toughest part, it will still rise — though not so steeply — for another mile and a half. The gradient lessens just as you pass the Haylie Reservoir, and then it's a case of recover as best you can, as you head straight south for the next section of road, which has higher, craggy slopes to the left, and a high stone wall to the right. This, unfortunately, blocks out the view of the Clyde and its four biggest islands, but you can get glimpses of this vista from time to time at gaps in the

Re-crossing the Clyde back to Wemyss Bay, and passing the other ferry en route to Rothesay as it passes Toward Lighthouse. Another great jaunt round the soft lady is over, and the pleasant, warm deck of the Cal-Mac is being enjoyed to the full. However, there are quite a few steep miles still to be ridden and thoughts soon turn to the home run, which for me is a toss-up between going via Greenock or Largs.

wall where it has crumbled; it just lets you know what you are missing.

The road will now swing to the east after about half a mile or so, but the large stone wall guarding the Kelburn Estate remains your constant companion on your right flank, and still the road rises. All this is on good, fairly new tarmac, and once clear of Kelburn, it's onto the open moors. You are now heading inland due east on the A-760, and this part of the trip is one of the finest. That's because more often than not you will be assisted by, if not a good westerly tailwind, then at least a tail breeze, be pumped up by your exertions on the Haylie, and in full flow. On top of all that, the upland mixture that awaits, of both heath moor and reservoir, is very much to my liking.

If the sun is out, it is a heavenly stretch of road to ride, knowing too that you're homeward bound. The whole road toward Kilbirnie is either flat or slightly downhill, which means a high speed can be maintained for the most part. Soon the first of two large reservoirs is reached; both sit to the right of the road. Muirhead, with its old boathouse and all, is the first, and this is followed almost immediately by Camphill. This is a longer and more slender dam than its stockier, shorter neighbour.

On either side of this high glen are the Muirshiel hills and laws, rough sheep pasture and crags, giving a real rugged feel to the whole scene. Though pleasant on a warm summer's day, it's a wild and raw place in spring and winter.

You literally whizz by both dams, feeling on top of the world, as you shortly reach then pass the Boag Road down to Dalry on the right. Continue descending gradually and swiftly, curving some fast bends, til eventually the moors cease and away to your right, Ayr bay is just visible. Then a fast banking descent into Kilbirnie begins. It's full concentration, even when you enter the town, for it's straight and fast all the way to the centre, where you have to brake hard for the small mini roundabout. Sturdy stone cottages and solid buildings are the make-up of this small town, lining both sides of the street, guiding you through this somewhat forgotten corner of North Ayrshire.

Its right at the roundabout, then left at the next, to go straight ahead and take your leave. As you do depart, you have a choice as to whether to take the cycle track or the road. Staying on the road, it's now double bends that lead you away after the initial lift out of Kilbirnie, and the elevation this small climb gives is enough height to allow you to enjoy a view into the Garnock Valley. It holds Kilbirnie Loch and also the Barr Loch, followed by Beith, which soon becomes visible on its hillside perch across the valley. This is one of the few Ayrshire towns not to nestle in a hollow. I'm less than an hour from home now, and it's only around 5 miles or so to the next town of Lochwinnoch.

This will be reached by a road that dips and rolls more than the upland Largs road, though any tail wind will still assist. The valley green has a softer touch than what has gone before, and the road to Beith is soon passed on the right just after entering Renfrewshire. Again it is one more climb and descent before slicing under the old railway bridge and then passing Barr Castle, before

If going home via Largs, it does mean a hard climb up the Haylie Brae, though there are splendid, if all too brief, glimpses of all the Clyde islands to be had through the gaps in the Kelburn Estate's wall.

flowing and bending down into Lochwinnoch. To enter the village proper, turn left at the lights and enjoy heading up its delightful Main Street. Pass the post office, then the Brown Cow Inn, before going over the zebra crossing, and making straight for the climb and the derelict old church dead ahead.

All the while you are hemmed in tight on both sides by well-worn buildings of a real good age. The village itself looks very picturesque, nestling as it does below the rugged Muirshiel Hills, and a feeling of homeliness and warmth is given by the solid white houses, many of which still have coal fires. John's Hill (the B-786) is the name of the long climb that waits at the end of the High Street, and it is a great pull-up of length and gradient, taking you up past some splendid housing and leading to the top of the village. As you leave, the gradient lessens, at which point the next right turn takes you onto the road to Howwood, and there isn't much respite from the climbing.

Very quickly the road rears up again, and it's one more dig in to get to the top. No sooner have you got there than it's a plunge down, then another climb immediately begins where, if you get it right, your momentum will carry you well up onto the opposite side. One or two false summits finally bring you to the crest of the road, from where it's a long straight stretch of very fast downhill and then bends and more downhill, til you are just about entering Howwood itself.

It's quite an exhilarating descent and one to enjoy after all the previous hard work to get there. Cross the River Black Cart, then the road and rail bridges, before swinging left at a quaint and broad V-junction, which would do any village proud. After passing the village store and then the Howwood Inn, you're on the road to Johnstone and back on the flat to boot. Just a few hundred metres of Howwood remains, then it's time to leave this delightful dwelling, where the next mile or so brings you into Johnstone. Here, it's proletariat housing schemes and so-called bog-standard secondary schools that greet you.

Continue in on the Beith Road, all the way to the lights at the Thorn Inn in 2 miles time. Then the back road is taken, up past the Abbey Cemetery and down onto the Glenpatrick Road, just skirting the village of Elderslie again. A right turn and it's up the Glenpatrick itself, as twisting, tough turns lead you up alongside the Brandy Burn. Stone wall, stream and woodland are to the left, as is the Leithland Road with its hump bridge start. With fields to the right, the Gleniffer Braes show a steep front ahead, and then the deceptively tough, short climb up onto Foxbar Road is taken on the Mackiesmill Road.

Ahead, well it's a straight road back to Glenburn and I'm almost home now. Regardless of how tired I am, I always feel contented at this point and very lucky — mostly for getting back safe. And I always thank my guardian angel for getting me home in the one piece.

The most important thing in any run is not your performance, how well you went, or any of that. No, it's returning intact and living to fight another day. Good thing to remember that

Liam Boy.

Another fine view from the Haylie Brae, and this time it is a much closer look at Hunterston Ore Terminal and Little Cumbrae, as they sit still in the shimmering Clyde. At this point, the steepest part of the Haylie has been climbed, and ahead lies one of my favourite stretches of road, the one from here all the way to Kilbirnie

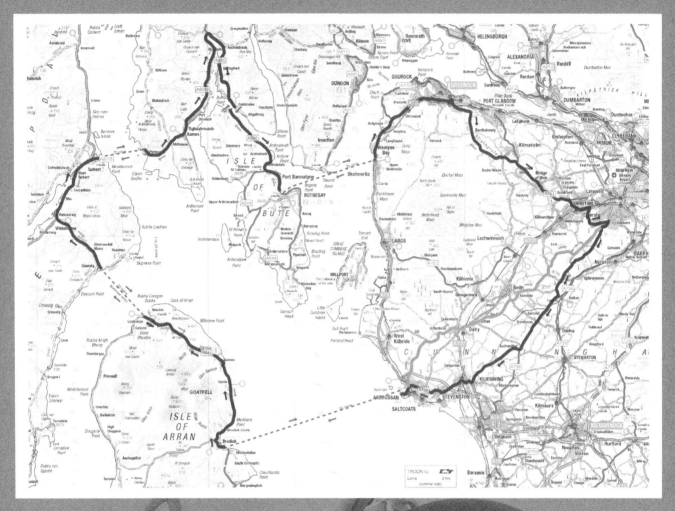

THE FIVE FERRIES

VIA SERGEANTLAW

102 MILES
6.33 HOURS
ASCENT 5520 FT
4211 CALS

VIA DALRY

102.6 MILES
6.36 HOURS
ASCENT 5880 FT
4350 CALS

FROM ARDROSSAN/ WEMYSS BAY

70.4 MILES
4.30 HOURS
ASCENT 3540 FT
2712 CALS

O'S LANDRANGER MAPS 64, 63, 69, 62.

ROUTE SUMMARY

CLOCKWISE	CLOCKWISE VIA DALRY	ANTICLOCKWISE
Gleniffer Rd B-775	Gleniffer Braes B-775	Elderslie
Sergeantlaw Rd	Mid Hartfield Cottage	Johnstone
Lugton	Rowbank Reservoir	Kilbarchan
Auchentiber A-736	Gateside	Brig O Weir
Kilwinning	Dalry	Quarriers
Stevenston		Greenock
Ardrossan Harbour	Ardrossan Harbour	Wemyss Bay
	Brodick	Rothesay
	Lochranza	Rhubodach
	Cloanaig	Colintraive
	Tarbert	Portavadie
	Portavadie	Tarbert
	Colintraive	Cloanaig
	Rhubodach	Lochranza
	Rothesay	Brodick
	Wemyss Bay	Ardrossan
	Greenock	Dalry
	Quarriers	Gateside
	Kilbarchan	Rowbank Res
	Johnstone	Hartfield Farm
	Elderslie	Gleniffer Braes
	Paisley	Paisley

BLAW WEARIE*

This is a classic. This one has it all. From the distance, to the scenery, to the climbing, and then sprinting for at least one of the handful of ferries that will carry you onto two islands, two peninsulas, and the Clyde coast thrown in for good measure. It will provide you with one memorable day out that won't be forgotten in a hurry, and will also provide the challenge of wanting to do the run in the opposite direction, when wind and weather are favourable. So what is all the shouting about? What could constitute the word 'classic' to be used with such confidence and without fear of contradiction?

Well, you don't get onto just Rothesay or just Arran; you do both on the one run, along with the Cowal and Kintyre peninsulas. The views down the Kyles of Bute from the Tighnabruaich road are as equal and awesome as Pladda lighthouse and its partner in crime, Ailsa Craig. The climbs are many, constant and varied, with flat coastal

respite intermittent and welcome. Stitching together all of this pattern of fields, sea lochs, mountains, islands and glens, are five magical Cal-Mac ferries and a slender elegant strip of tarmac, that will most finely guide you round this lengthy loop, starting in earnest from Wemyss Bay round to Ardrossan Harbour; or vice versa, if you prefer.

Now mark my words here! If you decide to start from Ardrossan, then ensure you are ably assisted by a descent south to south westerly airflow, which will not only be desirable when going from Brodick to Lochranza, but will be absolutely crucial when going from Claonaig to Tarbert. That is, if you want to connect with the very next ferry sailing in the chain.

Admittedly, it's not the end of the world to be stuck in Tarbert for an hour or so, but it does tend to lose the momentum of the day and take the icing off the cake somewhat. The same south west wind can be a great aid

---

* - **Blaw Wearie is an old Scots saying that means literally puffed out.**

and most welcome companion on the long pull-up out of Tighnabruaich, especially after the all-out effort to cover the 10.8 miles to Tarbert from Claonaig in less than 45 minutes, done on the previous leg. Half of this is done on a tough, dipping, single track road.

Likewise, should the plan be to start off in Wemyss Bay, it is equally desirable to get the wind behind you when needed, with a north to north westerly airflow being ideal. Not only will this assist in the road over to Tighnabruaich in the opposite direction, but more importantly, help in getting to both Claonaig and Brodick. Time for both ferries is not in great supply, and the routes to both destinations are fairly challenging. Personally, coming from Paisley, I will aim for the old stalwart of the 9.45am sailing from Ardrossan to Brodick if going clockwise, or the 10.15am sailing from Wemyss Bay to Rothesay if going anti.

There are plusses and minuses with either direction, and it is a somewhat difficult call to make as to which, if either, is the easier or harder way to do it. What is good to know from the outset, however, is that although the two larger mainland-based ferries normally operate very strictly to their timetable, the two smaller ones feeding the Kintyre peninsula are not always so pinpoint. Sometimes they can arrive and depart several minutes behind schedule, and this can really put you under pressure for what is already a tight timetable. This is probably most damaging when doing the run anticlockwise, for should you dock late at Lochranza and therefore miss the 4.40pm sailing from Brodick, then it's a fair old wait till 7.20pn, for the next boat home.

Likewise, it would be a real downer to miss the connection at Claonaig, when coming down from Tarbert, as there is nothing there except a bus stop. This would not provide much in the way of entertainment for the one hour and 15 minutes you would have to wait for the next one.

The tightest time, however, is the aforementioned leg going clockwise from Claonaig to Tarbert and, as already stated, an hour spent waiting in the pretty Argyllshire town isn't the end of the world. And there is the added advantage of knowing that when you finally do get going again, the Bute ferry times are a lot more flexible and accommodating than the Arran ones.

For me personally, to tilt the balance back in favour of going anticlockwise, there is double the recovery time on the ferry back to Ardrossan as there is to Wemyss Bay. One hour, compared to 30 minutes. This at a time in the day when you really need it, and also the route home from the former is slightly shorter than the latter, with slightly less climbing involved. I would say, however, that as great a day out as it as and as glorious a run as it is, it would be best to leave it to not only a scorcher of a day, to add to the pleasure, but also to a time when you are going fairly well and preferably not carrying too much extra weight. The reason I say this is not because it can't be done when you're not in top nick. It can, but I say it because it will make the sprints between some of the ferries a lot less stressful, thus adding to the pleasure.

This is not a day of carefree plootering. Far from it. No, clock watching and skilful judgement are continuously required to keep you on track, which even when going to plan, will require an all-out effort for at least one ferry. Add to that a total of 5840 feet of ascent and it's obvious why the lack of weight would be preferable.

It doesn't really matter which way we go here, for I will describe each of the six legs of the journey in both directions when we come to them. So that is the overall

Heading up the Sergeantlaw Road early doors, making for Ardrossan via Lugton and Kilwinning. It's the start for the Five Ferries (clockwise), and I often take this route as it is marginally shorter than going via Dalry. I only found this out by accident, much to my surprise.

structure of this outing — five ferries and six legs. It sounds more like a military manoeuvre than a cycle run, and when you first sit down with a Cal-Mac brochure to work it all out, it can get a bit higgeldy-piggeldy, as you constantly flip backwards and forwards, trying to figure out the most suitable ferries.

On this run we will also, for the first time, be covering ground that we have already covered. This will happen from time to time throughout the book, as several runs will use the same stretch of road for part of the way at least. I will try and keep that to a minimum, and that is one of the reasons that I will use a different approach to Ardrossan this time, going via Lugton and the A-736. Not that covering the same ground will in any way detract from this marvellous outing, but here goes.

PAISLEY-ARDROSSAN

Off we go then, clockwise to get us started. Which means Ardrossan, here we come. It will be just before 8am that I will leave for the boat and, if our summer is playing ball for once, it will already be a pleasant warm morn as I start up bonnie Gleniffer. These are not my words to describe the Gleniffer Braes, but the words of Robert Tannahill, our local poet; a friend and acquaintance of Rabbie Burns. Both men admired one another, and had the title of national bard not been placed on the Ayrshire man's shoulders, then it would have been given to Tannahill.

So, much huff and puff as the hill is started, and instead of going straight on up this day, I will turn first left, after first grinding up the early right hand bend, then regaining some composure on the short flat section before the steepest part of the road is reached.

The fairly straight and steep section of the main braes road (the B-775) has its gradient intensified by being hemmed in on both sides by a near vertical   bulging, plant-covered crag on the left, and a stone wall of character right-side. Then just as it starts to open up, it's time to make what at first feels like an Alpine manoeuvre, by turning hard left and starting the climb up the ramp-like Sergeantlaw Road. 16% gradient in the first brutal section, it feels like you're in the Tour de France ascending the Alpe d'Huez. But hang on for a bit, for it soon relents as you round the first corner, bending right then lying back, with all the charm only a single track road can deliver. It straightens up, becomes gentler, but still climbs, with intermittent softer rises, leading you up into and through the conifers to the road's highest point.

Just about to go through the Middleton Farm crossroads, still on the Sergeantlaw (going clockwise). It takes another tough wee pull-up to reach here, after taking the initial steep ramp right at the start. However, it now puts you in a very advantageous high position and it is all downhill from here to Lugton.

All this is done, at least part of the way, by going between rough pastures, containing some Highland coos, all grazing behind old rustic, wrought iron railings. This really does add to the feeling of the land which time forgot, and who's complaining? Not me. It's about 15 minutes to this spot, and it affords quite a view of the surrounding fields and all, with the main back of the braes road away and down to the right.

It would be great if the Sergeantlaw kept this height, but unfortunately it doesn't. For no sooner have you reached Seageantlaw Farm itself than it's a bolt straight plunge down, which would also be great if the lowest point in the road was not so potholed and stone-strewn. This admittedly has been improved recently, so it's not the shake, rattle, and roll, bottom-out that it once was.

At this point you pass Mossneuk Farm, the very farm the street took its name from, with one or two other nearby farms giving their names to Glenburn streets also. Dead ahead lies a tough wee climb that is testing and barren, ascending as it does beside windblown trees which line fields' edges, and guided by barbed wire fencing, not quaint wrought iron. It tops out and levels out just before the crossroads at Middleton Farm, which is a great spot to be in at this point, as once again height is gained and it means all the hard work is done.

Superb riding all the way down to Lugton lies ahead now, with the knowledge that the taxing wee pull-up to the junction with Sergeantlaw, which has to be done if you take the main road, will now be by-passed. As this little climb is one that is fairly testing and more arduous than it looks, I can't really describe the feeling of contentment I get when I know it doesn't have to be taken.

Now I know what you are thinking here. Why on earth is Liam boy going this route to Ardrossan, when the normal one of being a back road Bob to Dalry will do the job sufficiently and get us to the ferry on time. Well, the reason is thus. Not that long ago, after years of taking the Dalry road to the Arran ferry, I decided to do a Clyde coast training run that would not include going round the island. As I wanted to get as many miles in as possible, I decided to take the long way down and go by Lugton and Kilwinning to Saltcoats, and then onto Ardrossan.

I was under the impression that this route would add an additional 4 or 5 miles onto the run easily, and it just so happened for a change of scenery I took Sergeantlaw at the start, and Saltcoats town centre — instead of the coast road — at the finish.

You could have knocked me down with a feather when I looked at my computer, and found out it was actually over half a mile shorter to Ardrossan Harbour going this way. I would never have believed it. On closer inspection of the O/S map on my return home, I could see how the road ran, and how indeed it was shorter. There is also a lot less twisting and turning on this route, and therefore more chance to maintain a higher average speed, which is an obvious advantage when chasing a strict ferry time. There is admittedly a slowing down as you negotiate Kilwinning town centre, as there is with Dalry on the other route, though Dalry is not so time consuming.

As both routes also have their great descents and views — the Kilwinning one being the B-778, the road that comes into the town off the Irvine road — then it's fair to say their even Steven as to which is the best one. I may take either route on the outward journey, but always return by Dalry and Rowbank on the home leg, that just being my personal preference.

So, as I was saying, it's tally-ho from the end of the Sergeantlaw, right down to near enough Lugton, as the long, undulating descent past the ruinous looking Hall Farm is flown with glee. The buildings of this old house and adjoining barns practically make up the roadside boundary, so I can't help but think it must have had more hits than John Lennon over the years, though remarkably it's still more or less in one piece.

After turning right onto the Irvine road, it's now busy, busy time. So as always keep your main A-road wits about you, as you get the head down and get on with the serious business of making that crucial connection at Ardrossan. There are one or two gradual rises on this stretch of road, but as you're well warmed up by now, they are for the most part a glide-over job, most of which can be done in the large front chain ring.

However, if you remember back to the Turnberry run when I gave the first tip about smooth pedalling, then this bit of road is ideal for using another exercise to achieve a similar supple action. Don't go onto the large front chain ring, but instead stay on the inner one, as this will increase your cadence (i.e. how fast you spin your pedals).

Keep in as low a gear as possible, which will minimise resistance and allow you to reach a high cadence of well over 100RPM. Some computers will tell you this. If you don't have one, don't worry, just go as fast as you can til you feel yourself start to bounce in the saddle, then ease off a bit and spin as high as you can for as long as you can. Relax your toes again, to give yourself as even a balance as possible in both legs.

This speed workout is best done on a long gradual descent, so the Irvine road is ideal. This will increase your ability to accelerate quickly, and also has the major plus of getting you using both your pins with equal amount. Once you start doing that, you will notice one hell of a difference.

This speed drill can be done on any shallow descent and can easily be incorporated into longer runs, with the advantage of being quick to recover from. So it can be done numerous times, along with the ability to break up a bit of monotony on a long stretch of straight road during lengthy endurance runs.

Talking of which, after approximately 5 miles on the Irvine road, turn off right just before the Blair Tavern, and head down the wonderfully vast and open B-778, taking you and your machine into range of the coast. The feeling of limitless space on the early part of this road is added to in abundance by a number of factors, not least the height of the road, as it soon opens up the sight of Ayr Bay away in the distance to the left.

Sea and sky make for a wonderful arena of openness, with the vast air bubble being jagged into on the right by the Arran peaks themselves, no less. It's a pity that this great stretch of road must come to an end; it really is one that is enjoyed, as there should be a tail wind to assist, thus making it a sing-along-a-Liam stretch. But the descent into Kilwinning does it justice; this is the

Having made the ferry at Ardrossan (clockwise), it's across the Clyde we go with Arran's peaks
showing well beyond the flying saltire on the bow of the Caledonian Isles.

one I mentioned earlier, as you fly down through wood and bend, then into the town itself. Turn right over the Garnock, and right again at the lights, which will take you past the rail station and you're on the road to Stevenston.

It's not long until you find yourself on the edge of this former North Ayrshire mining town and, like most of them, it's now hard to imagine what it must have been like in those days. There's now no hint of this once great industry here, but every now and again you bump into a miner from Ayrshire or abouts, and it's interesting to hear their tales.

I would have imagined that with such an unhealthy and dangerous number, most guys would have been glad to see the back of the pits. Not so; far from it. On one occasion on Brodick pier, I got chatting to a motorbiker who had approached me to lament about the Arran road

surface. At first I thought he was a Fifer, but it transpired he was from Muirkirk and had worked in the Ayrshire coalfields.

After they closed down, he then pursued his trade in the remaining Fife pits and had even travelled further afield as further closures dictated. This was due to his love of the job, along with all the camaraderie that went with it. I learned that working at the actual coal face paid more than a guy further back, who was either taking coal away, or passing up wood and the like. The more dangerous the working position, the better the pay. I asked if it was such a difference as to make it worthwhile. "Most definitely," came the reply.

So shortly after leaving Kilwinning, a large busy roundabout must be crossed, where the Stevenston road meets the A-78. The mayhem at this point is now added to, as the new bypass feeds from the other side. After a quick sprint and dash, however, it's into the safety of a bus lane that takes you into the town and down the wonderfully named Boglemart Street, heading then into sunny Saltcoats, with the rail line for company on the left. This is soon crossed soon by a steep, hump bridge where, for the shortest route to the ferry, the town centre road is taken, passing the station where my memory lies long and fond. I still have the photos of me as a kid on Saltcoats beach.

I must say that Saltcoats centre does look tough and lacking, as does a lot of this area, which appears to be in need of cash and regeneration. From here it's a short ride down and round South Crescent Road, skirting the South Beach itself, before turning left into the harbour and riding down with great expectation.

That was your first close-up look at the open sea, with the salt air and island backdrop really getting you fired up for what's to come. At around 22.5 miles, that's the first leg over and now it's recovery time on the Brodick boat for an hour. But first it's ticket time. After that, you must wait your turn to board.

ANTICLOCKWISE

Had I done the run in the opposite direction, then I would be at this point around 5.40pm, having caught the 4.40pm in Brodick. The return journey home would be

Just about to pass through pretty Corrie on the second leg of the journey (clock) between Brodick and Lochranza. You're not under too much pressure on this leg; as there is ample time to cover the 14.6 miles between the two places. That said; there isn't too much time either to slow down and admire the quaint wee harbour; along with its Viking longboat.

the same as for the Arran run, with the pull-up off the coast perhaps even more arduous than it would be for the island run alone. With a west wind being a most welcome team-mate at this point, you simply have to dig in and get through the sixth and final leg of the outing. Often the only thing that has kept me going on this stretch in the past has been the fact that home awaits at the end of it, which makes the pull-up out of Dalry and the big haul up past Rowbank Reservoir just about bearable.

PAISLEY-ARDROSSAN

Cal-Mac Ardrossan Tel No. 01294 463 470

Adrossan ferry dep 9:45 AM or arr 5:40 PM to or from Brodick (Check CalMac website as ferry times may be subject to change.)

Via Dalry	Via Sergeantlaw	Return Via Dalry
23.1 Miles	22.5 Miles	23.1 Miles
Ascent 1220 Feet	Ascent 880 Feet	Ascent 1420 Feet
1.29 Hours	1.34 Hours	1.40 Hours

It is pretty obvious, as you approach Arran, why the Vikings named Brodick the broad bay (Breidr vik). However, as you depart Ardrossan, it's not so obvious, from the boat, where its name came from. It isn't Norse, but instead comes from the Gaelic, A`ird Rosain, and describes the town's physical position, which translates to small headland. Only later when you study the map can you see the accuracy of the description.

So off you sail out of Ardrossan Harbour, just like many have done since 1834, and like them you feel the thrill of an adventure coming on. It can be advantageous to have filled your water bottles in the Cal-Mac cludgie, so you are ready to proceed without stops on the run over to Lochranza.

BRODICK-LOCHRANZA

The second leg of the day should not put you under too much pressure, despite the fact that the imposing Boguillie has to been done enroute. There is approximately 1 hour 20 minutes to cover the 14.6 miles, which again should be wind-assisted if old Mother Nature is playing ball. There is also a nice flat warm-up to get you going again once you disembark, and what a stretch it. You could not wish for a more idyllic setting than the ride out of Brodick, heading north round Brodick Bay, with the morning sun on the salty blue. The road goes so close and flat to the shoreline that basking seals may even give you an odd look, while all the time, high above, the sentinel of Goat Fell watches all below it.

So you're off to a flyer, and that's how it stays as you continue along the east shoreline, at times passing strange-looking rock formations, which bring young groups of geologists here in their droves. You'll find yourself motoring well — it's hard not to along this wonderful stretch — before shortly arriving in the village of Corrie. This will delight as always, for it simply has too much for it not to.

Today, however, there is no time to slow down enough to appreciate it all, for your mind is focused first and foremost on making the next ferry. The tight curve over the stone bridge in the centre of the village will demand a slight slowing down, but that's alright, as it is a most pleasant spot to swerve round.

More coastal riding follows, and it does for a total of 7.7 miles all in, til the end of Sannox is reached. Once there,

Corrie's aforementioned harbour and longboat, which just about puts the icing on the cake for this most picturesque of villages.

the road turns sharp right, crosses the burn by another delightful stone bridge, then the climbing starts. Not totally in anger at the start, for this is a small pull-up that will shortly level off, but it does get you warmed up for its big brother who resides just up the road.

High above on the left, the lofty perch of Suidhe Fhearghas (Fergus's seat), sits side by side with the Ceum na Caillich (the witch's step), which makes the entry in the grand bowl of the North Glen Sannox corrie all the more dramatic, then the serious climbing begins once the bridge over the North Glen Sannox Burn is crossed.

Up the hillside the road snakes, barren and bleakly, not too steep at first. But in the middle section it gets to a testing 11% for a time, before starting to lie back, thank God, as the summit is neared. This is reached when my computer tells me I've done 700 feet since leaving the ferry, with things made a lot easier by the long needed new surface. It was on this very stretch of road last year, while trying to make the Brodick ferry as I attempted the five ferries anticlockwise, that I wrecked my rear rim. Fortunately, it somehow held out to the ferry, but required the train and bus home.

Now I've already mentioned the best technique I find for climbing, but what is also good to know, especially when trying to make a tight deadline on a long climb, is not to panic. Stay calm, don't rush, and therefore blow up. It will cost you a lot of time and anxiety if you do.

You're not watching the clock too much on your way north, for I can normally cover this leg in under an hour, and with the ferries spaced at 1 hour 20 apart, it's a pretty good comfort margin. So when you reach the top of the Boguillie, you can just about see a chink of Lochranza through the criss-crossing ridges of the Chalmadale Glen, and that's the cue for bombs away.

It really is one hell of an exhilarating charge down. It's quite technical into the bargain, with the first test of your high speed bike-handling skills coming into play as you cross the bridge over the small hill burn. But it gets more open and straight forward after that, til near Lochranza, when caution needs to be exercised, before… plonk! You drop delightfully into the village itself. Phew! Or words to that effect; it's suddenly all tranquil now. It's gentle time again, making the most of the pleasant trundle along this quaintly nibbled-edged road, down the salt side. First by its curving small estuarine river, then past its magnificent castle, where boats on sandbanks keel sideways half asleep.

Then it's round the headland to the ferry terminal itself, where the openness and freshness will be a great antidote to any stifling heat you encountered in your climb out of the Sannox corrie. Timewise, you should be okay, with a good 15 to 20 minutes to spare, and should you wish a

And now for the big fly in the ointment on the second leg (clock) — the Boguillie. For me, this is the second big climb of the day. Despite this, there should still be plenty of time left to make your second ferry, but I'm always glad to get over it regardless of which way I am going.

nibble or coffee, there is a small snack bar just opposite the pier. It's not the cheapest, though. Just beyond it, the public toilet sits with a great tap outside, perfect for filling water bottles.

So the second leg has been successfully covered, and now it's rest time as you await the smaller and admittedly quainter Cal-Mac. This is where it can get a bit anxious on this run, because now you watch the clock closely. As I said at the start, this ferry does not always keep as strictly to the timetable as the larger ones, and every minute will count on the next leg, the tightest of the whole day.

ANTICLOCKWISE

If you were doing the run in the opposite direction, you would also be watching the clock, even more closely perhaps, as you prepared to disembark the ferry when it comes into Lochranza. The timetable says you have 1 hour and 5 minutes to go from one terminal to the other, but at Brodick the big ferry likes everyone to be on with five minutes to spare, so in reality you have one hour

The ferry just arriving in Lochranza, and now the clock will be watched very, very closely. The next leg from Claonaig to Tarbert, when going clockwise, is the tightest leg of them all. If you are coming from Claonaig going anticlockwise, then you will be watching the time just as closely. You only have in essence one hour to get to Brodick if you are aiming for the 4.40pm sailing, so you want to be on top of the Boguillie no later than 4 o'clock. I can usually manage to do it in about 54 minutes, if slightly wind-assisted.

exactly. That is one advantage you have when chasing one of the smaller ferries, for it's good to know that you can practically embark right up to the last second, and even more so if your sprinting because time's getting tight. It can be psychologically advantageous to tell yourself that it may be running late, and so give yourself some hope to keep going flat out. It's been known to make a difference.

So that's what you're faced with. You've got one hour to cover the 14.6 miles from the top of the island to its capital[1]. On the flat that's no real problem, but there is around 700 feet of ascent on the way, so it's stay calm, don't panic, and don't blow. Once you start riding, watch your computer like a hawk and gauge your effort accordingly.

Even if the ferry docks on time,[2] waste no time, get off first, and start riding straight away. The good news is that you have a mile of flat road going through the village to warm up on before the hard climbing starts just as you leave. Don't forget that the Boguillie is at its toughest right at the start. Soon you have a chance to recover and get organised for the remaining bulk of the climb. I can normally do this stretch in about 54 minutes if I'm on my top bike and wind-assisted, so that leaves me just five minutes to spare.

---

1   If you're doing the run anticlockwise.

2   At Lochranza, that is.

If all goes according to plan, I reach the top of the climb at about 3.57pm. You don't want to be there any later than 4.02 pm, for that means it's right on the nail. Even so, with all going well, there's no room for complacency. After what is now a smooth dive down from the top of the Boguillie, it's full steam ahead. First over the North Sannox Burn, followed by a slaughter of the next climb, then drop like a stone to Sannox.

Now it's 7.7 miles of flat ahead, which will be done in near time trial mode. If you're like me and find it hard to get motivated in a normal time trial, then you're just about to surprise yourself. When actually faced with a situation when you need to go flat out and your sub-conscious mind knows this, then boy, oh boy, you find you can ride faster, suffer more, and pull out all the stops when it really matters.

With a bit of experience you will soon be able to tell how much, if any, time you have to play with and can then adjust your speed accordingly. Admittedly there is no time to appreciate the delights of the east coast road this time, not even pretty Corrie, because your only concern is staying focused on making the 4.40 ferry.

The trip round Brodick Bay always seems to take forever on this leg, as you can now actually see the ferry, but then have to swing away from it to cross the Rosa Water. But make it you must, and make it you will. When you do, it is a really satisfying feeling of achievement and relief, for all your chasing is now over.

On disembarking at Ardrossan, you can now amble home at your leisure. The hour long sail and the well-stocked big cafeteria feel like heaven, as more often than not I treat myself to a really good feed on this crossing, to make the final leg back to Paisley a damned sight easier.

The MV Loch Tarbert berthed at Lochranza.

Once again we're off, this time leaving Lochranza slip behind (clock), and it is more than fine to relax and recuperate for the first half of the sailing before thoughts turn to the frantic time trial that awaits on the other side.

BRODICK-LOCHRANZA

Brodick ferry arr 10.40 am or dep 4.40 pm to or from Ardrossan.

14.6 Miles
Ascent 700 Feet
54-61 Minutes

LOCHRANZA-BRODICK

Lochranza ferry dep12.00 am or arr 3.35 pm to or from Claonaig. (Check CalMac website as ferry times may be subject to change.)

So, returning back to the Claonaig crossing. You now find yourself enjoying the views looking back to Arran, which become more dramatic as the boat enters the Kilbrannan Sound. Her engines churn up foam as the high hills start to show again, as does more of the isle's top coast. With her stunning green curves, sandwiched between the solid blue sky and the ever-moving and glistening blue brine, she is a most bonnie island.

The red and white tub, however, is steaming toward the Kintyre coast and thoughts now turn to Tarbert and time. Here comes the big challenge of the day, for the first half of this leg is on a steep and demanding single track road that you hit straight off the boat.

If on time, you should land at 12.30pm, having left Lochranza at midday; and if on time, I'll eat my hat. It's only 45 minutes till your ferry leaves Tarbert and its 10.6 miles away, with a total ascent of 720 feet to boot. So you can imagine my despair when we once docked eight minutes late on one occasion and I didn't think I had a cat in hell's chance of making it. For the record, I did.

Looking back at bonnie Lochranza, the village and the castle, as the ferry heads out into the Kilbrannan Sound (clock).

A glorious view looking back from the ferry across the Kilbrannan Sound towards Arran (clock). This just happened to be an out of this world glorious day, and the views were immense because of it.

CLAONAIG-TARBERT

In contrast to the dramatic and rich-looking shoreline of North Arran, the Kintyre shore looks somewhat barren, and this look is further enhanced by the sparseness and lack of facilities at the Claonaig slip. The only things keeping the bus shelter company here are a phone box and a large, light blue, tin toilet that does appear fit for purpose, it has to be said.

Landing even a couple of minutes late puts you under pressure, which is usually the case. So coming off down the ramp like a marine on D-day, you mount your steed like a cowboy who has a dozen Apache breathing down his neck, and with no real warm-up to talk about, you start attacking the pedals for all you're worth.

Despite the fact that you do have 10 minutes more to play with when coming the other way, one big advantage of going this way is that it's a much faster, less technical descent when diving back down to sea level on the single track stretch. This is when you are descending on the other side down towards the A-83. The majority of the twisting and turning is done at this end of the road as you climb and climb, up to and above 127 metres, going to 14% on one tight bend, which I always seem to manage quite effortlessly.

The big drawback and slowdown is when having to constantly pull in to let oncoming vehicles through. You lose a lot of momentum then, and have to use a lot of energy to get going again. Talking of getting going, when you leave the slipway, turn left onto the single track (B-8001), ignoring the right, as it is a dead end leading to Skipness.

It's a quiet one today as it's a midweek run. Just the way I like it.

Approaching Claonaig slip (clock) and now it's pressure time. The barrenness of the place will hit you right away, and is in complete contrast to pretty Lochranza which you've just left behind.

This is your lot at Claonaig slip, so try not to miss the ferry there and get stranded. The big blue shed beside the shelter is a toilet, which is more than able to do the job, so it's not totally bereft of facilities.

The road sign says 11 miles to Tarbert, but it's slightly less than that at 10.6. Shortly you arrive at a quaint old T-junction, where we take the right this time and suddenly you are being told it's only 10 miles to Tarbert now. To add to the character of the place, the road signs here are so battered by the elements that you can hardly read them until you're very close up.

The climbing starts here as you pass a derelict old kirk and head up on this, as expected, very barren moorland road. A good road surface greets you, though, as do pointed, very solid, wooden black and white hand-painted poles that mark the laybys, making for an even more backwater feeling. The place is all the better for that, in my opinion.

After the initial climb, the road dips down and sweeps past two or three isolated houses. All the time, rising away in the distance can be seen the rest of the road, as it leads up and over the low lying ridge away to the northwest. The road straightens and remains so

for the most part once you begin on the climb, but there is a tight wee double bend in the road shortly after you begin on it, and the O'S map says it gets to 14% there, though it must be said I barely notice it.

The land all around is typical Kintyre — low lying and rolling hills, rough grass and fern for the most part, and sheep-filled in places. You now dig in deep and keep as good a momentum up as possible, while watching the clock like a hawk. This part of the run can be very frustrating, as it is the slowest and toughest part and, as already mentioned, approaching vehicles force you to stop and give way. Continually restarting is not only frustrating, but also a real energy-sapper as I mentioned.

Straight and rising, straight and rising goes the road, til a ridge appears in the distance and this means you have almost topped out. The ridge in question sits across the other side of West Loch Tarbert. Now there is one more final dip and gentle rise in the road to come, as you skirt the edge of a conifer plantation on the right and come to a fairly modern-looking house on the left.

This rather large and grand-looking pad is a bit unusual, in that its outhouse and garage look more striking than the house itself. At this point the downslope begins — at last, you think — and wasting no time, you throw yourself

The Five Ferries isn't always done in glorious sunshine, as this photo of Arran shows while I await the ferry at Claonaig (anti). It poured from the heavens the moment I landed on Arran, but that is to be expected from time to time.

Okay, so it's -in time big time now as the tough wee single track road from Claonaig is started (clock) just after leaving the ferry. There is no time to hang about and no warm up, as it's straight onto the attack. The sign says 11 miles, but I make 10.6 miles which is good to know, more for psychological reasons than physical.

onto the early open straight. This is before taking on a tight upper double bend, again the sign showing 14%.

Ahead and below the quiet West Loch Tarbert, containing as it does the usually empty Kennacraig pier, sits patiently awaiting the ferry from Islay. Down towards it you plummet, banshee-like, straightening out through some lower cultivated fields, before meeting the junction with the A-83. A bit of relief is always felt at this point, for now you can really motor on this stretch and you know that the half-way point is reached and an accurate time check can be taken.

That is, of course, if you are hell-bent on making the next ferry. I usually am, but it is perfectly fine to aim for the ferry after that (in an hour's time) and meander up this road, enjoy it, and have a good feed in Tarbert when

This is the wonderful view you get of Arran and the Kilbrannan Sound when you are approaching Claonaig (anti). It is a fantastic long descent to the ferry, which is great respite after the tough long climb up from the A-83.

The third big climb of the day for me (clock) is the long, arduous, and time-scarce pull-up on the B-8001 single track from Claonaig to the A-83 at West Loch Tarbert. Having to constantly pull over to allow cars coming towards you to pass can be a time consuming and frustrating business. It's amazing just how busy this quiet looking wee road can be.

Approaching the high point (clock) on the B-8001, and the hand painted black and white passing place poles simply add backwater charm by the bucketful to this already delightful stretch.

you get there. That is actually a good way to do it, as you will normally be hungry at that point and it's a pleasant spot to spend an hour, to be honest. I personally, however, like to give it laldy the whole way and get into full time trial mode for the next stretch.

Tarbert 6 miles says the road sign beside the bus stop, and the first of numerous fast, flat bends is taken on the road north. In no time the sign for the Kennacraig to Islay ferry is passed, and then it's more of the same swooping bends and gentle rising straights to get the machine round. This is done mostly on the big chain ring, as the challenge is accepted, by me at least, to make the 1.15pm sailing from Tarbert.

Despite being a more modern road, which are usually lacking the scenic charm of their older counterparts, the 83 is very enjoyable to ride and picturesque in places. Mostly it sweeps round and straightens through tight, tree-lined terrain, but on occasion you will get a dramatic glimpse of Loch Tarbert to your left, showing off its ruggedness and bays as you hurtle along. There's not a lot on this stretch, though you do pass a large sort of bus garage/goods yard-type place on the way, followed by some holiday homes further up. But the main point of interest for the bike rider is that just about 1½ miles outside of Tarbert, you hit a tough wee rise.

This can fairly slow you up, just when you don't want it, but thankfully it only lasts about 0.3 of a mile. So once again another wee dig-in is required to take you up and over this rise, going under the pylons and passing the cemetery, before bending down to the head of the West Loch, and entering the town itself. On passing the top mud flat bay, the rather striking grey tower of the parish church heralds your arrival into this most pretty fishing village. It really comes into its own when the final slope is taken down to the waterfront, between its old buildings, and the scene that greets you when you get down at the harbour won't disappoint. Tarbert is a most picturesque port, at one time having a small fishing fleet, which nestled safely in this natural rocky haven.

If you expected an eye-pleasing scene of stony slipways and harbours, fishing boats and yachts, bobbing moored vessels and colourful buildings lining the road, then you've come to the right place. Tarbert has all that and more. Beautiful wouldn't begin to describe the place, as the surrounding rocky slopes protect and shelter all below them.

The view you would get from the highest point on the B-8001 when making for Claonaig (anti). A glimpse of the Kilbrannan Sound is just possible, and then the fun begins. But be warned: this descent is a lot more technical than the one going down to West Loch Tarbert, and even frustratingly begins to climb a little just before the ferry slip is reached.

If you're not aiming for the next ferry, then grab a bit to eat at the Lite Bite Café at the top of the bay, and just sit by the water's edge and enjoy every minute of it. Looking out to sea, or Loch Fyne to be more accurate, is also stunning. Especially the way that the wooded headland of Rubha Bhadan curves round as it protects the port and all her craft within it. This includes a sizeable marina now based off the north shore.

For us, it is the south shore road to the right that will take us to the ferry, and down it we must charge if heading for the 1.15pm sailing. We ride through what feels like an older part, as the buildings keep everything narrow and tight, and the pier to the left actually still services small fishing boats and not modern pleasure craft, as far as I can tell.

When you make it on time to your vessel, which will be the 1.15pm sailing for me, it's another great feeling. More than most, it's the prize of them all. Park up, sit down, and await departure, which won't be long. And, like leaving Lochranza, you'll find yourself looking back until you're well out into the loch.

ANTICLOCKWISE

When coming the other way, the arrival into Tarbert is always a pleasure, too. The warm-up along the shore road, along with the extra time you have to make the 3.05pm Claonaig sailing, makes for a much less frantic arrival on the Kintyre peninsula. You arrive — hopefully at 2.15pm, having caught the 1.45pm ferry at Portavadie — and the

flatness and smoothness of the A-83, means that soon you are settled in and making good headway. However, that wee bump in the road at the head of West Loch Tarbert can cause as much disruption going south as it does going north. To be honest, we could do without the wee bugger. The rest of the A-83, though, purrs by with no problem and there are some great views down Loch Tarbert heading south. It always seems to be looking good when you get to the halfway stage and turn left onto the single track. Often, this is when things start to get tough, for the first mile here rises up like a rocket and it's very easy to damn near hit the bonk.

All that climbing you did on the road over to Tighnabruaich will now start to tell, so you just have to dig in and get up and over it. Easier said than done, and it can take so long that suddenly you realise that time is now getting tight again. You're wondering as you go southeast: *Just when is this bloody descent going to start, after all that climbing I've just done?* However, once past the high white house, and with the clearing of the conifers on the left, the sight of the mighty Arran comes into view and the great

Another shot of the B-8001 and its attached passing place poles. This is the scene at the very top of the road when going anticlockwise and Claonaig-bound.

road down starts pronto. When it does, you often have to brake hard for tight bends, and oncoming vehicles and even slight road rises will slow you down again.

Despite all this, it is a great sight coming down towards the Kilbrannan Sound with high Arran beyond. And once all the long dives and bends and turns have been taken safely, then finally — and I do mean finally — the salubrious site of the Claonaig bus shelter comes into view, normally just as the ferry is docking. It is with great relief more than anything that you stumble on, glad to get a break, but you know it's not over yet. The road to Brodick contains the Boguillie, so you're going to go from the gun one more time yet.

Doing the Five Ferries can be a real test of endurance and mental toughness. But if you've done enough miles and trained hard enough, then it is rewarding to do. As I've said before, if I can do it, you can do it. I'm no speed merchant; far from it. I'm often passed and dropped by other riders when I'm out on the road. So take heart, don't be afraid to take it on. If you do miss a ferry and have to wait for another, or even get the train home, so what? Welcome to the club. We've all had to do it at some time or another; it's a pretty big club.

CLAONAIG-TARBERT

Claonaig ferry arr 12.30 pm or dep 3.05 pm to or from Lochranza.

10.6 Miles
Ascent 700 Feet
38-45 Minutes

TARBERT-CLAONAIG

Tarbert ferry dep 1.15 pm or arr 2.10 pm to or from Portavadie (Check CalMac website as ferry times may be subject to change.)

Right enough of all the morbid stuff, for so far so good. We've made all our ferries and now are sailing across Long Fyne with the wind behind us and the old currant bun (sun) upping the feel-good factor big time. As you cross, the view south to Arran now takes on a different but equally dramatic silhouette. Even the island itself appears blue, with perhaps only the white of any present cumulus clouds breaking the stranglehold of what is in essence a fantastic all-encompassing blue heaven.

West Loch Tarbert only comes into view when the B-8001 is climbed (clock), and then it's a great gung-ho descent, none too technical, all the way down to sea level where the A-83 is met. The single track road takes up as near as damnit half of the 10.6 miles of this leg, with the remainder being made up by the much flatter and faster 83.

Just 25 minutes of sailing takes us across the Fyne to Portavadie, which couldn't even be described as the middle of nowhere. That simply wouldn't do its remoteness justice. Despite this, someone had the idea of building an all-singing, all-dancing, upmarket-type marina-style complex, along with likewise associated accommodation. It is a most impressive development, with even the staff quarters being somewhat salubrious, and time will tell if it will be successful. I wish them well.

Picturesque Tarbert harbour is reached, and there's usually no more than a few minutes at least to wait for the ferry's arrival if you are aiming for the very next one. But if not, it's no great hardship to aim for the one after and spend just an hour in this most delightful of spots. I've been known to do that on occasion myself.

The small Isle of Cumbrae ferry approaches Tarbert Slip and, although the wee man was fit
or the job, it has now been replaced by a larger, brand new vessel.

Looking back at Tarbert as the ferry pulls away and enters the deep
broad blue of the Fyne. You are now crossing the country's largest sea
loch. It is a most enjoyable 25 minutes
across to Portavadie.

A lone yacht navigates its way towards Tarbert. Many will be seen
if you are out for a jaunt on a sunny weekend, as well as many bike
riders. I often do the run midweek, and never see
another rider all day long.

PORTAVADIE-COLINTRAIVE

As you arrive onto the Cowal peninsula, the first thing you come to will be the small but welcome sight of the Cal-Mac building, where it's possible to refill your water bottles if needed. If you've studied the timetable enough, you will realise that a challenge now presents itself, should you wish to accept it. According to my computer, it is just under 19 miles, 18.8 to be pedantic, from Portavadie to Colintraive. The time is now 1.40pm. On paper, the next realistic ferry you could catch to carry you over the Kyles would be the 3pm sailing, which will of course deposit you at Rhubodach North Bute, in roughly five minutes.

Not much to look at, but don't let that fool you, because the wee Cal-Mac hut at Portavadie is well able to cater for your needs and a real godsend on a wet and windy day, with warm rooms and good toilets. It has come to my rescue on at least one occasion.

Heading for Portavadie (anti), and the loch you see in the distance is the Fyne, with the Kintyre peninsula beyond. At this point you're on the road between Millhouse and Portavadie itself. It has a really remote feel to it, and this is just magical. If going clockwise, you will be climbing to a point above Millhouse.

The ferries leave Colintraive every 30 minutes for most of the day, for what is one of Europe's shortest car crossings. It's frustrating if you just miss one, for it's a half hour wait before you can then get across a stretch of water you could probably swim in half the time.

When I said on paper that the 3 o'clock ferry is makeable, that's because most riders could cover 19 miles in the 1 hour 20 minutes available on an ordinary stretch of road. The problem is that this is no ordinary stretch of road. This is the most magnificent and toughest leg of the entire journey by far. There is in the region of 1600 feet of ascent between the two terminals; that's a lot of climbing to slow you down, which makes for hot work on a warm day. The reward is tremendous, however, with a view of unforgettable beauty looking down the Kyles of Bute from

a very high vantage point, from where your next ferry can be seen plying its trade on the Kyle, toing and froing between Cowal and the isle.

The reason I mentioned a challenge, if you so wished, is that I reckon the 3 o'clock ferry could be made if you went from the gun and made no stops. This would mean a fairly frantic dash, which might appeal to you if you've done the run several times and want to test yourself. By all means have a go. It's much more pleasurable and less stressful to aim for the 3.30pm sailing, thus giving you 1 hour 50 minutes to cover the road and therefore enjoying it to the full.

Start off by going away from the Portavadie jetty, up a pretty awful stretch of road — no doubt, purpose-laid to service the pier — and in less than a mile you meet the real road, thank God. When I say real road, it's only a single track, but it's in good nick, which makes the fairly gently climb that follows very pleasant.

Away to your right, the waters of the Fyne can still be seen, shimmering beyond the brightly lit green fields and farms. And the sheer quietness of this setting reinforces its feeling of remoteness, which I must say, is something I really do enjoy. It's a gently curving climb up through ferns that look five feet tall in places, through an area of forestation that is now coming to cutting age (25 years), and a lot of it was being felled at the time of writing.

Ahead the road rises a bit steeper, as it heads for a clear gap between two large conifer plantations. On reaching the top of the climb, you find yourself looking down a steeper, bolt-straight stretch of road which fires you straight into the small hamlet of Millhouse.

As you shoot down, the view across this rough hinterland further reinforces the feeling of isolation, which always made me wonder why they built a mill here. I was under the impression it was either a textile mill or baking mill, and couldn't figure out why they put it here.

The high point of the road above Millhouse is seen from a fair distance away when going anticlockwise. It is particularly unmistakable as it sits between to plantations of conifers. At this point you've just climbed out of Kames and are approaching Millhouse itself on the B-8000.

Surely a more accessible location would have reduced transport costs, etc. The most likely answer was safety, for it turns out it was in fact a gunpowder mill and I suppose the more isolated the better.

There is apparently still a powder-testing gun in one of the nearby fields, along with a memorial to those killed whilst working there. God knows how old the mill must have been, but I do know that for men working a cannon itself it was a very precarious operation, just as dangerous for them as it was for those they were aiming at.

This is the aforementioned high point above Millhouse, and now begins a screamer of a descent down to that village. Then it's on down to Tighnabruaich and the Kyles of Bute no less (clock).

On the big pull-up of the day (and that is saying something on this run), when you leave Tighnabruaich on the A-8003 (clock). It goes on for about 4 miles before the viewpoint is reached, though thankfully it isn't sustained.

Your reward for all the climbing is the classic view right down the Kyles of Bute from the high point on the A-8003 (going anti & clock). What a spot it is, and you will have a helluva hard job trying to pull yourself away and get going again. I would defy anybody to ride by here and not stop, as it's got to be the highlight of the whole run.

A closer look at the Kyles from the A-8003 viewpoint, and the Colintraive to Rhubodach ferry can be seen berthed at Colintraive. This picture also shows just how short the crossing really is. Away in the distance is the Ayrshire coastline round about Largs.

begins. 3.5 to 4 miles of climbing now lies ahead, sometimes on single track, sometimes not, by no means sustained. Far from it.

Like a lot of this area's roads, it will level then dip in one or two places, but also rear up hard to test you well, especially mentally, when you may have thought the worst was over. The ordnance survey map says that at no point on this climb does it get to 1 in 7 or 14%. My computer tells me different, a lot different, but I can't guarantee this features accuracy, so will go with the map's assessment.

Our own James II came a cropper during the siege of Roxburgh Castle in 1460, when he personally attempted to fire off a large cannon known as the lion. So there you have it, mystery over. And with that, you arrive at the Millhouse crossroads, where the road straight across will take you curving and climbing gently back through some more high rough meadows, before it descends down delightfully into Kames. Turn left at the next crossroads (staying on the B-8000) and before you know it, you've glided into the land that time forgot: Tighnabruaich. Keep your eye open for the *SS Waverley*, for she still plies these waters from time to time, a reminder of when this now quiet shorefront was once a holiday hotspot.

The blueness and beauty of the Kyles hits you as you descend down onto the shorefront, which is one you want to savour. Yet you don't stay on it for long, only a minute or two. You will still be trying to take in all that is around you when you come to the hotel and must turn left, up the A-8003, and this is where things get tough. It's a short ramp-like start to this one, from the second you come off the shore road, and it might be an idea to get out of the saddle to give yourself an extra bit of oomph!

After that, it's into the routine of sitting down and spinning low gears, as the longest climb of the whole day

As height is gained, what I can tell you is that the view away to your right will get better and more stunning with every few feet gained, so you're constantly looking away to admire it, which helps take your mind of the dog fight you find yourself in.

The climb finally ends at a very obvious official viewing point, complete with information plaque and all. And what can I say? It's a most awesome, uplifting spot to stand on. Your eye is drawn right down the Kyle to as far as the mainland away in the far distance, as the slender strait acts as a natural draw to hold your gaze and admiration for quite some time. The gentle hills on both sides slope away from you, to add to the effect. And in-between, small craft dance in the pool below, amongst the islands and bays, lost in their world for a few hours, as I am in mine.

The one thing that is sure to pull you away is the thought of the great descent to come, and when you do start down, it seems to be an almost mirror image of its opposite number — the side you've just come up.

First you're flying down, then levelling off, then down again, then levelling again, and even a bit of a rise, before finally the bulk of the descending starts and it's payback time for all the suffering. You eventually drop down to the head of Loch Riddon and into a most pretty part — perhaps the most charming of the entire run.

The road now meanders north towards its meeting with the A-886 and in doing so enters deciduous woodland, always a delight, which is complemented perfectly by the meandering River Ruel, as it mimics the road's route back up the glen. It feels so nice to be able to hold a steady pleasant pace now, as this flat stretch of road makes for a welcome break from all the slogging up and manic diving down that you've just done in the previous few miles.

But I must say, it is the presence of the woodland, aided and abetted by the quaintness of a stretch of single track road again, that makes the scene so special. Whoever decided to cut down our native woodlands ought to have been shot. It is one of the few things our scenery really lacks in this era, along with all its associated plants and wildlife. The few buildings at Ormidale couldn't be in a more idyllic setting, you can't help but notice, as you continue to pedal your way north. And in doing so you are actually heading, for the moment at least, in the opposite direction from where you want to go. This can be a frustrating part of this route, especially if you are tight for time when trying to make the ferry at Colintraive.

Colintraive has been successfully reached, and our fourth ferry (if going clockwise) will be the Loch Dunvegan which waits above. No more than five minutes will be required to ferry us over the kyle and deposit us on Bute for the easiest stretch of the whole run, which takes us to Rothesay.

The Kyles of Bute again, though this time in black and white.

You feel you can almost touch the damn thing as you stand looking down the Kyles from the high vantage point, but the minute you leave there, you start going away from your intended target. On top of that, and to make matters worse, despite the fact that it's wonderful on the single track stretch at the head of Loch Ruel (Loch Ruel and Loch Riddon are the same loch), all the hard work is not yet over. When you turn right and start to head down the A-886, it's still scenic, though the charm is lost somewhat by being now on a slightly more imposing A-road. It's roughly just over six miles down to the ferry now, and there is still around 520 feet of ascent to be tackled, which comes in the shape of three fairly lengthy muscle-bound climbs.

Not steep, no. More long and arduous. So it's get into the Jan Ullrich mode, which means hands on the brake lever hoods, select a slightly higher gear than previous climbs, and grind your way up. You want to tackle these climbs like a diesel engine, not a racy fuel injection. The final pull-up is the real daddy of them all, but it can be totally by-passed by a small road on the right, that will be indicated by a rusty old sign post. This, the B-866, follows the shore of the loch, and rejoins the main road

Before you board, however, let me take this opportunity to recommend the Colintraive cludgie that doubles up as the local bus shelter. The water in here is always wonderfully cold, even on the warmest of days, and I always pour some over my head and down my back on a really scorching hot day if I am doing the run clockwise. In fact, I actually look forward to this, as I overheat on the climb over from Tighnabruaich.

on the other side of the climb and, while doing so, takes you most charmingly curving round bends and bays, as it winds past hidden houses and beached boats enroute to Colintraive.

The road surface is, of course, fairly poor in places, and it does meander so much as to slow you down a touch. So if racing for the ferry, stick to the main road, which has the added advantage of a wonderfully exciting descent which deposits you right at the ferry terminal itself. There you go, how was that for a run?

The view you get of Colintraive from the ferry as you cross the kyle when going anticlockwise. Don't forget to fill the water bottles in the Colintraive cludgie when you disembark, as the longest, most arduous, though most scenic leg is just about to begin.

ANTICLOCKWISE

The route over to Portavadie is, of course, the reverse of the way we have just come, with all the equal delights, thrills, and spills of the clockwise journey. You will arrive at Colintraive at 11.45am, after catching the 11.40 at Rhubodach. I thoroughly recommend filling the water bottles in the excellent wee toilet they have beside the slipway[3], before setting off and aiming for the 1.45pm sailing from Portavadie. This gives you a very good cushion of two hours to complete the 18.8 miles over to there, with the early big pull-up from the terminal getting you back in the swing of things early on. Not that you will have cooled down on the crossing, anyway, as it's so bloody short.

Heading north on the A-886 does afford wonderful views up Loch Riddon, ones you can't appreciate as you head south, with even a glimpse of Tighnabruaich itself across the Kyles early on. When you turn left to double back on the A-8003, you come face-to-face with one of those electronic Cal-Mac signs that tells you if the ferry is running or not, and whether it's on time or not. You don't really notice this coming the other way. Then, after the delights of the Ormidale stretch, the big climb is started, where the toughest part will be in the middle section, where my computer shows it going to 13%.

Needless to say, the view is equally as stunning when going in either direction, with both Tighnabruaich and Kames as equally quaint. The pull-up out of Kames is fairly steep, but it curves and climbs delightfully, so is not a chore. The previous monster climb helps to make it feel easy. As Millhouse is approached, the steep straight road leaving it and the gap between the conifers is very telling and acts as a guide drawing you west. It's a pleasant hinterland beyond there, which curves downhill on the remote single track road, with fields, farms, and Loch Fyne showing ahead.

This stretch is a damn sight more pleasant than the road leading down to the terminal itself, but it's always nice to arrive. The aforementioned Cal-Mac hut can be a godsend if the weather turns, and even on the nicest of days it can do very quickly at this point. You should have around 20 to 30 minutes to wait for the ferry arriving, and the last time I was there I noticed the new marina complex had a café attached. Despite the fact it looked wildly expensive, I went in for a coffee and cake. Turns out, it wasn't too bad, no pricier than the hut over by Lochranza.

3 - This is on the Colintraive side. There's only a bus stop at Rhubodach.

PORTAVADIE-COLINTRAIVE

Cal-Mac Colintraive Tel No 01700 841 235

Portavadie ferry arr 1.35 pm or dep 1.45 pm to or from Tarbert.

18.8 Miles
Ascent 1600 Feet
1.19 Hours

COLINTRAIVE-PORTAVADIE

Colintraive ferry dep 3.30 pm or arr 11.45 am to or from Rhubodach.

Now to get back to the clockwise run. If you aimed for the 3.30pm sailing from Colintraive, you will have a wee 20 minutes to yourself here, which is best spent topping up the water bottles in the previously mentioned nearby toilets. And, bearing in mind the water in there is always fantastically cold, if it's a scorcher then also use some of it to cool down by letting it trickle over your head and down your back and front. Oh my, how the simple things in life bring the most pleasure.

As you wait for the boat, you can't help but feel that you've just completed your own mini Tour de France all in one day. There's been rolling terrain, coasts, mountain stages, and time trials, all thrown in for good measure. If

The MV Loch Dunvegan is seen crossing the kyle as you wait for it at Rhubodach (anti). Be warned, though, there is absolutely nought at Rhubodach, not even a bus shelter, so try to time your arrival well so you don't have to wait too long if rain looks imminent. There is nowhere to take cover. On a warm sunny summer's day, however, there is no problem as it is a most wonderful spot to linger.

The long flat road down to Rothesay now begins, and this is you right at the start at Rhubodach (clock). The only slight rise will be as you pass Ardmaleish Farm before you drop most delightfully down to Kames Bay and Port Bannatyne.

that's the case, don't worry because the next stage will feel like a rest day.

The leg from Rhubodach to Rothesay is the easiest one, whichever way you go. For not only has it the least amount of climbing, but it's also the shortest, and going in either direction will not put any time pressure onto your already stressed shoulders.

RHUBODACH-ROTHESAY

So sit back on the ferry and relax; crossing, of course, is done in no time. Then off you spin, taking advantage of the near flat road by gently breaking the old pins in again and looking forward to a wee visit and bite to eat in Rothesay itself. You have 1 hour and 10 minutes to cover the almost totally flat stage of 8.2 miles, so no great hurry, unless you're dying to get in and stuff your face.

As you can imagine, it's a pleasant enough saunter down the kyle, going in and out of some woodland, and continuing the shore ride til the rise is met just before Ardmaleish Farm. This wee bugger is a rather rude interruption to your canter, for it's tougher than it looks,

Flying round Kames Bay and heading for Rhubodach (anti). The skirl along Port Bannatyne's Main Street has just been completed, and with a bit of time to spare and mostly flat road in front of you to the next ferry, it is easy going for now.

rising for about 80 to 100 feet and gets steep to about 10 %. What it does do for you, however, is to give you the elevation to appreciate the tranquil delight of Kames Bay, as down you drop to the shoreline in an effortless glide, and continue in the heat and sunshine to circuit round the bay's curve and into Port Bannatyne itself.

Here I'm met with some old familiar faces — hotels, inns, and stores, that I've ridden past, God knows how many times. But each time it feels better when I do, for I'm never disappointed by this friendly old front, before I disappear quickly up its main street or round its shore road and on towards Rothesay. Down the home straight now, no rush, take it all in again and enjoy it.

There's plenty of time before the ferry docks and plenty of time for a nibble, which is nice, because plenty of time is one thing that is missing from this run but it's the only thing missing from this run. A little bit more of that elusive stuff here and there would most likely add to the pleasure of this outing, but there is time aplenty on all the other runs, so this one is unique in that respect.

You'll soon now find yourself sitting close by the pier enjoying your food. Herring gulls will noisily let you know that they'll have what you don't want, while still keeping a respectful distance. Savour the island's quaint charm. It's too soon for thoughts to turn to mainland climbs off the coast; all that is still far in the future, as lost you sit, not really wanting to be found. Why should you? It's not often you meet these moments

Only with the arrival of your ship in the bay will you part. Til the next time, promise. The ferry itself adds its own presence to the occasion, as those big Cal-Mac diesels send heat-shimmering plumes out into the hot

Rothesay air again, quivering the houses beyond. Raise your coffee cup, tilt it forth, and again promise a return.

Savour the boat's speedy departure. Who knows how long til the next rare Clyde coast scorcher? The grand Glenburn Hotel, an archaic old relic of a bygone day impressing above all others, is shortly passed on starboard. And with it, the island is soon gone again.

Heading down Ardbeg Main Street making for our fifth and last ferry at Rothesay Bay (clock) that will carry us back to the mainland at Wemyss Bay. As always, you will be well under Rothesay's disarming charm by now, and most likely you've eased up a bit to enjoy it, having taken your foot off the gas. I recommend it.

ANTICLOCKWISE

When doing this leg coming in the opposite direction, it is also one which is not too taxing or tight for time. Arriving in Rothesay at 10.50am, having caught the 10.15am at Wemyss Bay, the Rhubodach link-up will be at 11.40am, so giving you 50 minutes to make the 8.2 miles this time. You will still be full of running at this point, and often have to make the journey up into a fresh northerly airflow. Nothing too terrible, just enough wind to aid you in the climbs over to Tighnabruaich and the Boguillie back to Brodick. Even so, shelter can first be found by the protection of Rothesay Bay itself, then by the buildings of Ardbeg Main Street, before the north end of Kames Bay does likewise.

On cresting the rise out of Kames and passing Ardmaleish Farm, any northerly breeze will be felt full-on, as you look in awe up and into the massive Loch Striven. Passing the junction where the Striven meets the inner Kyle of Bute, you are well on your way to your second ferry of the day, which is gained by following the flat shore road and waves. This leg will also prove to be

the easiest, if going anticlockwise, but it gets you warmed up nicely for the hardest. However, that is all behind you now if you're going clockwise, so let's get back to the mainland and the home run.

RHUBODACH –ROTHESAY

Rhubodach ferry arr 3.35 pm or dep 11.40 m to or from Colintraive

**8.2 Miles
Ascent 100 feet
33-35 Minutes**

ROTHESAY-RHUBODACH

Rothesay ferry dep 4.45 pm or arr 10.50 am to or from Wemyss Bay.

WEMYSS BAY-PAISLEY

Another Cal-Mac cup of coffee sees Wemyss Bay approach. The old railway station is a most familiar sight. So here we go then. For the last time today, it's once more unto the breach, dear friends[4], though not for the aid of either England or Saint George. No, it's more personal than that, and more pragmatic; it's the one to get you home.

So big effort time now, for ahead is a fair old way and ahead is a fair old climb. Largs is an option, certainly, but the Greenock route is the one I usually take, being just slightly shorter, bearing in mind it has been a long day. If you've done the run clockwise, chances are you will get a welcome bit of wind assistance as you head off, tootling under the rail bridge and up the short, steep hill to get you out of Wemyss.

Take it from me, it's good to get that one over with, for it's a bit of a pecker, and then you're off. Settling down quickly, you get used to the traffic again on the busy A-78, before shortly diving down into the Inverkip section of the trunk road, which always feels busy and tight. My, how you're missing the quiet island roads already, as they make this stretch feel like a bloody motorway. It always has a bit of a frightening feel to it at Inverkip, but it doesn't last long, as it's flat and fast.

---

4 - **A nice bit of William Shakespeare there.**

And so it's once more goodbye to the islands for another day, as the ferry steams out of Rothesay Bay and heads across the Firth of Clyde (clock). A long look back will be given as always, and so, too, will the promise to return. So far I've always kept my word.

The sanctuary of the big roundabout is soon reached, the one that feeds left into Gourock, but we're going straight across and heading uphill at first, through the Spango Valley. It's dual carriageway here, with a bit of an unofficial cycle track to the inside of the white line, so suddenly there is now plenty of room.

The traffic volume doesn't merit such a wide road in this area; it was built just to accommodate the massive IBM factory that we are just about to pass, which now employs very few. Rising above the Spango is the outliers to the Muirshiel Hills, which at their lip houses the meandering Greenock Cut. And with all this space suddenly upon you, it feels like fresh air fortnight. The gradual pull-up is rhythmical, not brutal, and is mirrored on the other side as the much enjoyed long glide into Greenock.

From this point to the top of the Auchmountain Road will be the toughest part, which starts off with the pull-up past Branchton station, followed by another identical descent on the other side down to the roundabout.

Come off the A-78 here by turning right up Dunlop Street (the B-7054), and shortly start climbing up into the Drumfrochar. You soon hurtle down its lengthy slender gradient, passing the old Tate and Lyle site as you do, before bending left at the bottom, which plunges — and I do mean plunges — down Baker Street. White knuckles grab the brake levers here to make a stop, an abrupt stop. One that must be made halfway down this hill at the traffic lights, to enable the right turn to be made onto Ingelston Street, which is also part of the B-788. This will carry you high out of town. To stay on it, turn first right at the church, before going under another rail bridge and then… Gulp! It's real eyeballs-out stuff, as the start of the Kilmacolm Road rears up on a brutal 15% ramp, and its only saving grace is it's a short one.

The level stretch of road beyond is a godsend, where the long, lengthy climb leading up onto the Auchmountain Road now starts. Forget Jan Ullrich here, this is a real

A look back over the shoulder is more than warranted from near the top of the Auchmountain Road the B-788 (clock) to see Inverclyde sitting still in the evening glow. The last big pull-up of a long and memorable day is now coming to a close, and it is time for a little reflection. A well-earned pat on the back is due, for no more major obstacles are in the way for most now on the home run.

It's almost all over as the top of the Auchmountain Road is neared in glorious evening light (clock), and it's a job well done.

The sharp-eyed among you will have noticed that this, the last leg of the Five Ferries, is simply a re-run of the first leg of the Rothesay run in the opposite direction. That would be correct. Similarly, the first leg of the Five Ferries anticlockwise is the same as the start for Rothesay, with the only difference being the time that I leave Mossneuk Drive. Instead of 10am it would be 8am, to give me plenty of time to catch the 10.15am sailing from Wemyss Bay.

Obviously, as you approach Paisley and the roads become more numerous, then several variations are possible from the route I used to

But I'm going to leave the last word to the anticlockwise run, for this is the fantastic view you get when descending the Gleniffer Braes, usually just after seven in the evening. The hard work has all been done, as all the upping and downing from Ardrossan is behind us now, and I hardly need to turn the cranks to reach my front door. This makes the descent of the braes all the more enjoyable for me. For the record, I actually only got the opportunity to get this shot when I punctured, otherwise I would have flown right down and missed it.

Tommy Voeckler job (read "hang on by your fingernails"). The bulk of the climb isn't too bad, however, and a good wee cadence can be maintained, as you settle into your rhythm and dour it out.

Good views of the Clyde will shortly be exposed, but not great ones. The real dramatic sea lochs and hills will all be over your left shoulder, and thus out of site. Bends and curves, along with a slight steepening in the gradient, means it's almost over, and when the small reservoir, rough grazing, then electric sub-station are reached, it is all over.

Curve and plummet down into the softness of the Renfrewshire dairy fields now, heading for Bridge of Weir on the Auchenfoil Road (still the B-788). Leave it at Gateside Farm and follow the minor roads from there all the way back and through Quarriers Village. The whole pastoral scene will lift and delight just about all but the most exhausted of riders, and if your fitness is up enough by now, you will still be enjoying every minute of it. Leave Quarriers and enter Bridge of Weir by the excellent Torr Road, where dry stane dykes guide you, and pretty cottages on the right hand side welcome you.

gain Bridge of Weir on the Rothesay run. One will be the cycle track, which you pass under coming in on the Torr Road, and is a good, flat, sheltered return route, especially if you are totally canned or the weather has turned real nasty.

Linwood or Johnstone centres are also options if you decide to travel down the flat but busy A-761, but Kilbarchan is quiet and direct, so I tend to go that way, with the only fly in the ointment being the initial steep pull-up out of Bridge of Weir. The great payback is a brilliant descent down into Kilbarchan Village itself, which is now a lot quieter since Paul Gascoigne left.

Carefully you negotiate the heavily parked main street, with its constantly changing quaint names, and then shortly you'll find yourself in Johnstone. To the Beith Road we charge, and thus the top of the Thorn Brae, before heading up the back road into Elderslie, going via the Kings Road and then Abbey Cemetery. The speedy ride down to the Glenpatrick Road is sandwiched between white houses left and fields right, which is always a delight.

It's not all over yet, for the Glenpatrick is a tough wee climb in itself, but it's a pretty one, soon running beside the Brandy Burn's protective stone wall, its shallow waters skipping and jumping neath wood and rock. Then, as rural Renfrewshire is left behind on the Mackie's Mill Road, finally — I repeat, finally — you take the day's last climb, the deceptive wee nipper that takes you up onto Foxbar Road.

I can actually remember when I first climbed this hill on a bike, back in the Seventies, riding my Raleigh Chopper. It took me by surprise then and still does, as it turns out to be a damn site harder than it looks every time. Perhaps being the last real climb of the day might have something to do with it.

ANTICLOCKWISE

If doing the run anticlockwise and heading for Wemyss Bay first, simply follow the return route in the opposite direction, which if you remember is the identical route we took on the way out on the Rothesay run.

WEMYSS BAY-PAISLEY

Cal-Mac Wemyss Bay tel no 01475 520 521
Wemyss Bay ferry arr 5.20 pm or dep 10.15 pm to or from Rothesay

Outward	Return
26.4 Miles	26.4 Miles
Ascent 1440 Feet	Ascent 1360 Feet
1.45 Hours	1.42 Hours

I'm soon at my front door, and first thank my guardian angel for keeping me safe on all those miles once again. Pleasure and satisfaction are always present, and I urge you to attempt the Five Ferries run the first chance you get.

And if that doesn't tempt you to buy a top end machine, I don't know what will.

Liam Boy.

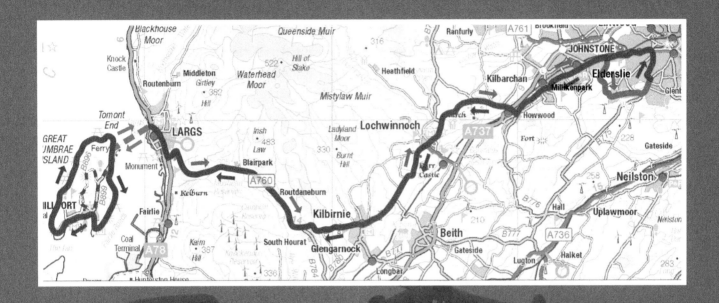

GREAT CUMBRAE

FROM PAISLEY	FROM LARGS
60.3 MILES	14.3 MILES
3.53 HOURS	0.58 MINS
ASCENT: 3300 FEET	ASCENT: 500 FEET
2315 CALORIES BURNED	535 CALORIES BURNED

O/S LANDRANGER MAPS. 64, 63.

CAL MAC LARGS TEL NO 01475 674 134

ROUTE SUMMARY

Elderslie
Johnstone
Howwood
Lochwinnoch
Kilbirnie
Largs Pier

Isle Of Great Cumbrae

Largs Pier
Kilbirnie
Lochwinnoch
Howwood
Johnstone
Elderslie
Paisley

THE MILLPORT RUN

If you just so happen to stay too far away from the Clyde to reach it with a bike, then driving down and parking before beginning the run is a good option. It is done most noticeably on the Arran run, but that tactic can be used anywhere, anytime, whether for this neck of the woods or even somewhere further afield. The reason that I mention this is because the island run that I'm about to describe is perfect for a family man or woman who has young kids and wants to introduce them (and yourself) to the delights of a Clyde island while being perfectly safe. The gentle smooth loop round Great Cumbrae is as near as dammit 10 miles in total, compared to 55 round Arran, with the smaller isle having a total ascent of 20 feet, compared to its big neighbour's 2940.

For the most part, the tarmac is in a damn sight better nick than either Arran or Bute's, so there is less chance of little ones coming off unexpectedly after hitting a bump. This should allay the fears of even the most anxious parent. Apart from the pleasant surprise of a smooth road for once, the other thing that hits you about this place is just how quiet and tranquil it is the moment you leave the ferry. Millport, as the isle is universally known, is again different to that of either Brodick or Rothesay, for the ferry does not dock in the main town, but rather at Cumbrae Slip, several miles round the coast and directly across from Largs.

This means that on disembarkation from the Cal-Mac ferry, there is no hustle and bustle awaiting. No kids, cones, cabs, candy bars, or chuck bars. They're actually waiting in Millport itself, along with some hillbillies, should you land when the Country and Western music festival is on. No, Cumbrae Slip is usually just an orderly queue of cars by the roadside, waiting to board the ferry back to the mainland along with the foot passengers. That's it; all low key to begin with.

Then you trundle off in the direction of the town and find you've got the place to yourself. "So how in God's

113

Passing Barr Castle just after leaving Lochwinnoch on the A-760, and it's taken a tough climb on the Bridesmill Road from Howwood to get here. However, the flatter and safer cycle track can be used to get this far, and also as far as Kilbirnie. It runs just the other side of the castle.

neighbour lying just offshore to the south — previously had small farms or settlements of their own, with Little Cumbrae last showing a population in 1991 of 6 people. This is in complete contrast to Millport's population of around 1400, which makes it the most densely populated island we have.

Still, this isn't in anyway obvious. Like both Bute and Arran, the majority of residents are all situated in the main town and, once out of it, it's solitude again. Along with its most pleasant coast road, the island also has an excellent wee inner hill road, taking you up to its highest point.

name can a flat 10 mile stretch of road be called a run, Liam boy?" I hear you scream.

Well firstly, sticking to the coastal road is only for the wee bambinos, or for anyone — any age or gender — who hasn't been on a bike for a long time. This would also stretch to people who don't even own a bike, for there is more than one bike hire shop in Millport to cater for such clientele. That's just fine by me, as a lot of people go over with the plan of hiring a cycle for a jaunt round the island in mind. You're sure to meet more than your fair share of day trippers as you cruise round the far side of the isle with not a care in the world. Secondly, let me assure, that doing the Millport run from my front door is no stroll in the park.

Far from it. The distance involved of over 60 miles, and the amount of climbing involved, over 3000 feet, make it long enough and arduous enough to be a good summer day's run in itself. But is still short and flexible enough to be done on a calm winter's day, when a trip round an island is required to lift jaded, short-day blues.

Of all the islands in the Clyde, Great Cumbrae is the smallest inhabited one, though it wasn't always the case. Both Inchmarnock and Little Cumbrae — the next door

This gives a testing wee climb in its own right and also provides a view of the Firth of Clyde unequalled by any other, making you feel you've had your money's worth from the ferry fare. This in itself was actually cheaper than was advertised in the Cal Mac brochure at the time of writing, but the service was also different from that advertised, being every 30 minutes instead of 15.

However, it's such a frequent service and such a short waiting time that there is no need for anxiety about missing or catching any particular boat. There are no refreshments on this ferry, as the crossing is so quick — about 10 minutes — and gives just enough time to fire off some photos, or to get out on deck and admire the view.

So that is what awaits you at the end of a 22 to 23 mile, fairly tough run down from Paisley. On a really blowy winter's day this can actually be nigh impossible to do. For when you get up onto the moors above Kilbirnie, the wind can be so strong that on occasion I've been forced to turn back and dive down the Boag Road to Dalry for shelter.

With a lot of great but tough road ahead of us, we better get cracking. Just for a change, I'm going to head out directly west, not by the Foxbar Road, but by going down and out of town by the Ferguslie main road. This, for once, means no climbing to start with, but instead a fast dive down passed the Royal Alexandra Hospital (RAH) and then along the Mill Road. This is a fairly new road and slices through what was the grounds of the old Ferguslie thread mills. I only mention this as it was my father's last place of work. Thomas Coats latterly had two big mills in Paisley — the Anchor and Ferguslie. Both have long ceased trading, though the Anchor Mill, over in the east end at Seedhill, is still there and this magnificent building is now fully restored and has been converted into flats.

As you leave the former Ferguslie Mill site, which is now a modern housing development (surprise, surprise!), you'll notice that the house builders thought it a nice touch to preserve some of the old stonework, which has the Ferguslie Thread Works name on it, thus providing a reminder of what was once there. Let me assure you, however, that Coats were notoriously poor payers right from the word go, with some of the stand-offs between the striking mill girls and the police the stuff of legend. My old man would turn and laugh in his grave at the thought of anyone wanting to be reminded of the place.

This quaint old direction sign is stuck on the side of a house in Kilbirnie just at the start of the Largs Road (Cochrane Street). For me, this is the real start of the run to Millport.

And with that thought, I'm shortly out of there and onto main road Ferguslie. I call it that to prevent any confusion with the nearby housing scheme of Ferguslie; the correct title of the main road is simply Ferguslie, the same as Calside is just Calside. As I head west under the old rail bridge, it's onto Main Road, Elderslie, now and an exacting gradual pull up gets the old heart and lungs finally working, as an attempt at a cycle lane is followed. The main off-road cycle lane which follows the old Canal Street rail line, is on your right, hidden behind an imposing, slanting, big grey wall.

Large houses of mixed style, but all impressive, line the left of the road, as does the clubhouse of Elderslie Golf Club. This was a real playground for me in my youth, as I actually grew up in the Foxbar housing scheme, which sits cheek-by-jowl with the far end of the course. The main cycle route must leave the protection of the old Canal rail line and join the Main Road for a short stretch, before cheekily diving back into cover down to the right, at the appropriately named Canal Street.

I don't take that, but instead I continue along the road and shortly pass a memorial to that great Scottish patriot William Wallace. Elderslie likes to lay claim to being the birthplace of the great man himself, though in all honesty it's impossible to be certain. Wallace, we believe, was brought up in the lowlands in a place called Ellerslie. Certainly that is similar in name to Elderslie, but the place has a rival in Ellerslie Wood in Ayrshire. Some scholars believe his father's name was Malcolm, but others think it Allan. An Allan Wallace was a crown tenant in Ayrshire about that time. So both sites have equal claim.

Descending the big left hand top bend of the famous Haylie Brae, and it's white knuckle time for a few exciting seconds. In fact, you've been plummeting fairly fast for quite some time already to this point, though nothing quite like what is to come.

Elderslie Main continues in a similar vein for about another mile or so, flanked on the left now by neat little cottages, before it comes to the Y-junction which is the top of the Thorn Brae and the start of Johnstone town. It was the birth place of William Farrell, my father; that one I can be sure of. The old Thorn Inn stands guard right in the apex of the Y, sporting an exterior of neat grey and green paintwork, an exterior of a once hard drinking man's pub, which gives a very good accurate first impression of the town, in my opinion. This is where this start route joins the other one coming down the Elderslie back road, and with that it's off down the left fork and out the Beith Road. The going is fairly flat, as first you pass on the left, the bulky Johnstone Castle housing scheme, whose front row of neat houses and gardens does it proud.

This is immediately followed by the Rannoch Wood, whose mature trees separate the Castle from Cochrane Castle — a much smaller estate whose former grey, square, low rise flats have just been demolished, and we await their replacement. This in turn is followed by the high school, whose grounds put the sprawl in sprawling.

Just across the road on the right side, is the somewhat old and rundown Howwood Road scheme, whose ending comes at the roundabout ahead at the top of Cochranemill Road. Beyond that comes the two outlying schemes of the town, Spateston and Coresford. Spateston is the larger of the two, sitting on the left, across the road from its smaller cousin. Despite wearing a grey 1960s concrete uniform, its hillside background does give it a sense of the rural, and is a saving grace.

With the clearing of those two, it's out onto the flat and straight country mile or so to the village of Howwood. This road, for the most part in its early stages, is lined by trees and broken stone walls. Going into the village you meet the white line of solid built houses, straight and true, which line the left. They used to have uninterrupted views across the fields on the right, down into the shallow valley of the River Black Cart. Not so now, as the new development of Torbreckon, directly across the road, somewhat spoils the view. Soon the village centre. Here the village inn, thc Howwood Inn, stands on the right; tall white and welcoming, just as it's always done since it was built in 1770. A more quintessential looking village pub would be hard to imagine.

This is equally matched by the quaint and wonderful village crossroads, whose staggered junction gives the

option to turn left and climb, via a hairpin bend start, the long and pleasing Bowfield Road. This leads up to the loftily perched Bowfield Country Club, which was once a bleaching works; one of two such works in the village that served the Paisley mills. Below Bowfield Road, down to its right, is the ground of Muirdykes, which saw action in 1685 when the Covenanters fought Royalist Jacobites. This has been described as a very bloody encounter. The Covenanters were led by the prominent Cochrane family of Johnstone, whose name survives in the places and roads of that town to this very day.

Back at the crossroads, we want to bank down right, passing the village store and running out of the village on Station Road, where we shortly cross the rail bridge close to the modern station. Although welcome and needed, like all new stations it lacks the charm of its earlier built counterparts, with Howwood's last one closing in 1955. Next comes the stone hump bridge that takes us over the River Black Cart and onward to the first big climb of the day. As you leave Howwood, there is a gradual rising of

More hard braking at the bottom of the Haylie Brae, though this is the last of it, thank heavens. It is a very dramatic arrival to this great seaside town.

Just departing on a fairly choppy sea from Largs pier for the short but scenic jaunt over to Cumbrae

the road at first, before hitting the main climb, then you cross over the cycle lane that follows the route of the old rail line west.

This can be a good alternative to the road should certain circumstances dictate, for it is direct, sheltered and flat. However, as we've just started out and are full of running, we'll stay roadside and tackle the hills. They begin in earnest when you double bend round, and ahead begins the long pull up on the Bridesmill Road. A wall of back-breaking proportions[1] on your left keeps you constant company for the whole duration of this fairly lengthy rise, which isn't too fierce at around 6% gradient. Remember not to attack a big climb early on; stay seated if you can, and get into the right gear and into your rhythm as soon as possible. Get out of the saddle if you must, but again remember that you will be less efficient, as a moving upper body requires oxygen.

Still by standing and moving your hands around on the handlebars from time to time, it spreads the workload around and eases pressure. I personally like to have my hands on top of the bars about a thumb's length away from the stem.

So, green patches of fields make a pleasant partner on the right, as you make the first and therefore usually the hardest climb of any day. If you are in the mood to attack it, leave that till near the top. The Bridesmill then dives down and immediately rises up again, giving the opportunity for another climbing tip: when faced with such a scenario, try and use the momentum from the descent to take you as far up the other side as possible.

1 - For the men who built it that is.

Then, just as you start to lose momentum, having selected the right gear (which is the tricky bit), stand up and give it some welly till you clear the top. This will minimise the overall effort used, and now you're well warmed up.

The Bridesmill dives down again and then it levels out. Look way ahead in the distance, and what a sight awaits. The eye is drawn down into the valley, right down to Castle Semple Loch, with the green fields above rolling away to add to the effect. The loch, incidentally, was named after the large powerful Semple family once prominent in the area. Shortly the high T-junction with the B-786 is reached and, after turning left, the descent down into lovely Lochwinnoch begins, and what a descent it is.

You're in for a very fast treat here, as John's Hill goes down through very salubrious houses near the top, before it will first curve gently and then bend sharply right, dropping down to the long straight Main Street. The buildings lining it are old and solid to a man, giving away their great age. And behind Main Street, there are rows of equally solid white houses. Unlike the ones sitting up on John's Hill, these are all straight and identical, giving away the fact they were purpose-built workers' houses for the nine mills which once operated here. Lochwinnoch was therefore a planned-out village, and not one that developed naturally. It was something akin to an early new town, but one I'm glad to say that is a damn site prettier than East Kilbride.

So, as you roll over the zebra crossing and pass the Brown Bull Inn (one that matches the Howwood Inn for rural rustic), it's up to the junction with the A-760, where you turn right for Kilbirnie. To do so, you must first cross the River Calder by a metal bridge, which has been purposefully narrowed by road markings to keep traffic flowing in only one direction at any given time. This is done by a set of traffic lights, and it's here that I'd like to discuss the subject of traffic lights and cyclists.

I know some bike riders who dutifully wait at red lights and others who charge through with gay abandon. Me? I'm somewhere in the middle. If I think it's safe to go, I'll go. I don't wait at red lights per se. I don't like traffic lights, whether I'm driving or riding. I think they are outdated, inefficient and, worst of all, badly managed.

In Germany, after a certain time at night, they switch off the lights, except at major junctions, and they leave a flashing amber light instead, to warn you to proceed with caution. That makes sense. If they can do it, why can't we? The only time a lot of our junctions move freely is when the bloody lights pack in.

Bridge of Weir and Barrhead are classic examples of this; they used to be great to drive through, but now it's queues, queues, queues. Some drivers take the hump when they see a biker run red, but they're just pissed they have to wait. The road safety brigade will be screaming blue murder here, but that's just my take on it. To a certain extent it has an element of risk but, if done right, is normally okay; well, let me put it this way, after all these years I'm still in one piece. The Prime Minister David Cameron was clocked doing it on his way to the House on one occasion, so if he can do it, I can do it.

The initial short stretch of the A-road, as it leaves the village, is quaintly known as Newton of Barr. It bends left and climbs gently under the trees before passing the sturdy Barr Castle, nestled in its moaty pond overlooking the Barr Loch. This was not a dwelling of the Semples, but built by the Glen family in the 15th century. Its square build gives away its age, as only the earliest castles were built in this style. Later ones were more rounded, to better withstand the impact from cannon balls. Barr, incidentally, is an old lowland Scots word meaning crest of the hill; it's not a place named used anywhere other than the southwest.

The road continues west, firstly by a classic little chicane under the old rail bridge, which now holds the earlier mentioned cycle route, and then begins a tough wee stretch with one or two small testing hills. They push the old heart rate up and let you know you're alive, as the cut-off road to Beith is shortly passed and into Ayrshire you go. The taking of the next rises enters you into some great curving farm road, passing by farms, through fields, just as Kilbirnie Loch now appears in the valley down left. All this just before the bending descent into the old North Ayrshire town begins, with the moorland hills beyond making it quite a pretty scene as you do.

There are still old mill buildings down by the Garnock, to give this former textile town some attachment to its past. You'll see them on your left as you approach the roundabout near the centre. But go right, then left at the next mini roundabout, where a great old road sign attached to a building lets you know you're on the Largs Road proper.

One or two yachts dance on the waves on the horizon of the Fairlie Roads, as this stretch of water is known. This is the view looking south from the ferry towards Hunterston.

Now you're talking. Nine magnificent, but fairly arduous miles will get you to this old Clyde coast favourite and, as we start out, it will have occurred to some of you at least that we have already covered this road as we returned from the Rothesay run. Well, now's as good a time as any to explain why I am going into such detail on a road we have already covered, admittedly in the opposite direction. And that's because some roads, though not all, are completely different animals when done one way as opposed to the other. The Largs Road most definitely falls into that category for several reasons.

Firstly, heading west will most likely be into a headwind, which you soon learn makes it a lot harder a lot of the time. Second, the gradient runs in the totally opposite way, and therefore gives a completely different slant to the ride (if you'll pardon the bloody awful pun). Third, the scenery going out west is quite different in places, thus making it appear an entirely different road altogether. And fourthly, heading out as opposed to heading home, especially when returning after a very long run, is a completely different mindset and therefore totally different again.

So an uphill slope takes you and the road up and away from the centre. And as you go, you'll notice on the left what appears to be a new development of houses, some for rent. These, I think, come with a built-in no buy clause, courtesy of Cunninghame Housing Association, as Maggie's[2] right to buy your council house policy wasn't the best or the most balanced, though neither was she.

2 - Thatcher of course.

So, with a bit of cheer in my heart, I head out west. As you pass the golf course, the serious climbing begins in the shape of a long rhythmical pull up onto the moors themselves.

Soon the familiar trappings of that terrain will be encountered: the rough grazing; the sitka spruce plantations (in various shapes and sizes); reservoirs; and now, unfortunately, wind farms. The Largs Road is no exception, with one of those ugly buggers appearing and sitting on the left, just after you pass that old stalwart of a bolthole, the Boag Road (the B-784). The worst of the climbing is over now, and from here you turn your attention to getting the head down and tackling the remaining miles to the top of the Haylie Brae. All the while the road still continues to climb at a gradual gait, going from about 170 metres at the Boag to around the 230 mark at its highest point.

Kilbirnie itself sits around the 50 metres mark and, with the A-760 being just short of 2 miles to the Boag and with 120 metres of climbing required to reach it, it will give you some idea of the climb up. It's a fast road for cars now, but isn't too busy to make it unpleasant, as both Camphill and then Muirhead Reservoirs mark your progress west. The approach to Muirhead in particular is quite striking in the way that the dam wall cuts bolt straight across the landscape, defying nature of course, which does nothing in a straight line. On a warm summer's day with a gentle westerly wind, it's great to ride this high moor road, especially in rare baking heat, as the closer to the coast is, the greater the expectation.

When the road suddenly becomes free of cars, there is silence. Hot, high, moorland silence, a special silence. One that requires the inclusion of high ground exertion to lift you into that special place, a place one can't get to on lower ground.

You do need some vehicular noise first to provide the springboard to the place of appreciation. Rather like when you deliberately tense your muscles then relax them when you want to attain a certain level when doing some relaxation techniques. A bit like the relief you feel when a neighbour's alarm stops ringing; the Largs Road is often like that. The peacefulness hits you. The stillness hits you. Enjoy this special moment of health and appreciation. The cars won't be long in returning, of course; in the meantime, enjoy.

Being in such a great state now, the prize of the descent down to the coast with all its magical moments will soon be upon you, and with it, all hard slog and effort will be instantly forgotten. But before we get there, I want to talk about another important aspect of the endurance game and that is nutrition.

In the modern day western world, we have and are making some great advances in numerous fields, and at one hell of a rate at that. However, in one important area in all our lives, we seem to have lost our way and could even be described as going backwards. That area is food and nutrition. In my schooldays back in the late seventies and early eighties, there was hardly a fat kid in the entire school.

Not so nowadays. A very well marketed fast food industry, computer games taking over from active outdoor games, cars providing school runs, and busy parents relying more on quick-fix dinners, have all meant a gradual rise in obesity in juveniles and adults over a period of time.

If you come to cycling fairly young, you get into it enough to race and you're in pretty good nick, then a balanced protein and carbohydrate diet — one that is specific to your events — will be appropriate. For others who arrive on the scene, weight loss from cycling is an attraction or even a necessity. To them, I'd say first of all congratulations, you've just made a good decision. Life is all about decisions.

The key to good sustainable weight loss will be bike riding and a high protein, low carbohydrate diet. You do not need to go strictly Atkins here; far from it. When you are on the bike, it's fine to have high energy food, whether it's in the shape of drink additives or its food bars. In the winter I usually have some chocolate bars — just bog standard, nothing fancy — in my back pocket for longer runs. In the warmer weather, when the chocolate would melt, I have similar bars that aren't chocolate-covered.

You can invest in some specially designed power bars and such like, which do contain additional benefits. But remember, the body simply breaks down whatever you're eating to sugar to use it as fuel. No matter what it is, the body will do the same with it. It doesn't matter if it's a Kit Kat or an expensive energy bar, it goes through the same process.

Don't forget what I said earlier. When you stop riding, it's okay to eat carbs for the first 20 minutes, for they get stored in the liver as glycogen and replenish the depleted energy stores. After 20 minutes, the carbs get stored in the body as fat, so that's your cut-off time. When you eat food, it releases insulin from the pancreas which the body

Heading for Millport on the island's inside road, having just come off the ferry at Cumbrae slip, and the quiet charm hits you straight away. The fact that the road has just been resurfaced and is bowling green smooth, makes it even more of a pleasure.

uses to provide energy. This is fine when you're doing a high workload; when you're on the bike, in other words.

However, when you are sedentary, most of the insulin that is produced will store the unused energy as fat. High protein foods produce less insulin than high carbohydrate foods, because they have less sugar, so when you're not riding, stick to the protein not the carbs, it will make the fat come off quicker.

The glycaemic index was a system designed for diabetics to inform — and thus help — them to avoid high glycaemic (sugary) foods and help them stay balanced. It's a good idea to go online and get a copy or some knowledge of the glycaemic index to help you avoid weight gain, even if you're not diabetic. The foods you want to avoid are white bread, potatoes, pasta, and such like. And just cutting out

the food that you know is crap — the crisps, sweets, fizzy drinks — will make a real difference.

A specifically made cycling recovery drink can be good to have when returning from an especially long run, and does help, as these contain ingredients which replenish what the body loses in sweat. Drink additives can also be useful if you intend to do a ride of more than an hour's duration.

Obviously drinking pure water, with no additives, will mean that your body will call on the energy stored in fat to propel it and thus make weight loss quicker. And yes, when you get used to doing longer runs, the body does become more efficient by using more of your stored fat for energy. But not all drink additives contain carbs. I like to use the Zero High 5 tablets, which contain electrolytes but no sugars.

Keep your eye open for the big lion-shaped rock which you will pass enroute to Millport; it really does resemble the big cat, in all truth. So much so that I was completely taken aback when I first saw it, as I had never heard of it before I set eyes on it.

and I admit I find water hard to adjust to, but again, gradually going over to it is best. This is especially true if at the moment you are a fizzy drink fan, whether it's low cal or not.

If you are changing or are in the process of changing your diet, be aware of how you are feeling. If you start feeling unhappy for any reason, it might mean you are trying to do too much too soon. Re-adjust slightly back to the old diet and go again. It helps to know yourself here, and to be able to go inside and workout what's wrong. That's not easy for some to do, but that's where the morning pages will help, more of which later. And with that lecture over, we arrive at the top of the Haylie Brae.

You would have seen the magnificent high peaks of Arran as you approached the back end of the Kelburn Estate which, with its trees and wall, shortly obscures the great view west. The descent starts right from the moment you come level with the old locked east gate, and then it's time to relax and get a well-earned breather as the force of gravity alone will do the work.

Here we go then: Toro-Toro-Toro, hands on the hoods as the now smoothed surface swings right and the long straight road ahead pulls you down. Far in the distance, the blue of the Firth of Clyde can be seen. But that's about

This means I get some energy, but still get maximum fat burn. 1½ tablets per water bottle, I find, is sufficient. So during and just after a ride, carbs are fine, but try not to eat them just before a short ride of less than an hour or so, because by not doing so it will encourage the growth hormone. The growth hormone is what makes you look muscular and gets you into shape. Eating before a short run and activating your insulin will cancel out the effects of the growth hormone, so leave the grub out on the short ones.

If you are used to a high carbohydrate diet at the moment, gradually bring yourself off it, but don't try and stop eating carbs overnight. You simply won't be able to handle it. I'm speaking from bitter experience here. You will quickly become one unhappy bunny, so no Kamikaze tactics. A gentle wean off is best.

Water is the best drink when not exercising, as it also helps with the reshaping process. I am a right tea and coffee hand,

The shimmering Clyde shining aglow just as you pass Keppel pier. Soon the swing round into Millport Bay will be made, but don't worry, as your tranquillity won't be disturbed by any great rate. Anyway, the gentle old look of the town will provide its own unique charm as compensation.

Before you swing away from the inside road, a really good look can be had across the Fairlie Roads to Hunterston Ore Terminal. This, like the rest of the mainland, is close enough for you to appreciate in detail. This is the big difference between Cumbrae and the other two Clyde islands, Arran and Bute, which are too far from the mainland for you to notice.

all, as that bloody great big wall on the left hides the rest and the best of it, away to your immediate left.

There's no time for admiring the scenery now, as you literally scream bolt straight to the start of the steepest part of the Haylie and, thereafter, even more acceleration as it gets technical. The first big wide left hand sweeping bend is hit and it can be an awkward bugger to get right. Remember, the body stays low and centred as the bike leans in, and don't steer into the corner.

Inside leg is best against the top tube, but some guys — even the pros — like to let it swing out. Soon you're round and then speedily down to the bottom right hander, which is tighter and just as fast and awkward as the top bend. This is followed in a split second by the hairy hurtle down to the lights at the bottom, with the old hands hurting from the constant braking.

Not too far to go now, and it's a much gentler ride down into the busy streets and town of Largs itself. Quickly a roundabout, then a second small roundabout are reached, and just beyond on the left is the rail station. The ferry terminal is almost dead ahead now, but what really strikes me is that no matter how quiet the place is, this part always seems teeming and mobbed.

It's only a couple of hundred metres or so to go now, as you navigate your way through all the hustle and bustle. Add to this the usual seaside suspects of calling gulls, salt air, and even the smell of fish and chips on occasion, then finally Cal Mac, with the Loch Shira being your host ferry.

As it backs away from the shore, Largs always show an

impressive front, with its colourful carnival and striking church spires. The non-sandy, pebble beach right in front of you was most likely the spot where the Battle of Largs itself took place, and not where the monument to the conflict was erected about half a mile to the right, in the shape of the pencil.

The conflict was over ownership of the Western Isles, which had been in Norwegian hands, in one guise or another, for over 400 hundred years. The Scottish King at the time, Alexander III, had tried unsuccessfully to buy back the islands, as had his father, Alexander II, before him. In fact, his father almost succeeded in winning them back by force, but died unexpectedly, just as victory was in sight.

When Alexander III therefore found himself in the position of main man, he was still only a boy, so everything got put on hold. Thirteen years later, when the now Norwegian King Hakon refused to sell, the III followed in his old man's footsteps and went on the offensive. This forced Hakon into action, and he assembled what was described as the largest fleet ever to leave Norwegian shores.

Eventually, after a bit of island hopping, the Norwegians found themselves anchored off Great Cumbrae, roughly where Cumbrae Slip is now positioned. On the last night of September 1263, a storm forced about four of their boats onto the coast, which the Vikings then set about trying to salvage. On the 2nd of October, the main Scottish force — under Alexander of Dundonald — arrived on the scene from the south, to give battle.

And with a swing right at the south end of the island, the approach to Millport is made, which requires you to skirt round its rather stunning looking bay, I might add.

Arran's peaks sit behind the bobbing boats in Millport Bay, and they say that the big island looks its best from this viewpoint. You make your own mind up on that one.

It seems that the Norweegies were in two positions. A smaller force of about 200 men were on a mound just inland, led by Ogmund Crouchdance[3]. And the bulk of them, 700 to 800 men, including Hakon himself, were on the beach. The mound men feared being cut off from the rest, and so decided to join their comrades in arms down shoreside. However, their tactical retreat soon became a rout, which caused a bit of panic among the beach-based Vikings.

They retreated to their boats, where fierce fighting now took place, with swords, bows, axes, and even stones (thrown by Scots slingers) all being used. The Scots now occupied the mound, though to the Norweegies credit, they won it back by the day's end[4].

At night the Norsemen boarded their ships, but returned next morning to pick up their dead, before sailing north to the Shetlands, where old Hakon shortly passed away. The issue of the islands themselves was settled three years later in the Treaty of Perth, which finally saw the Scots take sovereignty over all the Hebridean Isles and the Isle of Man (Mann).

Don't forget that negotiations were constantly going on between the two sides, before, during, and after the whole conflict, and it was skilful, protracted negotiations by Alexander III that kept Hakon's fleet anchored offshore till

3 - The Vikings often gave men names due to their features or characteristics. I can only assume that Ogmund was a demon on the dance floor.

4 - This mound is now topped by a monument called the Three Sisters that has nought to do with the battle.

123

This time it's Little Cumbrae that looks good across Millport Bay, and it can look stunning from various vantage points around the island.

The fertility of the island's landscape often comes as a surprise, as you approach, for it's difficult to imagine such a small isle having as much dairy land as this does. As you trundle away from Cumbrae Slip, suddenly all is charming. Now, mark my words here. It doesn't matter which way you tackle the island or which permutation you do any or all the roads on the isle; every way — and I do mean every way — will be an absolute pleasure and delight.

Turn right coming off the boat, and it's round the top of the island and down the back road. You really are coast-side here, down touching the water's edge, giving you such a low viewpoint, that the blue of the firth and the blue of the air seem to totally overwhelm you.

The blueness at close quarters is further enhanced by the shoreline rock, striking deep red sandstone, which encompasses most of the island, except around Millport itself. Looking up the Clyde will be the first great flat blue that delights you. You should be able to make out the tall tower of Inverkip power station, just after passing the monument at Tomont End, which (although hard to read) was erected to remember two drowned midshipmen from HMS Shearwater back in the 1840s. The rest of the firth, and then the adjacent Isle of Bute, provide the eye candy

the storm hit. This was a good tactical move, for the odds were not in the Scots King's favour.

So with that historical knowledge now firmly rammed down your throat, it's time to lean against the ferry's bannister and admire the rising rounded Largs hills, which make a superb backdrop to the town. The cut of the Gogo Glen, sitting deeply and directly behind, is very noticeable and striking, as the boat goes quickly across the Firth. As eye-catching as the mainland is, you're sure to find your attention quickly turning to where you are heading, as the Cumbrae Slip quickly approaches. However, before you get that far — in fact, just after the boat departs— you can't help but notice that the horizon to the south on the Clyde, almost seems to have a line drawn along it from Hunterston to the top of Cumbrae. Shimmering waters, with high, long-sailed yachts, provides an enchanting and mesmerising view that quickly seems to move left and is gone.

Skirting round the streets of Millport Town, with the bay slightly aglow with good light. The combination of sea, light, and land, can often keep it all interesting at every corner turned.

If you decide to head for Millport by coming down the far side of the island, as opposed to using the inside road, this will be one of the many great views of Arran and Bute you will get as you make your way down.

as you start making your way quaintly down the back straight.

I say quaintly because of the road's situation, condition, and particularly the single pavement that accompanies it, which is void of street lights. It really gives the feel of old time transport, a land that time forgot — and who's complaining? Widely across the Clyde lies the Cowal Hills, sometimes clear, often white-topped, but at times too far away to see Toward lighthouse.

Bute (Rothesay) lies closer and at first provides a gentle, but classic canvas to the performing white-sailed yachts on their watery, wavy stage. It certainly holds your gaze, and just as well. The far end of Cumbrae itself is a rather uniform and drab affair, with first of all the shoreline and its dramatic red sandstone rock. Sometimes, but not always, there is some wild machair between it and the road.

Then comes the road and pavement itself, which has on its inside a rather wild fields-width of overgrown machair heather and gorse, which ends in either a steep ramp of trees or crags. It does remind me of the far side of Arran in places, but it's fair to say that the view of the firth is so stunning, that it totally overwhelms the island for scenery at this point.

So this is what greets you as you head south down the west road of Cumbrae, passing numerous named bays — White Bay, Wine Bay, the unfortunately named Stinking, the delightful Skate, then Little Skate. Below Bell Craig there is Bell Bay, and next comes Fintry, which has a much visited café, should you be so inclined.

I don't, as a rule, so I trundle on which is no great hardship, because the view simply gets more stunning by the wheel turn. Not only does the slightly more dramatic South Bute put in an appearance, but right behind it comes real drama in the sky, in the shape of Arran's mountains. When they're clear, they are an awe-inspiring sight. When they are cloudy or misty, it adds to their mystery.

The southern tip of Bute holding the Relic of Saint Blane's Church is its remotest part, and cuts a fine silhouette in the shape of its prominent Hawks Nib Crag. This is somewhat overshadowed, not surprisingly, by what is a full broadside of the Arran armoury; it is a scene that would put most others in the shade.

The road down continues past Deadman's Bay and then, once past the bay of Sheriff's Port, another scenic twist is added to the pot. This comes as a bit of a stunning shock to the system; it will feel like you have really been in a hypnotised state, as the going was slow and the view mesmerising. When I say the going was slow, what I'm really saying is that Cumbrae's only fault is that it is simply too small. It's only natural to slow down and make it last when you finally do get on it, and only then do you realise just how good it really is. The gaze is held westward, constantly and trance-like, as you trundle south on the island's outside road.

Arran provides, as always, a sharp, high show and then, totally unexpectedly, Little Cumbrae has the audacity to try and steal, if not the show, then certainly the scene. I

Once the climb up to the island's trig point begins in earnest, the views really do open up. This is a look up the Clyde from the high road, with Inverkip's power station chimney very prominent.

say unexpectedly, because nowhere else on the Clyde does this small isle appear so close or as dramatic as it does when you near the town of Millport from its west side.

The slanting diagonal crag that rises away from you, sitting as it does above the Wee Man's Long Bay, tries to be the equal in seascape drama to the mighty Arran itself, no less. This is helped greatly by its close proximity and its rugged garb, as it rises up to its highest point of Lighthouse Hill. So now it's the almost touchable little one that holds the gaze as, swinging left, just a flat field's width in from the coast at Nupkur Point, you near Millport itself.

First, you will unexpectedly encounter some wooden chalet-type houses that would not look out of place by the side of a Norwegian fjord. But that's only temporary, as soon the strongly-built, aged buildings and tight pier side streets are entered, and you're into the town proper. To reach this destination from the Cumbrae Slip direct, or should I say by the inside shore road, the going is mostly sheltered from any westerly breeze, making it pleasant and peaceful, It isn't too misleading to say idyllic. Even the road surface, normally an island's Achilles heel, is as smooth as a baby's. No need for any exertion either; like the rest of the circular shore road, there's not more than 20 feet of ascent in sight.

It begins at the slip, of course, and quickly passes the outdoor centre on the right, then shortly thereafter the old pier and white cottage at Down Craig, which nestles below its woodland copse. Just past that is the magnificent B-899 road, sloping away and up into the woods to the

Often after making a full circuit of the island clockwise, I will then cut inland after I've repassed Cumbrae Slip and start to make my way to the top of the island. This is done on the B-899 which eventually runs into Millport Town as Ferry Road. To reach the top, however, we take a right turn off it at the lovely wee junction you come to just after Ballochmartin Farm. In its early stages, it is very leafy lane.

This is you looking Northwest from high on Great Cumbrae, towards Loch Striven and the Cowal hills. It is an awesome sight. The broad blue of the sky and firth can put you in your place

right, heading southwest, on a slightly more direct line toward old Millport Town itself. It's a road we will be taking later, but in the meantime continue heading on down the shore road, where Farland Hill's high ground — prominent and pastoral in the distance with its soft sloping green jacket — is in complete contrast to the two blue tall cranes of the Hunterston Ore Terminal, sitting directly opposite, across the narrow strait of the Fairlie Road. This is the name given to the short stretch of water between the isle and the mainland at this point.

Right down by the water's edge, the road bends and curves in concert with the shoreline. It sits only feet above the waterline and is protected from the ravages of flooding by a rather antiquated and, to be honest, ineffective looking shallow concrete slope. To its credit,

The trig point is just about reached after the tough wee final ramp on the road has been forced up. The Glaid Stone is the big rock sitting to the right.

this does have an element of charm attached to it and blends in very well with just about everything else on the island. Just about everything else on the island has an element of charm attached to it.

The mainland feels so close at this point that you want to reach across and touch it as you pass the bays and points of the inside road, which have even better names that the west roads. Names like Stinking Goat, Clashfarland Point, Davy's Dub and Butter Lump.

This continues so smoothly and delightfully until you come level with the Hunterston Ore Terminal on the opposite shore and it's then you can appreciate the length of the pier there. Having once driven to the end of it, I can assure you it is of awesome proportions. The size of one of the massive coal scoops — the smaller versions you see on JCBs — could have easily swallowed up my vehicle and then some.

It's also at this point that you spy yet another pier; this is the Keppel, which is immediately right after the Millport Town sign. Before going any further, look behind you and you will see a rather strange sight in an unusual rock formation, known as the Lion. This is assuming you haven't seen it already; it could not be more accurately named.

Across from Keppel Pier is the old Marine Research Station, whose splendid buildings give away its ripe old age. The road bends right, and as it does it takes you round into Millport Bay and the town itself. What a magnificent sight greets you as you do, both aquatic and ashore. The bay contains the Eileans — a couple of small, low lying islands right in the heart of it, which provide even more shelter for small craft in what is already an ideal natural haven for them. This is emphasised by the amount of yachts and small boats anchored there.

Only just further out sits the splendid Little Cumbrae, behind which is the star herself, just waiting in the wings for the clouds to clear her high peaks — the sharp Arran at her best.

Looking north up the Clyde from the highest point on the island. It is reputedly the finest viewpoint on the whole of the Clyde coast, and even if you personally have another favourite, you must agree that this is up there with the best of them.

Looking Northwest from the top of Great Cumbrae, with the famous Glaid Stone in the foreground. It is very easy to linger here for ages.

If so, this they say is the place to see her, for it is reputed that from Millport Bay the very best view of the Dark Isle is to be had. You make your own mind up on that one, and you will have some time to do it as there is the sandy Kames Bay, which is the inner top right hand part of the larger Millport Bay, to ride round. What a ride round it is. The whole of Millport's dwellings — some white, some grey, some red, two high, three high, but all solid — sweep in an arc. The road sweeps in an arc, as does the brilliant white iron railing that separates road from rock at this part. It's a sensational sweep, sitting as it does between the blue of the bay and the green of the woods and hills above.

Head round and do your utmost to take it all in as delight comes at you from all angles. This is one of several prominent Kames Bays in this neck of the woods, and

as far as I can tell Kames is just an anglicised version of Camus, the Gaelic word for bay.

This is another slow down stretch here. You can't help but feel you've reached your destination, despite the fact there is still a long way to go. The solid villas that line the right hand side are all of impressive character, which is also the word I'd use to describe the majority of buildings on the Millport shorefront. As you clear the end of the small sandy beach of Kames, the prominent road coming in over your right shoulder is the B-899 and is an equally fitting way to arrive here.

Round the bend and it's Glasgow Street, with the road sitting back from the shore just a little now as you purr along trying to take in the whole scene. This may include numerous American and Confederate flags that fly from lampposts and the like, in support of the now well-known

Still on top of the island here, but just beginning to make for Millport. Even at its highest point, the island is still fertile enough to support cattle rather than sheep grazing.

Millport Country and Western festival. Some buses have displayed destinations like Nashville as they waited for the ferry at Cumbrae Slip in the past, just to get you in the mood for some hillbilly shindiggin. The buses themselves also had a bit of turf war going on back in the eighties, when Maggie struck again with her deregulation of bus routes.

As hard as it is now to believe there was a no-holds-barred-whacky-races episode, with buses vying for business from the town to the ferry and vice versa, it got so dangerous at one point that visiting cyclists would stick to the outside road for safety reasons. Nowadays, thankfully, that's not the case.

A massive white marquee tent sits in the grounds of Garrison House when the festival is on, and as you ride past it's banjos and take your partners by the hand. A hot dog stall (snack bar) conveniently sits to the left. After passing numerous cafes and a couple of bike hire shops, the small sunken stone harbour and old wooden pier are reached.

The pier is worth a ride onto if you fancy it, giving good views out across the bay and Eileans. Come back past the Royal George Hotel and climb slightly out onto the West Bay Rd, bending left as you do. Straight ahead is the road climbing up to the golf course, which promises much but offers little, a bit like a dating agency. The West Bay then drops slightly and as it does it opens up a coastline of sand, rocky shore, and Little Cumbrae, with a run out past classic grey stone villas that mirror those on the run in. The panorama of Little Cumbrae, Arran, and the tail end of Bute, all dutifully sing harmoniously in the view, as you swing out onto the Valhalla of the west coast road.

I like to head on up the back straight and be totally engulfed in the big blue. Sunglasses hopefully fully needed, sun-creamed limbs basting, and low gears spinning. All this continues right up to the top where, coming back round to and approaching the Cumbrae Slip, Largs comes within sight and touching distance again. However, it's not ferry time yet. No visit to Millport would be complete for me without a climb up to its highest point at the trig point and Glaid Stone. To get there, first ride past the white cottage at Down Craig, then take a right up the B-899.

The climb is a fine one and not brutal; far from it. It is chocolate box pretty, as you ascend up through the leafy lane, enjoying views of the Clyde and its accompanying hills through the hedgerows and across the long sloping dairy fields to the left.

The farm of Ballochmartin is cut through as the landscape opens up, with the hedges giving way to the dry stane dykes of the upper road. This quickly leads to the junction with the road coming down from the top. Double back hard right and climb just a little bit steeper at first, as you round the side of Tonnel Hill, with the view up the Clyde starting to appear and making this a very worthwhile effort. The blue channel of the upper river draws the eye northwards, guided in by the low-lying Cowal and Inverclyde hills on either side.

A comfortable cadence can be kept as the road narrowly bends left again through some stumpy wind-clipped trees, and soon the view west is in the ascendancy. Now it really does start to get seriously glorious, as the broad

A fantastic view of both Arran and South Bute just before the screaming steep descent down to Millport begins.
Every twist and turn of the high road brings one amazing vista after another.

Looking down to Millport Town while still high up on the inner road, but the drop down to Breakough Farm is just starting and it's a bolt straight belter. Beware the bad road surface going through the farm, which is accompanied by a wicked bend

firth reveals itself in its entire splendid blue green garb, with white poised cumulus clouds above providing added radiance to the colours. These can come in neat if not perfectly straight layers, with the green fields of Cumbrae lying below them.

Then it's the turn of the Bute and Cowal greens, above which the lighter blue hues of the sky contrast with their cumulus cousins. The foreground colours are further added to by the red rusty tin roofs of Figgatoch Farm's barns and outbuildings, as it nestles safely in its dairy green garden, with a crop of fine mature deciduous trees to its credit.

The firth's width is further enhanced by our old mates, the Kyles of Bute, as they cut deeply and broadly away

Looking over Millport Town towards the Holy Isle, this time when approaching on the B-899 Ferry Road. This is another delightful way to make your entrance to the island's capital.

northwest toward the mighty Loch Striven. That really does give the whole scene an overwhelming feeling of space from the already airy and lofty perch, which is just about to be added to by climbing the ramp-like finish up to the trig point and Glaid. It's a 1 in 7 ascent here, which thankfully is as short as it is steep. When cleared, it does puff you out, but makes you feel you have earned the reward. Bang! The brilliant purple of the surrounding heather, absent on the ascent but now dominating the ground cover all around, throws additional radiance into the colour scheme. Dismounting then leaning the bike against one of the numerous green benches, you walk the few short steps up to the trig point and its partner in crime, the Glaid Stone.

The spire of the Cathedral of the Isles stands prominent in front of Arran's high peaks. This scene again is from the approach on the Ferry Road. This is often a forgotten route, but one I recommend you do even if it means having to ride another stretch of road twice. This is because it is such a beautiful road to ride, but to be honest there isn't a bad stretch of road on the whole island.

It's the view out west that holds court now, for it is just so mesmerising and stunning that it totally overshadows what would otherwise be a great view east towards Largs and the mainland. This, for the most part, is without the assistance of Arran, which at this point isn't shown at its best, by being somewhat hidden behind trees just to your left. If it's still and clear and bright and blue, what a job you will have pulling yourself away here. As I said earlier, it is reputed to be the finest view to be had in the whole of the Clyde coast. Linger as long as you like; no rush today. No big miles to be done. No long distances or big gears to be turned, just pleasure-filled miles, too few island miles at that.

As you do take your leave, you skirt round road and pond; riding through more high, hardy, stumpy trees which cling gamely and stoutly to the roadside, as a swing

The island has been ridden, and alas now it's time to return. The MV Loch Shira makes a fine sight as she cuts across the Clyde, with Largs town and its hills making a fantastic backdrop.

down and across Cumbrae's two cute reservoirs and out into the shimmering afternoon or, better still, evening waters of the glinting firth. Cumbrae's camel-backed, twin-humped Play Hill is prominent in the foreground, but it quickly falls away and tumbles down to the shore, over its lush green fields, and draws your eye flatly and bluely to the outline of South Bute.

There's no chance of picking out the dwellings or sandy beach of Kilchattan Bay in its dark silhouette, as the top of its outline slopes gently and quietly into the sea away to the left. Behind this, the mighty Isle of Arran does the same, where chances are her sharp peaks have snagged the clouds and held them captive in a line. Its ground falls away left and longer than Bute's, drawing the eye this time onto the closer-lying Little Cumbrae, now positioned right behind Play Hill's nearest and dearest highest hump. Young beef cattle graze in the fields even at the island's highest point, giving some idea of the lushness and temperate climate here, as the road starts to propel you down now; down straight and quickly at first, narrow and fast.

and a dip brings the south of the firth into view. This is when the most spectacular and grandest of all the island's scenes is encountered, and that is really saying something.

No prizes for guessing it's Arran that is the star attraction, now it has fully come into view, as you look

The MV Loch Shira glides into Cumbrae Slip. It's always a leisurely boarding, as the schedule isn't as strictly adhered to the way it is on the Brodick or Rothesay runs.

The Eileans in Millport Bay are just visible beyond the magnificent spire of the Cathedral of the Isles, as you hurtle down, hands on brake hoods, eyes ahead on the blue line of the horizon. All of a sudden the road gets technical. Up until now the road surface has been very good to excellent all round. But only at this point when you really need it, as the road itself turns sharply and steeply through Breakough Farm, does the road surface seriously let you down. It is so bad at this part that I would go as far as to say it is dangerous. So much so that unless you have ridden this stretch before and know what to expect, it is probably better and safer to first tackle this road in the opposite direction.

Even if you do know how lumpy and bumpy it is, you will still have to go round at a snail's pace, with both hands braking hard, and full concentration on the route

A great view of Cumbrae island from the mainland, taken on another run on another day. This one was from the high Routenburn Road that runs past Routenburn golf course, which can be accessed from Largs and gives great views of the Clyde as you run its length down to Skelmorlie. The start is easy to find, as it's signposted for the golf club.

you take, just to avoid the worst. Once through the farm, the road immediately returns to its usual high quality, where you quickly have a choice of two roads back into the town. Left will take you down to the start of the B-899, which at that point is known as the Ferry Road, or straight ahead will drop you back into the middle of Millport via the brilliantly stone wall-lined College Street.

On the way down you pass the Cathedral and its grand deciduous wooded grounds, before emerging onto Glasgow Street at the equally grand Garrison House.

Make a note where the road heads up to the inner high road at the edge of the Garrison House, because this would be the road to take should you wish to ride to the top of the island in reverse. A good plan would be to come along the shore road from Cumbrae Slip, enter Millport, then turn right at Garrison House and head up

College Street to Breakough Farm. Start the climb to the highest point by slowly climbing through the farm (much safer), then fairly steeply gain the top. The climb up from this side has a much more uniform steepness to it. The approach from the other direction is a lot more gradual til the final ramp-like section of the last part.

From the top going north, there are great views right up the Clyde, so much so that it's advisable to do this hill in both directions at one time or another. When coming back down heading north, there are great views across the Fairlie roads to the mainland, just before reaching the B-899, which will then be followed, with great anticipation, back into Millport. I say with great anticipation, because it is a most delightful ride to descend long and gradual down the Ferry Road to the end of Kames Bay, having the woodlands of the steep bank of Ninian's Brae to your left, while ahead it's a pleasant pastoral and subtle seascape.

The dry stane dykes that flank the inner road are made up from rocks of red sandstone and have a subtle red hue that contrasts so nicely with the surrounding greens. The Cathedral spire is again resplendent, jutting as it does above the trees in the mid distance, where beyond it's Little Cumbrae that holds court in the firth.

To continue your tour by this route, simply ride through the town again and then out the West Bay Road to the far side, where only the wind and waves break the silence. Don't be put off if the weather is not exactly ideal, because the seascape can often be at its best when the weather is a bit more changeable, and it does make for a more interesting and constantly changing landscape as clouds and mist play hide and seek with the sun and light.

There is no one way, as far as I can tell, to ride the island in a one-off and cover all the roads, without re-riding at

The MV Loch Shira is seen returning to the mainland on a glorious sunny day. Again, the view is from the Routenburn Road.

least one short stretch. Not that that really matters, for it is most likely you will find yourself doubling back and doing some bits twice, or even more, just for the sheer enjoyment. That's entirely up to you. It's that sort of place.

Sooner or later you will need to return, and will find yourself back at the slip and awaiting the ferry back across. It does make a splendid sight as it approaches, with Largs and its hills making a striking canvas behind it as it glides quietly towards you. Not much time for recovery on the way back, though it's not crucial on

And of course, once back on the mainland, the long slog up the Haylie Brae must be tackled. The climbing more or less starts the moment you come off the ferry, with only a little flat respite to be had as you start to make your way through the centre of town.

this one. Not much time for thought either, which is just as well, for the daunting Haylie Brae will need to be breached before you can ride the road home.

There are several variations to get me home and, to make it a more informative and interesting read, I could take any one of them. I will, I promise, cover them all later in the book. However, when doing this run, most certainly in winter and most likely in summer, I would return by the same route.

Before you start moaning and saying we have already covered this way twice already, let me explain why I am deliberately going back the way we came. That's because firstly it's one of my favourites and I like to do this stretch a lot, which you will soon learn will happen to you. You will come across roads and stretches of routes that you will never tire of riding for one reason or another.

Second, and most importantly, I said in the intro that this wasn't just a cycling book, but would also be about personal development, and so far I've kept all my tips and advice to simple bike riding or related subjects.

All that's about to change. On the run home today we are going to be looking at the bigger picture, so read on, you've nothing to lose.

Back at Largs terminal, the first challenge is to be able to turn right onto Main Street to get back up to the start of the Haylie. Easier said than done here, for it's always busy busy. When you do, it can be a bit precarious weaving through and round the traffic and the two small roundabouts, before starting to get the muscles working again, because the pull up starts here, not at the lights at the bottom of the brae.

The tough 10% grind hits you when you do round the corner at the lights, and up you go, the cemetery gates and the cottage on the left at the lowest bend synonymous with effort. Don't forget your climbing technique now, using both legs equally, staying seated if you can, though at the cemetery you may have to get out of the saddle to keep the momentum going.

Round the bend and settle into your rhythm, recover somewhat, and rock slightly from side to side if you feel it helps your momentum. You'll clear the steepest section soon enough, and after that the easier long gradual rise continues til past the Kelburn Estate.Usually its wind-assisted reward time, with the Muirhead Reservoir and its surrounding hills and laws providing a familiar and comfortable sight.

And with that, it's time to mention *The Secret*. *The Secret* is the book and DVD by Rhonda Byrne. It's been out a few years now, and you may have heard of it or even watched or read it. If not, I advise you to, and to make it your starter for ten on the way to improving your life and lot. I have to let the cat out the bag here and let you know what *The Secret* is all about, to get you interested and motivated to go and fully suss it out for yourself. *The Secret* is all about the law of attraction. In other words: what you think, you get. Whether you are aware of it or

As always, the high part of the Haylie brings with it the reward of the island view, this time a little late in the day with fantastic light for company.

With the clearing of the last gradient of the Haylie, there now starts one of my favourite stretches of road that runs from here all the way to Kilbirnie. It is predominantly slightly downhill, wild and scenic, and if you are wind-assisted, then it is very, very fast. Enjoy.

not, we are all using it all of the time, most of the time subconsciously, but effectively nonetheless.

In my experience, women are more open to this concept than men, so if you're a guy reading this, I urge you not to go for the off button, but to keep an open mind. The first thing a lot of people say when they are told about the law of attraction is, 'Eh! No way did I want that to happen, or to have her in my life or him in my life, or whatever.' Well, in a lot of cases — and I'm quoting wee Joe Vitale direct from *The Secret* here — I'm going to be a little bit in your face and say, 'Yeah you did.' It's just that a lot of the time you didn't know it.

The reason I say 'a lot of the time' and not 'all of the time' is because in my experience, and this is my experience alone here, as far as I can tell certain things happen to each of us on purpose, which are totally out of our control.

Why this is, I can't be certain. I'm only guessing that we are here to learn lessons and a lot of the adversity in life teaches us these lessons. Why? Again, I don't know. *The Secret* points out that we are all energy. Energy that vibrates at different frequencies and attracts similar vibrating energy, so in other words 'like attracts like'.

If you're not getting what you want in life, watch *The Secret*, it will tell you how to go about getting what you do want. Most people focus on what they don't have in life, they focus on their lack of, usually money, but not always.

What you focus on you get more of, in this case 'more lack, less money'. When you start to focus on what you want and not what you lack, you will start to get that. The trick is to add feeling to the thought, which will speed up the process of delivery. Once you learn how to apply the law of attraction in your life, things won't come to you randomly then — far from it — but you will be in the driving seat. The mind is all powerful. What the mind can believe, the mind can achieve. Make that your cumntra. I shall mention it again.

So with that first bit of worldly wisdom over, we should just be about descending into Kilbirnie and, with the fast bends approaching, it's back to the secular cycling tips.

On sweeping fast bends, keep low, keep your weight low, and spread it. The front brake should do most of the work to stop the back brake locking up. Your weight should be on the outside foot, with you staying upright as the bike leans into the bend, the inside knee either pointing into the bend or kept up tight against the top tube. Look ahead all the time in the exact line you want to go. And that's you down safely.

I'm only an hour from home when I reach Kilbirnie. The cycle lane is accessible from one of the streets on the right as you leave the town, and can be taken, if needed, usually in adverse weather conditions. One small point I will mention if you intend to use the cycle paths a lot, is that it's good to have a bell on your handlebars to warn walkers you are approaching from behind. None of my bikes have one, so I constantly have to slow down and shout warnings to numerous other path users. It's a real pain in the arse. It just so happens I really like the road between here and Lochwinnoch, so tend to stay roadside.

The old reassuring Main Street of Lochwinnoch is soon found, with its Brown Bull Inn, at the end of which comes the final big climb of the day over John's Hill. This makes a splendid near finish to the run. The gleeful charge down the Bridesmill Road is never dull, and neither is Howwood when reached.

On the road in through Johnstone, although being our shortest run so far, I just want to say that this is still a long one at over 60 miles, especially with so much climbing. Obviously, as I said earlier, you would start off with

A great broad view away to the west towards Irvine and Ayr Bay from the A-760, just before the fabulous fast descent down to Kilbirnie starts.

And finally when the top of the Bridesmill Road is reached, the last major climb of the day is over and the long luscious descent down to Howwood begins. Ahead, in the evening sunshine, can be seen Glasgow and it means I'm on the home straight.

shorter runs; some of my favourites, which I will give details of later on, are great to do if time is scarce or it's a winter's day jaunt.

The trick to successful building up is to add no more than 10% to your workload each week to stop you overdoing it. You will find this is easier said than done.

Another good idea is to judge your effort by time and not miles. That's because the same run could prove more arduous and time consuming in tough conditions than it would in calm conditions. For example, if you did a 20 mile run on a good day, it may take you (I'm using nice round figures here to emphasise the point) 1hour and 30 minutes. On a bad day, let's say it took you 2 hours. So if you went on mileage alone, both runs would be identical at 20 miles, but the time difference would be an additional 30 minutes, and a fairly tough 30 minutes at that. So go by time and build up your 10% by time, not miles.

And with the time it took to deliver that sermon, I'm almost home after making my way through Elderslie and then up the back road (the Glenpatrick) into Foxbar.

I just want to say thanks again for your company and I hope you enjoyed our jaunt together round the smallest of the Clyde's inhabited islands.

It has all the greatness of its larger brethren, and I assure you when doing it yourself you most certainly won't be disappointed.

Till the next time, take care
Liam Boy.

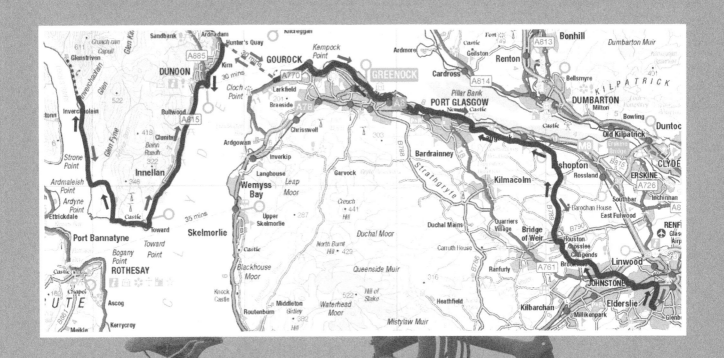

TOWARD LIGHTHOUSE, LOCH STRIVEN

FROM PAISLEY
80.8 MILES

5.02 HOURS

ASCENT 2360 FEET

2771 CALORIES/BURNED

FROM HUNTER'S QUAY
33.8 MILES

2.01 HOURS

ASCENT 480 FEET

1120 CALORIES/BURNED

O/S LANDRANGER MAPS. 64, 63, 56.

ARGYLL FERRIES   TEL NO 01475 650 338

WESTERN FERRIES TEL NO 01369 704 452

ROUTE SUMMARY

Linwood (Clippens Road)
Crosslee
Houston Village
Gleddoch
Old Greenock Road
Clune Brae
Port Glasgow
Greenock
Gourock
Mcinroy's Point
Western Ferries To Sandbank

COWAL PENINSULA OUTWARD

Sandbank
Kirn
Dunoon
Toward Lighthouse
Loch Striven Lodge

COWAL RETURN

Toward Village
Dunoon
Kirn
Sandbank
Western Ferries To Mcinroy's Point

RETURN ROUTE

Gourock
Greenock
Auchmountain Road
Quarriers Village
Bridge Of Weir
Linwood Or Kilbarchan
Johnstone
Elderslie
Paisley

TOWARD LIGHTHOUSE

THE LOCH STRIVEN RUN

I am going to declare myself here and admit right from the word go that up until I started to write the book, I had never before ridden down to Toward Lighthouse or up the side of Loch Striven. For years — and I do mean years — I had looked at this road run on the O/S map 56, and often thought about giving it a try, whilst countless times I'd admired the setting of the lighthouse from the closely passing Rothesay ferry. Once you've been riding for a good while, I guarantee that there will come a day when you do an old standard you haven't done for a long time which you really enjoy, and you think: why did I leave it so long?

Well, that's exactly how I felt as I made my way down the shore front heading south out of Dunoon, down towards this old shining sentinel. And this was despite the fact that one of the spokes went on my new Mavic wheels. This was the pair I'd splashed out on only that year, which were bought to replace my good Shimanos, the rear rim of which got wrecked coming off the Boguillie in Arran the previous October.

So for the fourth time in under a year, I had to limp back home with some sort of wheel problem or another, which I did successfully for the fourth time in under a year. Admittedly, this required the support of Argyll Ferries and Scotrail.

Insult was added to injury here by the fact that the lighthouse had just come into view, after riding for seven magnificent miles down from Hunter's Quay. But this did have the effect of giving me the desire to return and do the run in full. The reason I suppose I'd never done it before was because it is a dead end finish, if followed all the way up Loch Striven, and therefore didn't have the same appeal as a circular route. But don't let that put you off as long as it did me, because like the northwest road running up Bute, it is a delightful quiet corner that you can cover now and again, and should do so at least once. It has several strings to its bow, one being the completely different view it gives over the water to Rothesay Town, then the top end of Bute and beyond.

Heading down the Main Street (the B-789) of pretty Houston enroute to the high road above Langbank. This is a quieter, though harder, alternative approach to Port Glasgow and the Inverclyde ferries, but is an option I am known to take from time to time.

waterfront. I realise that the approach roads I am describing to get to the Clyde islands, and now Dunoon, won't be too relevant for a lot of people unless they actually stay in Paisley or close by.

For most people, the realistic option for a lot, if not all, of these runs, will be to drive and park at Ardrossan, Largs, or Gourock, etc. It would simply not be practical to ride the approach roads and then do the run over the water, before taking the long road back home in a single day, if you stay much further east of Paisley. However, some of the arteries that I use to access the coast are fantastic in themselves, and will be of

Going down only as far as the lighthouse will give an easy day out as it's flat, quiet, and ends very beautifully at the superbly positioned Toward Point. Being only seven miles from the Argyll ferry, it would be ideal for taking the kids out somewhere safe, and also different from Millport. This run won't suit say a team of guys out for a jolly, but is more suited to a solo rider who likes his solitude and tranquillity.

Loch Striven is mostly flat, mostly shore-side riding of about 34 miles long,[1] and to get maximum pleasure and scenery, it's best to start Loch Striven from Hunter's Quay using the Western Ferries from Gourock's McInroy's Point.

So first we have to get to Gourock, which has several options, though the three main ones I use all meet on Port Glasgow's Clune Brae if not before. I rarely use the route I take to Wemyss Bay for the Gourock ferries, though it is possible. Instead, I prefer to drop down to the coast early, around Port Glasgow, and go in via the Greenock

direct interest to some. Moreover, it can add to the day not to drive direct to the ferry terminal every time. For example, you can park short of the coast or even get the train to a destination slightly inland, and start from there.

When I first started out doing the longer rides, I once toyed with the idea of catching a train to Girvan and then riding home. I never actually did that one, but I did with Fort William. That gave a great day out on the famous West Highland Line, then a fantastic 100 mile run back through Glencoe, over the mighty Rannoch Moor and the like. Fort Bill would be way too much to do for most in a day and back, at just over 200 miles, so taking the train there is a good option.

If you, for example, live in Glasgow, it would be easy enough to drive or train journey to Dalry and then ride the high Moor Road over to the coast near Fairlie, if you perhaps wanted to make it more of a day out when doing Millport.

This would be just one good option of many, so for that reason I will include as many different approach routes as possible to spoil you for choice. With that in mind, the road that I will take to get to the West Ferries

1 - It's approximately a 34 mile round trip from Hunter's Quay.

in Gourock is slightly off the beaten track, but is quieter and scenically different from the more direct approach, with a good, tough climb thrown in just to get you well warmed up. And with that to look forward to, it's off out in a north westerly direction and heading through the old Ferguslie Mill grounds again, after flying past that bastion of medical learning the RAH (Royal Alexandra Hospital) on Corsebar Road.

Now I hit Ferguslie main road again, but at the roundabout before the start of Elderslie Main, I don't go straight, but turn right and am heading for Linwood on the Linwood Road itself, the A-761. This was once the site of the rather infamous Chrysler Car Plant that shut in May '81 and flooded the Paisley job market with nigh on 13,000 people, when the knock-on effect is taken into consideration. This was just at the very time I was leaving school, which is how I can be sure it shut in May '81. I say infamous, because it was notorious for strikes, which to my young mind seemed to occur on a weekly basis.

However, since then I have worked with a lot of former Chrysler men, who have explained that most of the problems stemmed from the guys in the K section, which became known as the crazy K. Being part of a production line, if one section downs tools then the whole show has to stop. This, to the best of my knowledge (though I never worked there), was a major part of the problem. So too, I was informed, were guys simply striking on a Friday night so they could go for a bevvy. Now that's what I call real work to rule. Having said that, the management could at times orchestrate strikes when it suited them so they didn't have to pay wages when demand for a particular vehicle was slow, or they had produced enough of that motor at the time.

It became a bit of a dirty business, I was also told, and the sad fact was that despite Linwood having only one production line and Volkswagen in Germany having four, the Scots workers still managed to produce more vehicles than their Deutschland counterparts; one a minute. It only goes to show what we can do and what might have been possible if we got our act together.

In the old days, a steel corridor went over the road you are now cycling down, which actually carried the half-finished vehicles from the north to the south plant. The old head offices are still there on the left hand side, but that's about all, for on the right are now the usual suspects of Asda, mucho car dealerships, multi-screen cinema, Pizza Hut, and all. The service sector here is totally

replacing the manufacturing base, as it has done since the early eighties.

As flat as a pancake the road now goes, straight ahead and under the concrete A-737, into Linwood itself, which is a sort of mini new town in its own right. This was a place purposely built, to a great extent, to house workers for the said car plant. And in keeping with the new town tradition, it has a look of square urban grey banality about it. This was particularly true for the small town centre which is just to your right as you enter. This has almost entirely been pulled down now, and who's complaining? We await the replacement.

So still heading northwest, we continue along just skirting the town on Kashmir Avenue, which was formerly known as Perimeter Road — a good name for a new town road — and in doing so, we also keep with new town tradition and go from one roundabout to another.

The one we come to now is the Clippens roundabout and it's in quite a strategic position. Turning left takes you to Bridge of Weir, by staying on the vaunted A-761, but we go straight ahead for North Clippens and the top end of Linwood. There is something about the gentle climb out on the Clippens Road that I like, and it is only now when you start to rise that you finally lift off what was the famous Linwood Moss. As you dig in slightly to get into a rhythm for the first slender climb of the day, you pass through the houses, shops, and schools of the north part of town, which includes the Clippens Inn and ends with right-side North Clippens and left-side East Fulton. All of

A fantastic view across the Clyde to Dumbarton is seen on this clear bright autumnal day from high above Langbank. This is good reward for all the hard climbing this wee back road requires, and why I like to use it a lot of the time. When all is said and done, it is a very picturesque run along the south bank of the Clyde.

these were built in support of the Hillman Imp, the first vehicle to be produced at Linwood.

The Darluith Road takes us out west, which is simply a continuation of the Clippens. This shortly ends abruptly at a severe bend in the road, where it slams into the side of the long, winding Barochan Road, as it makes it way from the foot of the Millbrae in Johnstone to the Houston hinterland. Charge straight ahead on this, through the first fields of the day, before dropping down over the Locher Burn, then the River Gryfe, and whizzing through tiny Crosslee

The first view of the shipyard towns comes just before you enter the Parkhill estate, Port Glasgow, just as you pass the isolated Parkhill House on the way in. Soon it's suddenly all change, when you leave the glorious green of Renfrewshire and slam into the tough urban block of the Port. However, the new house building programme softens the blow somewhat.

(well, it was before they started adding so many bits on). After this, a left turn at the big roundabout on the Georgetown Road finds you huffing and puffing a bit on a small climb, but not for long, as the right turn into the pretty white village of Houston means you're back on easy street.

It's a most pleasant short ride down the Main Street of the village, the modern version of which dates back to the 1780s, though the earliest records are much, much older. Two of the pubs displaying their year of birth — the Houston Inn (1779) and the Fox and Hounds (1784) — give the game away, sitting beside the rows of white weavers' cottages in North and South Street. Both streets were strategically placed alongside the Houston Burn to give the textile workers easy access for washing.

Leave the village heading north, which still finds you on the B-789 Barochan Road, despite all the previous turning and twisting, and make for the green fields above the Clyde at Langbank.

The journey there is one that shows Renfrewshire at its best, as first you ride straight, through the wheat fields, then turning and bending, as the road must, through a smattering of deciduous woodland. The terrain here is rolling hilly for the most part, but you will notice that

the ground rises and falls quite significantly around you, cutting sharp and deep in places in the vicinity of Barochancross. Beyond this, the road still holds a fair bit of height til the farm of Towncroft is reached, and it is possible to look over the pine trees within the old R.O.F.[2] grounds to the right and get a view across to the tower blocks of Glasgow, sitting away to the east.

Ahead, the Kilpatrick Hills also show up well as now you descend down the bends of the Barochan very quickly, then hurtle past the grounds of the well-known Monkey House, or Formakin Estate to give it its proper title. This house was a right bit of expensive folly, I dare say, and is so named because of the numerous stone monkey statues that adorn the roof and outer walls, which I also must say are quite a pleasing site. The house itself was started in 1903 but never finished, as the owner, poor old sod, ran out of dough before completion. The road is pleasantly wooded here, but also constantly wet with water running from the fields on the left. So unless it has been dry for a while, don't ride this stretch on your good machine or it will need a clean-up after.

2 - Royal Ordnance Factory.

This is the fantastic view of the Clyde that the former residents of Parkhill Avenue would have got from their rear windows. The new houses weren't built on the north side of the street the last time I rode through, which is why I was able to take this picture, but I'm sure the new residents will enjoy the view just as much when they move in.

Coming out of the woods, the whole scene opens up, especially after the Old Greenock Road is passed on the right, where after a little more curving through farmland, the Clyde itself now comes into view. Shortly, you part company with the Barochan, as it dives down to the right going into Langbank, but we continue straight ahead, thus continuing our journey now on the Old Greenock Road proper.

As the entrance to the Gleddoch House Country Club is passed, it signals the beginning of the tough climb I mentioned earlier, which will most likely find you out of the saddle and working hard, up through the trees and finally levelling out about 120 metres high, around the old farmstead of Undercraig.

The view across the Clyde to Dumbarton is glorious on a good day, as are the rest of the views as you continue west on this high plateau. But it'sonly for a short time, unfortunately, as now the road bends and dives back down again quite brutally, forcing brakes and caution to be used in equal measure. At this point you are behind the large leafy Finlaystone Estate, where the journey west will require a fair bit more oomph. The road continues to undulate through, then in and out of, more woodland, before passing the superbly positioned Parkhill House. The Greenock docks (what's left of them) can be seen in the distance, then it's back into leafy laneville, when all of a sudden… bang! It's straight into a very tough-looking Port Glasgow. Well, at one time it was.

What can I say? What a contrast, and all in the space of only a few metres. The hard look of the old derelict housing on the right hand side adds to the shock. To be

Running along the Esplanade on Greenock's waterfront with the Clydeport cranes behind. I think that this is the finest street on the whole Clyde coast and often make the slight diversion from the A-770 just to enjoy the whole setting.

fair, the new houses on the left look very good indeed, whilst at the time of writing the old houses sit empty awaiting demolition. One thing in their favour, however, is that they must have given their occupants a most fine view of the lower Clyde from the rear windows.

Continuing along to the end of Parkhill Avenue brings you and your machine to another famous Clyde brae, this one being the Clune. Coming in from this approach means you hit it almost halfway down, but don't worry, there is plenty of it left to get a good head of steam up as you turn right and plummet down banshee-like to the floor. Not straight away, though, as the gradient isn't too fierce at this point, allowing you to look up and admire the width of the firth and its associated charms, but then it flips down and it's full scream ahead.

The Clune isn't too heavily populated in its lower reaches — well, not on the actual brae itself — with only a small row of dilapidated buildings lining the left side and a now rarity of an old, white-painted Hibs Hall on the right. Behind this, the ground drops down sharply, so much so that you look down in amongst some real old tenements and an iron-railed school, which all have the look of the land that time forgot. Some nasty potholes at the lower part of the brae[3] make exercising caution a wise move, just before hitting the two big roundabouts that signal the arrival of the bottom and the A-8.

Busy but sane dual carriageway, is how I would best describe the next section of road, which will take us through not only Port Glasgow, but into the centre of

Greenock itself. Speed cameras and fairly common speed traps make sure for the most part that drivers stick to what must feel to them like a laborious 30 miles an hour all the way into the heart of Inverclyde.

The Port itself is quite a dramatic setting in the way that the houses cling precariously and steadfastly up on the hillside, overlooking the broad blue of the firth. It is this high ground so close to the sea that gives the area such a high rainfall, but in some way this is compensated by the fantastic views provided by living on such a lofty perch.

Carry straight on at the lights which are quickly reached; they are the gateway to the town centre, and have a rather impressive iron sculpture of a ship beside them. This a monument to the great trade of shipbuilding for which the area was once famous but now has only one yard remaining — Fergusons, which you've just ridden past at the bottom of the Clune Brae. This sits next to Newark Castle, which once gave the town, or rather the initial village, its name, before it was changed to its present title in the 1660s.

Much else has changed down on the waterfront in recent years, and this is very apparent as you round the bend, where the old road ran straight ahead into Greenock, with shipyards, dockside warehouses and suchlike, all sitting down on your right. These have all been demolished, literally to a building, in this area and replaced by an enormous Tesco, would you believe? So once again it's tatty-bye to the old heavies (industry, that is) and hello to the lights (service sector). So where you once got the Avenger in Linwood, you now get Asda; steelworks in Motherwell are now Starbucks; and in Greenock where you used to get the Titanic, now you get Tesco.

However, one benefit that did come from this major reconstruction was that the new road was thrown down towards the shore, which despite being modern dual carriageway, is in such an open and dramatic position that it is just a wonderful shoreside road to ride. It really is fresh air fortnight for a short time at least, as the journey on the waterfront finds you dwarfed by the magnitude of the setting, before you are forced back inland by a new housing development ahead, which was built on the old Kingston Dock. So the old road is regained all too shortly, with the aid of a couple of new roundabouts, and then takes you trundling in on the old A-8, happy as a pig in you-know-what.

3 - Ignore warning, as the Clune has since been resurfaced.

The reason I say this is because me and this road go back a long way, as I've ridden and driven it countless times, always going in on it flatly and joyously, soon passing the Norseman Bar, then the Greenock San Siro Stadium; I believe they call it Cappielow.

Unfortunately, new traffic lights have been introduced along the road to supposedly aid access to the docks on the right, which stutters the momentum somewhat. The docks still retain a lot of their old character, though, and are well worth a visit, if you are dallying through one summer's day and find you have the time. This stretch is great to cover, sitting in tight and safe among the traffic flow, looking long and flat ahead and feeling the seafaring character of yesteryear, despite the modern adjustments that have gone on in this corridor.

Kilcreggan and the Rosneath peninsula look serene and inviting from the deck of the Western ferry, though it's not our destination today. Our thoughts are further west as we head for Hunter's Quay, Dunoon, and Toward Lighthouse.

So many of the dockside buildings have been removed that it is possible to see the boats in dock from the actual road, though a lot of the right hand riverside is hidden behind a modern, slick-styled, red brick wall. This shields from view the former James Watt Dock when you reach the Cartsdyke area. The builders have, to their credit, made their new dockside flats look like old warehouse buildings, which enhances the area and keeps some sort of link with the past. This is a nice touch, for most of the redevelopment here is very modern and is in complete contrast to what has gone before. What the wall can't hide are the masts belonging to the yachts sitting in the new marina, which makes the most of the sea-faring facilities.

Things start to open up a tad as you approach the busy junction at the fire station, across from which sits

Harbour Bay on the right; this rarely contains any tugs nowadays. This is a pity, as they were always such a great sight in the past. You'll also notice here that the Greenock hillside tends to sit further back than its Port Glasgow counterpart and slopes away at an easier angle, making it less of a mountain goat existence for the Greenock inhabitants.

At the fire station lights, we want to go straight on, of course, but the turn left up Dellingburn, then Baker Street, would be the way you would go if you wanted to access the back road to Kilmacolm — the one we used to get to Wemyss Bay. Similarly, if you wanted to reach Gourock by that route, it's down Baker and Dellingburn you would drop, before turning left at the bottom.

So go through the junction and on into the town centre, which is situated ahead on the left and represented in places by some grand-looking buildings and towers. The most prominent of these is Victoria Tower, followed by the Mid Kirk spire. Two magnificent buildings are passed just before the large central roundabout is reached — one of which is the town hall and, just before that, the original James Watt College building, with a statue of the man himself standing grandly outside. Now just for the record, Watt never actually invented the steam engine, as is commonly thought (it was called the Newcomen), but what he did was to successfully modify it by the use of a condenser, to make it much more efficient.

His success and wealth from this breakthrough was almost certainly guaranteed by a patent of 25 years, which had been taken out by his business partner Matthew Boulton. This very lengthy patent prevented anyone else from manufacturing a like-styled engine, and therefore every mine in the country or anyone else who needed a pump for that matter, had to use the Watt/Boulton model. I want you to note this, for it's an important point that I will come back to later in the run and which has to do with personal development, but Watt's success was not so much the engine modification, but Matthew Boulton's belief in him. Boulton's belief in Watt gave him the springboard to success that we all need. I will return to this point later.

In the meantime, the run now finds us having to cross fully the busy big roundabout ahead, before we can continue on out to Gourock. And as we do cross, we part company with the busy A-8 and now glide onto the easier breathing A-770. It is a most fine route to take this one, as you head out west, and one which I can honestly say I

Another hard-working Western ferry passes in mid-water going in the opposite direction, Gourock-bound, with the unmistakable Inverkip power station chimney prominent behind.

continue ahead and bank hard right at the world's most awkward-looking junction and glide down onto the character-filled Shore Street. Every one of its small shops, numerous pubs and stores, look in the right place, sitting below grey, aged tenements, one of which is home to Paul's Food and Wine Store, where the purchase of ferry tickets is advised.

Armed with your ticket from Paul's Store, or one from a previous purchase, it's onward to McInroy's Point.

This starts quite dynamically by the road lifting slightly and then swinging left as it goes onto Kempock Street. Tight and busy with shops either side is the feel, whilst you drop the train station behind you. The long, grand curving Albert Road hurries you along the West Bay waterfront, out towards the end of town and the red vessels that await your custom. Gourock has always been known as a rather well-heeled area, and its frontline buildings seem to reflect this. They aren't quite like any other Clydeside waterfront, but always seem to strike me more like a Southern English port like Dover.

cherish. A long gradual, barely noticeable rise and descent carries the road eventually through a sandstone corridor of magnificent villas and houses, which once belonged to the rich of the town, the merchants, the shipbuilders and investors, hence the reason the dwellings are as grand as they are.

Battery Park and Cardwell Bay open up the view ahead and to the north, as the Fort Matilda area is reached. This is the point where you pass the coastguard station on Whiteforeland Point, which once held a battery of guns going back to Napoleonic times; hence the name Fort Matilda. Battery Park itself was created by filling in the sea with the landfill coming from the Newton Street rail tunnel, which feeds the track into Gourock station. Nowadays the park is used for playing fields, but during the war there was a torpedo factory on the site, whose merchandise was tested at the head of Loch Long. The old firing range can still be seen today, just across the bay from Arrochar[4].

Clearing the park signals the start of Gourock, as you enter the Cardwell Bay area where it's always tight and busy with the traffic's hustle and bustle. By turning third right down Tarbet Street, you come to the Argyll Ferries pier, but it isn't the one we want on this occasion. We will

The Kirn waterfront from the Western ferry, just as the boat is about to dock at Hunter's Quay. The steeple of Kirn's kirk, as always, prominent in the centre.

4 - It's only recently been removed.

They most certainly are a rich mixture of grandness and style, which is further endorsed by the Royal Gourock Yacht Club building — the only building to grace the coast side of the road further down. This stands out on its own in more ways than one, with its shapely, ornate walls and roof, being white and bold, with flying flags to signify its status. The backdrop of the Clyde is wide and wild here, with the hills and mountains now giving a real glimpse of their Highland character. The towns and villages opposite will show themselves small and discreet in the vastness, but with a bit more experience they will become familiar to you, even from this distance.

About this point, you will be able to see if a ferry is waiting or arriving, but hopefully not leaving. Even if it is, it won't be long til another arrives, as the service is very good, with sometimes up to three vehicle ferries operating at any one time. The Western is always running, even in the worst of weathers. If it has to stop operating due to bad weather, then as a general rule it would probably be too wild to go out riding anyway.

So on arrival at the pier, simply wait to get the nod from the crewman and then it's time to relax for a wee 20 minutes or so. Before boarding, take a look along the shorefront towards Gourock, and admire the line of the coast as it curves beautifully and gracefully back towards Kempock Point. It is a most calm and serene moment.

It is 23.7 miles for me going down via Houston, normally taking around 1 hour 30 minutes, which is slightly longer and harder than the most direct route, but was included to give you some ideas and options, should you so wish to use them.

After standing on deck to admire the view as we depart from the pier, it's then into the lounge to consume (your own) food and drink and also get some well-earned rest, which is done in the warm atmosphere of the Western's heated saloon (but don't worry, it's not the last chance saloon). There are very few, if any ships to be seen as you sail across the Clyde nowadays, though this wasn't always the case.

Having never known any different, it didn't occur to me that at one time the waters of the firth were like a huge game of X and Os, as ship upon ship criss-crossed each other, whilst making their way up and downstream. It was only on one occasion when I got chatting to an older lady at McInroy's Point and this was pointed out to me, did I then consider what a magnificent sight that must have been.

One magnificent sight that hasn't changed for centuries, however, as you align with the mouth of Loch Long, is the view north to the Arrochar Alps, with Ben Narnain and its partner in crime The Cobbler standing out boldly.

Equally striking, as Cowal is approached, is the nose of nearby Strone Point, which dives dramatically and diagonally into the deep cold water, right at the junction of the Holy and Long Lochs. The scene is enhanced by the jagged spire of the shorefront-sited Saint Columba's Church, rising sharply to make a most noticeable landmark. Likewise does the flamboyant Dunselma House, which sits above it on the hillside at Kilmun. Dunselma's tower could almost pass for a lighthouse, so grand is the structure. It was built for James Coats Jnr, another link to the far off Paisley thread mills. The Coates

A great view of Dunoon pier and a look out to sea are glimpsed as the Kirn/Dunoon waterfront is ridden. A real backwater, land that time forgot feeling is very much in evidence here, which is very much to my liking. But you may hardly notice anything shore-side as the sea view usually is just too good to miss.

family could afford it, considering the piss poor wages they paid their workers.

Hunter's Quay is almost upon us now, so it's time to disembark. The gentle rising ground above the road is wood-clad and fronted by white villas of age and quality, quite striking with their upturned V-style window surrounds. This seems to be a common building style in the area. The magnificent old Marine Hotel takes pride of place out front, but almost unnoticed, a small snack hut (the Coffee Ahoy)[5], sits across the road from the back of the car park, and can come in handy on the return journey.

5 - It's owned by a workmate of mine called John (Big Granville) Cooper. They call him Granville because he's open all hours (in his taxi, not the coffee bar, that is).

Once past Dunoon, the riding is simply superb with fast gliding swerves along the coastline all the way down to Toward itself. It is also flat and quiet, and so is a great road to take the kids along if you want a family day out as opposed to a solo endurance run.

Once the helmet has re-adorned the head, it's left turn and down the sea front, with Hunter's Quay continuing in a similar vein of white dwellings to the right and a grey railing to the left. This railing separates you from the drop to the water and will be an almost constant companion until you approach Toward Village itself.

It is a real treat to glide along what will be a much quieter shorefront, with a rather strange feeling as you look back to the side you are a lot more familiar with. You're still only getting into your early stride when you enter Kirn, which although a village in its own right, is now more or less a suburb of Dunoon. At one time however, it did have its own pier, though the last steamer sailed from it back in the 1960s.

The A-815 (Marine Drive) guides you quaintly and curvaceously along between the firth and more white

Another fantastic view down the Clyde, this one from Innellan. The whole way down is simply one fantastic sea view after another. There's never a bland bit of road on the whole stretch.

solid houses of this village, staying flat and perfect, till the Kirn Parish Church is encountered, sitting rather grandly at the bottom of the Kirn Brae. Built with glowing red sandstone, it is visible from across the water, if you know where to look, and has the most impressive solid, square steeple attached.

The churches here do the small communities proud, as do the rest of the buildings, always so sturdy and solid and putting modern day homes, often built on the cheap, to shame. This part of the village contains some commerce in the shape of a row of shops, but in keeping with modern trends, a lot of them are lying empty. Things then start to get seriously good as you round the next bend, where you start to feel the draw of the glinting Clyde as truly substantial. The going is flat and glorious at this point. The right side of the road is, as you'd expect, a procession of cottages and dwellings befitting such a seaside location, but that is not where your focus is concentrated, because ahead and sweeping all to the left, is a tantalising, glinting horizon that keeps you mesmerised in its jinks and glints.

Occasional palm trees adorn the road side and, with such a sun sparkling scene behind, you could be forgiven for thinking you were riding along a Spanish Costa. However, should you see any local wearing a sombrero, it's probably to keep the rain off.

Kirn, just as it enters Dunoon, has a space either side of the road, marked by a solid white line, to allow for parking, I think. However, this works very well as an unofficial cycle lane and is ideal to motor along in. It starts to open up a bit going into Dunoon itself, on Alexandra Parade, where the conifer-clad hillside of Tom Odhar sits further back, allowing more room for the town inland. Ahead is a mixture of old and new buildings, though the unmistakable shape of the pier will still be the one to catch your eye. There will be a bit more hustle and bustle around the pier itself, where the passenger-only Argyll ferry will dock, but this is to be expected.

Turn inland at this point and climb up slightly on the magnificently named Tom-a-Mhoid Road, where the greyness of the buildings is very noticeable. This, I assume, comes from some type of slate-like rock used in construction, for it can also be seen lying horizontally in the walls of the buildings themselves. Turn left and glide down Wellington Street, heading out south.

If you thought it was good up til now, just wait until you get going here, for that was only the warm-up. From now

on it really is "Hi ho, silver lining", for the next 7 miles or so is a bending, curving, shimmering seascape, to really make you feel good to be alive. The road rarely rises a foot, as it sticks to the contours of the shoreline, with the line of the Clyde being drawn across the surface from Little Cumbrae to the Holy Isle off Arran.

This is the magnet that draws you down, looking and hoping for more of the same; don't worry, you'll find it. The Gantocks Lighthouse sits level with you, just offshore out in the West Bay, as you continue on down and out by the Bullwood Road. Now if you thought you were heading for some remote, unlived in, quiet corner, then you're in for a big surprise. Most of the road down will be taken up by a variety of dwellings that seem to span several periods, and which are in many instances as grand as the setting they sit in. Funnily enough, the road that sits to their front seems to reflect in quaintness and character the same characteristics that the adjacent houses display, and this is a matter of interest as you cruise along. Well, it would be or most certainly could be, were it not for the distraction ahead and to the left of you, especially when the Clyde is a mill pond.

The bays are shingle curved delights, sloping onto their skerries and rocks, always curving further and further ahead, and shaping the road's path as it follows. And across the firth, the whites of the Inverkip houses are dwarfed by the power station's giant grey cooling tower and main building, which is also painted in pretty battleship grey.

Here, to make my point, the houses go from older stone villa types, sitting behind dry stone walls, to more modern detached bungalows with their more modern accessories. Also around this point, the hillside of the Tom comes in from the right steeply and dramatically, conifer-clad to the roadside, forcing the road to swerve out to accommodate it, leaving only a slight strip of flat land available for building on.

This is highlighted most spectacularly at the small water treatment plant you will pass, where the rock has been cut through on purpose and falls dramatically to the floor in slabs and sheets, making for a most striking sight. The riding is just as delightful, if not quite as rustic, but don't panic. Shortly on the horizon will appear Innellan, where you're back into the old stuff. As you enter, there is a very tempting-looking high road running up to the right called North Campbell Road. It is well sign-posted, as it leads to

The views actually get better and better the further down you go, believe it or not, and just to prove it here is one with Arran looking over Bute, which in turn sits behind Toward Point. The lighthouse is just visible if you know where to look

the golf course and which, appears on the map at any rate, to provide a high scenic route further south and therefore worth the effort to climb it. To be honest, forget it. The surrounding houses mar any view whatsoever and make it a lot of huff and puff for nought. So stay shoreside.

The red post office/general store will be the last place to stock up on provisions, should you require any, and is also where to get your ferry tickets on this run, should you require them. This will not only include Western Ferries, but also a 10 journey return ticket for the Argyll Ferries, which comes as a natty wee plastic card which gets punched every time you travel. The store is the only one left in this line of former shops, which used to number about fourteen. That is hard to believe, as is the fact that this was also once a holiday hotspot, especially as the former pier, which you've just passed, is no longer there. In case you need to fill the water bottles or use it, an old style cludgie (toilet) is situated across from where the pier once stood.

Some of the central Innellan buildings are pretty rundown and dilapidated, but this is not in keeping with the rest of the route, where they really are quite upmarket. This is most noticeable after leaving the store, where two large trees — one either side of the road — act as a sort of gateway to the southern half of this linear village, where for just about the first time, the jagged one herself (Arran) puts in an appearance. Depending on cloud cover, it may show itself earlier on in the run, but not always.

One thing that struck me the very first time I rode past here was that the houses, and particularly their gardens, are designed identically to some of those you find on Arran itself, usually in and around Sannox and Whiting Bay. Most noticeable is the very long and narrow front gardens, which is quite a distinctive feature, so I can only assume that style must have been in vogue at the time the houses and those on Arran were built.

By now the tower of the lighthouse will also have come into view, so it's full steam ahead as you spin and glide in the same vein as before, still being guided by the iron railing and still following the same graceful curves of the road. This shortly leads to the sign saying Toward, where the village of Innellan stops at the exact same time. Only at this point do the houses on the right cease and a rather rough-looking field takes their place. This cuts inland for only a short stretch before steepening onto a tree-clad slope. The high imposing ground that has for the most part tracked your progress south so far, finally falls away, leaving a gentler slope running up towards the conifers on Toward Hill.

The waters of the Clyde become hidden behind a procession of houses and backdoor gardens now, and for the first time the left side finds itself populated with an assortment of dwellings. The road is very straight at this point and at first telegraph poles mark your progress inward, with much anticipation. Experience tells you that lighthouses often hold splendid positions, and this one is no exception.

The main road itself swings away to the right, heading for Port Lamont, at which point a minor road goes directly ahead, leading straight to the lighthouse itself. Much to my surprise, I found another line of large houses — the usual modern development type — lining the first part of the road in, before finally reaching the spectacle of another whitewashed Robert Stevenson creation.

This is, to some extent, hidden behind a yellow two storey building, standing before it on the corner of the road, which seems a bit out of place and is typical of a lot of coastal dwellings the world over; it somewhat reminds me of the Normandy beaches. The road then becomes a track at this point, and a walk round beside the white walled garden is needed to allow the full view across the water to Bute and beyond to be fully appreciated. It just so happened to be the lighthouse's 200th birthday at the time of writing, as 1812 was its opening year. Just to put that into perspective, it means we're talking Napoleon here. She is still in great shape, as is the foghorn building that sits separate on the other side of the track.

And finally, the lighthouse itself at Toward Point is reached and it won't disappoint, I assure you. There are no facilities at Toward, which is useful to know, especially if you are out for the day with the little ones. And for the record, the store at Innellan is the last chance saloon for provisions. However, the whole setting makes it a worthwhile visit and you won't find a nicer spot to linger a while. But the decision as to whether to continue up the Striven will soon need to be made, and I recommend it.

Here it's common to see hard tilting yachts, with full filled sails coming screaming past — almost touching, it seems — as the mariners from the nearby Toward Yacht Club show off their skills. The rocky foreshore leads into the view of Rothesay Bay and Bute, with big brother Arran looking over its shoulder; a bit like that old photo of the Kray twins. But that is where the similarity ends, for there is nothing menacing about these two, only charming tranquillity as you linger, hopefully in the sunshine, among the whitewashed walls, buildings, and history of this splendid spot. Incidentally, the foghorn has now been removed, as with all lighthouses, and its building is now home to someone.

It would be very easy to linger an age here, but there is still a little bit of new riding left in the day, should you wish to carry on to the road end up the side of Loch Striven.

Before we start up, I will tell you right from the start that the finish will not be a spectacular one. Far from it. It will be just a road end, with a telephone box and a palm tree to mark the termination where the public road ends and the private one starts at the Loch Striven Estate hunting lodge. However, and it's a big however, the road up and down is well worth the effort alone, for the scenery, the setting, and the serenity (how's that for some tourist board flannel?).

But seriously, folks, it is as pleasant as it gets for most of the 8 mile run up, especially when you return back down to the shore again and go single track up the side of Loch Striven. It starts pleasingly enough, and there is no need to retrace your steps back to the main road, because the minor road itself goes in a loop. Therefore you re-join the A-815 further west, as it passes the last of the village houses, a short row of white cottages and then the primary school, before taking its leave of Toward. There is about a field-width of land between you and the coast at this point, but the road soon closes that gap and when you do meet the shore again, boy, is it beautiful.

The rocky shingle bays start meandering and curving up to Toward Quay, flanked on the other side by the grounds and woods of Toward Castle. As the road bends hard right, the grand old castle gatehouse is passed, with its turrets and stone-carved faces sitting either side of its ornate windows. Across the road, the quay houses the sailing club's buildings, with numerous craft perpetually up on blocks.

If you so wish, you can ride up to the castle, which isn't the original by any means. That was held by the Clan Lamont since the 1470s, and is a tower house that sits nearby. No, this one is a mansion built by former Glasgow Lord Provost Kirkman Findlay in 1820. This rich merchant was obviously a man of tremendous wealth, which is immediately apparent when you see the size of his pad. In fact, the gatehouse alone looks like it would have cost plenty to build, never mind the mansion itself.

It's here that the road runs uphill and turns inland for a couple of miles, and you find yourself in among the farms and fields. The height gained helps with the view over the flat land down to Ardyne Point and across to Bute. The road carries on almost bolt straight and flat, through the hedgerows, as it passes Killellan Farm, with the slope of Achafour Hill pulling up on the right, leading to highly-perched conifer swathes, while the lower fields hold sheep.

The road swings hard left and heads due west, and as it does the last of the high views over to Rothesay can be seen in the fields to your left, before a speedy dip in the road takes you over the bonnie wooded Ardyne Burn, which runs through the grounds of the rather splendid-looking Knockdow House.

The grand white walls of this Georgian-built mansion, easily seen from the road, was another, much later, family seat of the Lamont family. It was in their possession till 1949, when the death of Sir Norman Lamont ended almost two hundred years of occupation.

After passing this by a small climb, the road nose dives straight down, hemmed in on both sides by trees and walls, to the shores of Loch Striven. Then it turns right sharply, between two houses that seem to constitute Port Lamont. Now, if I hadn't told you that, you probably would never have known, for there is no name sign to tell you. This is despite the fact that the place gets a mention a few miles back on the road sign near the lighthouse. To be honest, it wasn't til I returned home from my first jaunt there that it struck me I hadn't noticed the place despite its mention on the sign. Only after checking the map did I realise that was it.

Not to worry, because now ahead is the single track road up the loch, where it isn't too taxing and is made

I recommend the run up the side of Loch Striven, despite it being a dead end, for the views and the remoteness you will encounter. Here you get a great look across the fields to Rothesay and Arran over Ardyne Point, just before you turn and drop down to the loch side at Port Lamont.

When I first saw this, I couldn't believe it. You pass a Royal Navy fuel and lubrication depot not long after leaving Port Lamont. I had no idea this existed til the first day I came up here on the bike. The base itself makes quite a sight when all light up at night. I only found this out when I was cycling to Rothesay in the dark from Rhubodach at the top end of Bute, returning very late one night from the Loch Fyne run (route 9). It in no way spoils the look of this magnificent rugged loch.

for quiet pleasure riding. This is slightly, and only slightly, interrupted by the unexpected sight of a Royal Navy supply depot; up until I first saw it, I had no idea it was there. The spartan pier, along with the battleship grey colour of its loading tower and lights, were a dead giveaway as to its purpose, which I think specialises in refuelling and lubrication. Its offices and buildings are fairly unobtrusive behind its fence, though, with the birch trees providing some blending and concealment. Beyond this, the road sits right down by the waterside, allowing views right up the length of this long and powerful broad sea loch.

Soon a very old and quaint iron railing is picked up, which was white in colour originally, but now is wonderfully tainted rust brown. The ferns cling round it like an old drunk would his buddy coming out of a Paisley pub late at night. The right side is wooded tight to the road, which leads forward and is, for the most part well, surfaced and slender. Lack of vegetation on the left

Talking of which, here we are firing up the east side of the Striven on as pleasant a stretch of single track road as you could wish for. No cars, no hills, no nothin'. Just free easy riding and usually a bit of wind for company.

still allows unrestricted views ahead, with bulky Cruach nan Capull showing well already.

The birches enclose and delicately smother the road here, which lifts and rises slightly more as you pass Brackley Point. Coming out of the trees, there is a stunning glimpse of Inverchaolain House as it sits by the lochside, brilliant white amongst its green trees and double bays that point sharply into the loch.

Above this, the cone-shaped hillside of Sron Dearg[6] elegantly sits, overseeing the rugged scene below, which contains the dark and delightful Inverchaolain[7] church. This is a very beautiful place of worship, in a very beautiful setting, and this building was constructed in 1912 to replace the one built in 1812 which was destroyed by fire. As 1812 was also the year they built the lighthouse at Toward, then it's safe to assume there was work aplenty on the Striven that year.

Outside the church gates there is a very informative noticeboard giving lots of info on the place and people of the surrounding area, and it has to be said that this building and its small graveyard are exceptionally well cared for.

After passing the church, the road briefly seems to be turning into a track, but it soon regains its tarmac status and in doing so curves round and behind Inverchaolain House, skirting a fenced field of big Highland coos. Usually at this point there will be an explosion of panic-stricken pheasants flying up and out of the woods on the right, screeching and screaming, wide and wild-eyed as they dive for cover again. Once you've gotten over your fright, the taking of the next bend more or less signals the end of the road, where just a slight dip and glide deposits you at the phone box and palm tree. Signs there let you know you're at the Loch Striven Estate lodge, and that the public road has terminated.

Through a gap between an overhanging tree and a gate, the eye is still drawn to the head of the loch, which it has been since you joined it at Port Lamont. You will find it impossible not to gaze continuously up the length of this snaking fjord, which is just so designed to have that effect.

It is not a long linger here, for there is nothing to hold your attention and there is still a good 17 miles back to Hunter's Quay. So the return starts fairly soon, and

6 - **It's pronounced Strawn Geerak, meaning red nose.**

7 - **It's pronounced Inver-hoolan, meaning mouth of the small stream.**

As you near the end of the public road, the big bulk of Cruach nan Caorach becomes ever more imposing. It makes a fine sight as you make your way up the loch side, as does the head of the loch itself. This is you at Inverchaolain, and from here you're inside the final mile.

with it the views down the loch match the ones up it. First to grab your attention will be the setting behind Inverchaolain House, different but just as dramatic as on the road up. This time the backdrop is of Bute and the broader, lower Striven, which enhances the foreground of the house and its elegant, curving, grey shingle bay. This one is lined with mature deciduous trees almost up to the waterline.

Sron Dearg also makes an impressive sight as you climb gently on the Inverchaolain stretch. The slender, elegant, steep-sided Striven impresses its full length and not an inch of the whole way is dull, til you reach the road end perhaps.

And after all the magnificent, stunning, sensational, scenic sea loch riding the Striven has just given us, what a fitting finish. Not (ha, ha, ha). I'm the first to admit that it is a bit of a disappointment, but that is about the only downside to coming all the way up to the entrance to the Glenstriven Estate. The road from here on is private and doesn't lead up to the top of the loch anyway, so the only option is to about turn. The road back down also makes it worthwhile, I assure you, in a more open style than the road up.

of day, but that often is the case as the sun will be sitting above the islands to the west, for the most part. If you are wind-assisted, with the effect of the airflow being further enhanced by the tunnel-like sides of the loch, then you will be positively flying along in and out of the breeze and the bracken at this point.

The Navy base is quickly passed, Port Lamont is soon reached, and then what a pain. A bit of climbing has to be done. This is the only bit on the entire run back and is needed to reach the wall and pond by Knockdow. Dip and rise over the Ardyne Burn again, then bank hard right before

After this, it is simply a case of enjoying the ride back along the lochside, where perhaps for the first time you might take more notice and pay a bit more attention to the opposite side of the loch. It would most likely have played second fiddle to the view directly up the loch, which can easily hold your focus on the entire way up. The west side has an even more remote look to it, with just a dead end single track road coming round the headland (another Strone Point) from Colintraive, to service the few dwellings that exist there. I've never come round that road, but will make a point to do so the next time I just miss the ferry for Rhubodach.

All in, the Striven is a shy, hidden loch and, due to having no through roads on either side, is a very quiet one which is rarely frequented. That, I like. I like my peace and solitude, and if you're like-minded then, believe me, you will enjoy your day on the Striven.

Fairly early on in the road down, the high top end of Bute will start to show, with its lighter colours in its lower fields contrasting starkly against the darker nose and hills of Strone Point and west side Loch Striven. This will depend, of course, on the strength of the sun and time

following the road, straight as a die, back down through the fields that have high views over to Rothesay. This situation is great for seeing the topography of the island of Bute, and really shows just how high its top end really sits, especially when judged against the almost sea level area behind Kames Bay. A very old, small, square mile sign, with finger pointing, tells you it's 9 miles back to Dunoon; these stone-made signs, I'm glad to say, are very common in this neck of the woods.

Following this, there is a great, flowing, straight drop back down to Toward Quay, whilst you stay about a mile inland from Ardyne Point. It was here between 1974 and 78 that three large oil rig platforms were constructed for the Cormorant and Brent fields in the North Sea. The construction basins, which are said to be massive, are not visible from the road but are well seen on the ordnance survey map. Apparently, this area has been marked for further development, but so far nothing has happened.

The original Toward Castle, as mentioned, was the stronghold of the Clan Lamont, who were the main players in this neck of the woods from probably as far back as the Norsemen. They had the misfortune to be

Returning back down through the birch trees and bracken. With all the flatness and foliage to come, along with the loch views and old rusty iron railing fences, it is a most pleasant purr all the way back down to Port Lamont.

Going up the Striven, the views are mostly of the ever-narrowing sea loch, and a most dramatic sight it makes. However, on the return leg the views are more open and pastoral, as this one looking over the mouth of the Striven and the inner Kyle of Bute show.

situated next door to the large and formidable Clan Campbell, who they never really got on with, despite having made several inter-marriages with and attempts at reconciliation. They had numerous bloody encounters against each other over the centuries, the final and most brutal coming in 1646 during the Civil War. On that occasion, the Campbells surrounded Toward and, despite assurances of safety should they surrender, they took the prisoners to nearby Dunoon and slaughtered about 200 Lamonts there, which was to avenge for earlier Lamont atrocities against Campbells. With such a heavy loss all at the one time, the Clan Lamont was never the same since.

The run down to Toward Village from the castle gatehouse is a very idyllic one, as across the water Rothesay Town sits patiently inviting you over someday soon. The bays on this side are most idyllic, as cormorants sit on the rocks darkly still, awaiting their next meal. The closer you get to the area around the lighthouse, the more appealing it becomes. Already across the Clyde, the hills above Skermorlie will be showing their softness and

pleasing the eye in the evening light, if you've left your return that little bit late.

The flat areas around Toward Village have a real low-lying coastal feel to them, and that I find most enjoyable. It's a feature that we lack in this part of the world, as quite often the land will enter the sea without easing its angle.

So the flat rough fields, with the white tower of Toward in the foreground and the gentle soft hills of the lower Clyde behind, make it a most pleasant return to the village. The Rothesay ferry will seem to come just as close as some of the yachtsmen, as she sails low and quietly past on her return to Wemyss Bay.

A great shot of the two ferries that service the Wemyss Bay to Rothesay crossing the MV's Argyle and Bute, as they pass each other in mid-water. This shot was taken just as Toward Point was reached again on the return journey. The ferries often make a splendid sight as they ply the blue firth in their dashing black, white, and red colours.

Returning along the waterfront to Dunoon, and as can so often happen things quieten down in the evening. With the breeze dying and the light softening, even Inverkip power station looks good, seen here across the Clyde from Innellan with the white houses of Inverkip marina standing out well.

Sticking to the main road this time, and ignoring the road down to the lighthouse, you shortly swing past the local church and find yourself on the straight stretch of road leading out of the village and back towards Dunoon. You know what to expect here and that's not a problem, for there is nothing hard or unpleasant to come, only easy riding and the Clyde for company on this first class return.

Soon the big guy puts in an appearance by your side, even before Innellan is entered, where a modern cludgie is situated on the right, should you need water or the other. Then its curve and bend, curve and bend all the way back along the shorefront, delighting in every single turn of the cranks. On the right evening, it has to be said, it doesn't get much better than this as the snaking iron railing, road, and shore bays, all carry you back quietly and safely to the ferry. If the sun is out and the Clyde is still, it will be a most gentle

run back, with glances over to the other side compulsory, always marked and dominated by the Inverkip power station tower.

It is one of those times in life that you don't want it to end, well, not too soon anyway. Dunoon does appear quite early on, but gets lost again as the road continually swerves in and out of sight of it. The side that Dunoon shows, as you approach from the south, is a fine sweep round its West Bay, jaggedly stopping at the waterfront as you ride through the grand grey houses of its southern suburbs. The slight climb back up Wellington Street allows a nice descent back down the Tom-nan-Mhoid Road, above which sits a monument commemorating the slaughter of the Lamonts by those dastardly Campbells.

If I've timed it right, I can jump on the Argyll ferry here and save myself some legwork either side of the Clyde, but that might not suit you. So I will take you back up along the Dunoon shorefront, which isn't a chore, and finishing off through little Kirn to quickly arrive at the Hunter's Quay ferry. It's a nice way to finish. The large Luss Hills across the water will be most prominent on the run up, which can be done at a nice pleasurable lick, to provide the ideal warm down that's always best to finish

The return back up to either Dunoon pier or Hunter's Quay is a most pleasant sway, at all times acting in concert with the shoreline. The road never leaves the river bank until it enters Dunoon town, and then only briefly. It is having the salt carpet for company all the way that makes this such an enjoyable stretch of road to ride, but so, too, does the procession of old houses you pass on your left side on the way in.

Another famous lighthouse is passed as Dunoon is reached, and this is the Gantocks. No chance of riding out to this one, as it sits offshore, but it makes a great landmark all the same and here a rare boat nowadays passes it, heading for the open sea.

with. Usually, there is a Western ferry waiting, but if not, replenish your stocks in the wee Coffee Ahoy snack bar and await the next one.

If the Clyde happens to be a bit on the choppy side, then there will be a bit of pitching and rolling on the flat-bottomed Western as you re-cross back to the mainland. This always adds to the fun.

The hills to the north will be that bit more photogenic in the evening light, making the parting of company that little bit harder for you. Still, you've got to get home, and if you've docked at McInroy's Point, then the good news is that there is a flat perfect warm-up to get you back in the groove. This constitutes purring along the Gourock waterfront, and before you know it you're round Cardwell Bay and back into Greenock.

For me, there are two main options on the return journey. The easier way is to join the A-8 in the centre of

One last look down the Clyde from Dunoon, before taking the ferry back across to either MacInroy's Point or Gourock pier. The long draw down the Clyde from here can have a mesmerising effect, and on the ride down it can be nigh impossible to take your eyes of the seascape and watch the road.

That grand old sentinel, the Cloch Lighthouse, stands guard, as always, as the approach to the south shore is made. In the evening light and with Arran behind, what a sight she makes.

Greenock, and follow it all the way back to the bottom of the Clune Brae in Port Glasgow and lift up off the coast from there.

The other is to follow the A-8 only as far as the fire station in Greenock, and then turn right to join up with the route I would take back home from Wemyss Bay. This is about a mile longer, with at least 400 feet more climbing involved. Still, sometimes I'm in the mood for the Auchmountain Road and will go that way for a bit of devilment.

For anyone wishing to return by this route and wondering how to get on it from this direction, I will take you that way this time, just so that you know. The return will be along the A-770, simply retracing our way back the way we came. Then after the big hectic roundabout in the town centre has been crossed, which is a lot safer and easier going this way, we pass the police station and also the statue of the great James Watt again.

I mention this specifically because I want to make a very important point or two here, especially to anyone who wants to improve and make changes in their lives. If you are at an age where you are quite happy with your lot, then the next bit of text isn't really for you, but I advise you to read on as you might like what you discover.

When we passed James Watt's statue earlier, you may remember that I made a point of telling you that it was his business partner's belief in him that was his true making. If you have any desire for self-improvement, then I recommend you read Noah St John's book, *The Secret Code of Success*. Noah is one clever guy, who will basically get you to use and maximise what you've already got. He is definitely worth a read.

He makes the point — very strongly early on — that for anyone to succeed they need someone to believe in them. This, in turn, produces belief in yourself, which is vital for success to follow. This can be a major stumbling block for most of us and can put you off reading any further, because you may feel, quite rightly, that if you had someone in your life who believed in you already, then there would be no need to read the book.

But you have two things in your favour with regard to that, in my experience. One is that whatever you need, the great power of the Universe will provide it just when you need it. This I have found to be true.

For those of you who are very secular and would prefer something much more down to earth, then I also strongly recommend using one of the many effective hypnosis downloads or CDs from a company called Hypnosis Downloads/Uncommon Knowledge. These are two guys — Roger Elliot and Mark Tyrell —based in Oban, who have turned out over 800 hypnosis tracks to cover everything from quitting smoking to being more confident, and from overcoming your fears to even improving your golf. They do a specific "Believe in Yourself CD" that I use myself, and thoroughly recommend you do, too. It will, if used, help to provide the self-belief that will allow doors to open.

The guys are very experienced and can help you overcome any social anxiety and problems that you have been plagued with ever since you can remember. If you are struggling in any area of your life, you've nothing to lose by giving the boys a try. And if you don't like the download for any reason, it's a guaranteed money back, no quibble deal. The boys can't say fairer than that. I will

Looking back after battering along Gourock's shore road in the evening light, and you won't find a better stretch of tarmac to warm up on any day soon. Being flat and a bit hustle and bustly, it always gets the old system up and running again in fine style after you've cooled down on the ferry crossing. You'll be raring to go again and attack the big pull-ups out of Inverclyde in no time.

A great shot of a none-too-common sight nowadays, that of a large ship berthed in Greenock docks. This is from near the top of the Auchmountain Road, where the subdued colours of the water and land beyond make the boat's bright colours stand out well.

give you more information about them at the back of the book, so you can suss it all out for yourself.

In the meantime, let's get back to the run, where we are just lifting off the Greenock waterfront. We do this by getting into the right hand lane at the big Morrisons supermarket[8]. When you do turn right, go straight through the next roundabout, under the rail bridge, and onto the very steep Baker Street, which isn't the one Gerry Rafferty sang about. As you head uphill to the lights where you want to turn left, try not to stop in a line of traffic, for the road is so steep you will find it impossible to get going again. When you do turn left, you are then onto Ingelston Street and already back on a previous return route[9]. The ramp-like start of the Kilmacolm Road is gained by turning first right at the church, and then it's dig in deep time.

Once clear of the big long climb on the Auchmountain Road, and having flipped down the other side, I have various options to return home, but all will have to go through Bridge of Weir by either road or cycle track. The fastest, most direct way onto the cycle track would be to continue on the B-788 (Auchenfoil Road), going straight across at the crossroads with the B-786 as it cuts across heading for Lochwinnoch. The road will then actually go under the old rail bridge just ahead that carries the track, which is where you would join it. The most direct way to

8 - You're right at the fire station.

9 - This was the way we returned home on the Five Ferries run and you are on the B-788, which you joined when you turned right at the fire station.

Bridge of Weir by road is to turn off the Auchenfoil Road at Gateside Farm and make for Quarriers on the windy minor road through the farms. After returning back through Quarriers Village, and entering Bridge of Weir by the Torr Road, you can join the cycle path there.

If you prefer to stay roadside, but don't want to go via Kilbarchan, ride back on the A-761, where after Brookfield at the Deafhillock roundabout, the choice to go via Linwood or Johnstone will present itself. Going through Johnstone town will find you, for a short stretch, back on that old stalwart of the Barochan Road — the one that took us away from Houston earlier in the day. It leads onto Johnstone's Mill Brae, at the top of which is a set of lights that never seem to be at green when you approach them. Of the countless times I have gone through this

Approaching the top bends on the Auchmountain Road (the B-788) and this is always a welcome sight, for it is a long arduous pull-up from Greenock, especially with a lot of miles in your legs.

junction, I think I can count on the one hand the amount of times I got green.

The town centre is always a bit tight and busy, but it isn't the biggest, so you're soon through and up the long Thorn Brae, passing the rail station and the Thorn Inn itself, from where the Elderslie back road provides the shortest way home.

For me, at least, it is slightly easier to return through Linwood from the Deafhillock, as it's a fast fly down into, then through this town, skirting along the edge of the place on Kashmir Avenue, before leaving on the busy dual carriageway of Linwood Rd. As I enter Paisley, I take my leave from the majority of the traffic by taking the right turn up Fulbar Road and going on a very personal trip down memory lane. Returning this way takes me past the

And with the cresting of the Auchmountain Road, you then flip over into rural Renfrewshire's inner fields, now on the Auchenfoil Road, but still on the B-788. There's still a lot of upping and downing to go, but a feeling of being on the home stretch is definitely felt.

very street I grew up in and the park where I used to play football, which now has a cycle lane running through it. Once the Foxbar Rivers area has been negotiated, I return home through Meikleriggs and the quiet Stanley estates.

So there you have it — our first time across the Clyde without touching an island, though the Cowal peninsula does have an island feel to it. I'm sure that didn't disappoint in the slightest, and Dunoon will be the base for the next few runs, all of which are equally good days out in their own right, with a fair amount of variation to keep up your interest.

Although the run across the water today wasn't the most taxing, the run up and down for me makes it still a long but great day out. Hope you enjoyed it, and don't worry we'll be off again soon. Till the next time, take car.
Liam Boy.

N.B. Noah St John: *The Secret Code of Success.*
Hypnosis Downloads/Uncommon Knowledge.

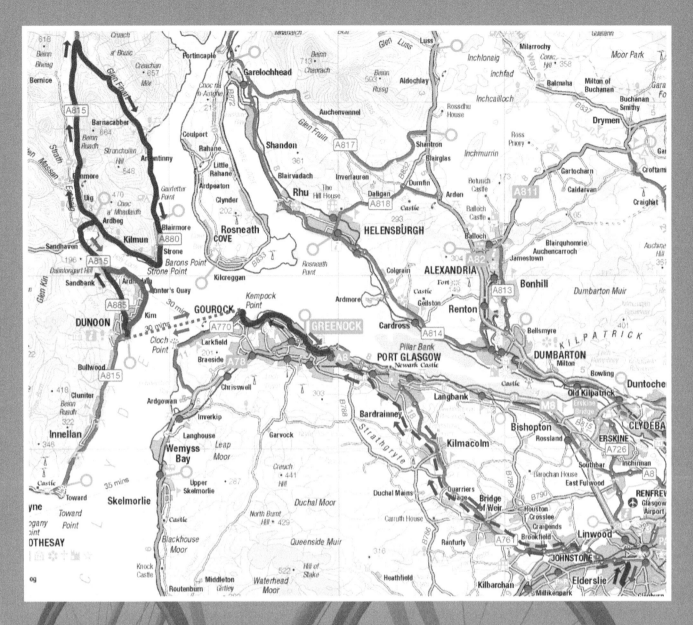

ARDENTINNY

FROM PAISLEY
72.5 MILES
6.55 HOURS
ASCENT: 1980 FEET
2811 CALORIES BURNED

FROM DUNOON PIER
30.8 MILES
2.03 HOURS
ASCENT: 720 FEET
1194 CALORIES BURNED

O/S Landranger Maps. 64, 63, 56.

ARGYLL FERRIES   TEL NO 01475 650 338

WESTERN FERRIES TEL NO 01369 704 452

ROUTE SUMMARY

OUTWARD ROUTE

Paisley (Cycle Track)
Elderslie (Cycle Track)
Linwood (Cycle Track)
Bridge Of Weir (Cycle Track)
Kilmacolm (Cycle Track)
Port Glasgow (Cycle Track)
Greenock (Part Cycle Track)
Gourock Pier
Argyll Ferry to Dunoon Pier

COWAL PENINSULA

Dunoon
Loch Eck
Glen Finart
Ardentinny
Strone
Kilmun
Hunters Quay
Kirn
Dunoon Pier
Argyll Ferry to Gourock Pier

RETURN ROUTE

Reverse of outward route

THE COWAL GAME

Until now, I have been a real roadie and strictly – well, for the most part – kept off the cycle tracks and used only the Queen's highway as my modus operandi. Now that's not to say that I have never or don't ever use the tracks, I do, usually when it suits me for some reason or other. Not least of which is the safe haven they provide when a very strong, usually winter's wind is blowing, and there is a real danger of danger, i.e. getting blasted into the path of some oncoming or following vehicle. They also provide an easy flat way back when you are returning canned from a long road run, when perhaps you bit off more than you could chew, or are simply out of nick. To the anxious parent, they also provide a good safe environment to let the little ones off the leash and allow them to roam freely for a bit, as you pedal discreetly behind.

So they have a practical use, not only for the recreational rider, but also the serious roadie. I mentioned in one of the earlier runs that cycle track riding does have its mellow pitfalls, which is true. But one drawback which I didn't mention was that a lot of the time they tend to be quite hemmed in and feel a bit monotonous due to lack of a view, as they follow the course of a once straight rail track. For a lot of cycle tracks this is true, at least in part, but that general overview does an injustice to the latter part of the track which follows the bed of the old railway line from Elderslie to Kilmacolm and beyond, and which once ran all the way to Greenock's Prince's Dock.

The stretches between Bridge of Weir and Kilmacolm, shortly after Kilmacolm and the section above Port Glasgow, are particularly dramatic.

This is more than a convenience route. This is a route of quality and pleasure that has a number of advantages over its road rivals which also head down into Inverclyde. It will provide a more relaxed, traffic-free journey for the scenic approach to the Gourock ferries. This time the Argyll ferry, leaving from the old Cal-Mac base of

The Glasgow to Gourock cycle track at Lounsdale Paisley. Joining it here in amongst the birch trees makes for a pretty start to our run out west where it will provide the easiest and for the most part safest journey all the way to the coast. Some of the sections to come are very unique.

Gourock's Kempock Point, will be the one we are aiming for. This will deposit us at Dunoon pier for our run north, up by Loch Eck and over to Ardentinny. This will be our second jaunt over to the former Clyde coast Mecca, and will give a day out of equal length to the Loch Striven run, but of totally different character.

The Striven was mostly flat, mostly shoreside riding of around 35 miles from Hunter's Quay, whereas Ardentinny will be slightly shorter at around 30 to 32 miles from Dunoon pier, but will be a bit more of a mixed bag. There will be some great shoreside riding, equal in quality and character to what we've done already, but there will also be – and I can't stress this enough – some out-of-this-world road to cover, which will be the black line of tarmac that follows the curves of Loch Eck. Now if that isn't enough, there is also a really tough climb up through the rugged Glen Finglas, and as the bulk of the run is circular, it can be done in either direction. It is equally awesome whichever way you go. No kidding!

So that is the next taster to tempt you onto your trusted steed and get into gear for some more of the same high quality road riding that you've now become accustomed to. On this occasion I will take you down and along the earlier mentioned cycle track, which I can thoroughly recommend as an approach route for the sheer charm and delight it provides in its latter stages, and as a good safe alternative to the roads for anyone, especially for those with youngsters who are at an age where they can start to put in some miles. At the point where it descends down from the high ground above the Port, you'll realise why I recommend it so highly.

I join the track just over a mile from my front door. It is once again reached by passing the RAH, for the track follows the course of the old Canal Street rail line that runs by the bottom of Corsebar Road. Nowadays it can prove to be a bit on the tight side as you pass the hospital, because staff are forced to park on the road due to extortionate parking fees in the hospital carpark itself. To my mind, whoever made the decision to charge the nurses and doctors a parking fee needs shooting, literally!

After scraping along the edge of car after car after car, turn right onto Craw Road and immediately left onto the cycle tack and head out west. If there is a south westerly blowing, you will notice the shelter which the embankments provide right from the word go. The tight closed-in sensation is very apparent in the early stages, which to its credit can be a haven for small birds and mammals; on occasion I've even seen woodpeckers in the trees here.

The young team making their way along this stretch will be oblivious to the fact that there used to be two major works either side, when it was a railway. One I've already mentioned – that being my old man's place of drudgery, the Ferguslie Thread Mill on the right – but less well known would be Balfour Beatty's on the left. It was a large sprawling area strewn with enormous reels of cables and associated vehicles and equipment, as Balfour's was a major supplier of support to British industry.

This large workplace was accessed from nearby Lounsdale Road, as was Balfour Kilpatrick's, a more electrical-based company, whose grounds were directly across the road from Balfour Beatty's. All three of these former bastions of our industrial might are long gone, and all three have been replaced by modern over-priced housing developments, which again highlight the change in our social and industrial landscape in such a short space of time.

The Canal Street line does exactly as it says on the tin. For the most part it follows the line of the former Glasgow to Ardrossan Canal which, despite its name, only got as far as the Thorn in Johnstone. The only remaining section of this once busy waterway can still be seen running through the old mill grounds on the other side of Green Road. It diverted at this point to service Ferguslie Mill on completion in 1811, before its closure in 1881 to make way for the railway itself.

It was in this section of canal that local bard, the great Robert Tanahill, drowned himself in a fit of depression back in 1810. Unfortunately this event was made all the worse by his burning of a lot of his work before he committed suicide.

Hurrying west, away from the scene, we pass under the Green Road bridge and before we cross the great wee bridge over Fulbar Road, we again brush beside another modern housing estate, this one on our right, and this one on top of the former large goods yard that once held court there; hence the name Station Road that feeds into it on the other side. At the bridge over Fulbar Road, there once stood a quaint-as-could-be signal box, and I can actually remember the night it went up in flames. One of the firemen almost came a cropper when he got a bit carried away on its roof as they put out the fire.

The old line is quite elevated beyond this point, as it approaches the start of Elderslie, but before it reaches there, it actually passes over another disused rail line running from south to north, and this was the line which went from here up to Barrhead. A lot of people might not realise they are actually on a bridge at this point, as it has been filled in below for many years now, but this was the very spot where I played as a kid and can remember it still. The Canal Street to Kilmacolm rail line lasted up until January 1983, which was quite late as most closures go, for the vast majority of our rail network disappeared in the mid-1960s after the commissioning of the Beeching reports.

Doctor Richard Beeching came across from ICI and was given the task of overseeing the entire rail network with a view to making it profitable, as it had been running at a loss for quite some time under the management of British Railways. This was despite massive development and modernisation in the early 1960s. The main report was produced in 1963 with a second less substantial one in 1965. The 1963 report came during the term of Harold Macmillan's Conservative Government and proposed a massive reduction in track (6000 miles), stations (2363), and jobs (70,000). This was in concert with a general overview to improve road links, especially the building of a new network of motorways. The Transport Minister at the time, who appointed Beeching to the post of chairman of the railways, was one Earnest Marples.

Marples, incredibly, was a partner and major shareholder in a company which built motorways. Despite the obvious clash of interest, it was never proven that he acted inappropriately at any time. And so at least a third of our great – and it *was* great – rail system was put to the sword. Admittedly, the railways were losing a lot of dough, around £300,000 per day, which is a lot of dough.

Is it art? This is one of several features to be found along the cycle track, though undoubtedly the most noticeable. It is rather well done I must say.

However, the cuts were very inflexible and money could have been saved in numerous other ways. As it turned out, the cuts did not put the rail system back into profit at any time, while our roads continue to get more clogged up by the day. It was a very short-sighted view and one taken by the two main political parties, because in 1964 a Labour Government was elected, led by Harold Wilson.

In the run-up to the election, they had promised to stop the cuts. But once elected, they reneged on these promises. As for Earnest – eventually Lord Marples – well, so much for his integrity. He finally left our shores one night by the last ferry across the Channel, with most of his possessions and money in tea chests. The floor of his Belgravia home was said to be littered with his clothes and possessions, as he bolted for safety, hotly pursued by the taxman who was looking for thirty years unpaid tax. It seems Ernie had no option but to cut and run. He ended up in Monaco for a while, and never returned to these shores.

So that is the reason, that to this day, if you're out and about and you know where to look, you will still find the remains of old track beds and station platforms in numerous quiet corners, though as already mentioned not this particular line.

You'll shortly find yourself running parallel with the main Glasgow to Ayr line, which sits behind a large wire fence on your right; Elderslie Main Road sits behind the large stone wall to your left, but not for long. Instead, you must join the road shortly and continue on it for approximately half a mile, before regaining the track by the end of a slip road which sits at the bottom of Glenpatrick Road, called Canal Street.

Although there are painted parts on the main road here to indicate the cycle track, it's normally very busy. That's fine if you're an adult, but not so good for little ones. The right hand pavement, however, will provide the necessary protection for the youngsters if needed.

When you regain the track, you almost immediately go under a bridge which carries the existing rail line, bending sharply right and then left as you do so. This bridge, incidentally, provides shelter for the Elderslie young team as they enjoy a small refreshment of a weekend evening. It's oh so nice to be back into the quiet of the birch trees again, as on we go cutting across the steel blue bridge over Malcolm's goods yard, then shortly crossing the tumbling River White Cart, after which it's decision time.

At this point the track splits into two. It's straight ahead for the old North Johnstone line or right for Kilmacolm. We want right. A back curving climb takes us over the Johnstone bypass, then down and straight, skirting the edge of Linwood. After a bit of undulation, it's onto the straight stuff ahead, and just after we go under Barochan Road, we meet the first point of old interest – the remains

of a platform, which was once the Houston/Crosslee station.

The track continues fairly level, staying in among the trees as it passes Brookfield, continuing to do so even after going under the stone and iron bridge which carries Sandholes Road. Things only open up briefly when we reach the fields after crossing Locher Burn, and then it's over Crosslee Road before returning to the roadside again, running beside the A-761 on the wooded approach to Bridge of Weir.

Nothing remains of the once busy and grand station building which stood here, though there is still a great air about the place, still enough of the old walls, bridges, viaducts and so on, just to give a feeling of what once was. Character is the word I'm looking for here; this spot has got it aplenty.

Leave by crossing over the Torr Road and River Gryfe, then again almost flatly out and under the first of many similar curved stone bridges. These bridges are so solid-looking and built to last; they've been there since the rail was first built, I dare say, and don't look like they're going anywhere soon. Real quality.

The track beckons you to follow it gently and curvingly onward, as – lightly hemmed-in – it passes under more bridges ahead. However, as it reaches Quarriers Village, it opens up and becomes very pastoral and it's

This is the view from the cycle track as you pass through the pretty Quarriers Village stretch and with no cars engines to shatter the peace it is as quiet as it looks.

time to relax and really enjoy the surroundings. The main road continues to climb up towards Kilmacolm running parallel with you on your right, especially in the early stages. And as much as this is a great road to ride, particularly when coming in the opposite direction, you can't help but feel a definite relaxing sensation as you purr more flatly and easily along the path.

Knowing subconsciously that there is no danger from traffic allows you to relax and enjoy the ride. Discarding the normal keep-your-wits-about-you tension is very noticeable at times. The gentle spreading tentacles of relaxation going down into your back and at the same time entering and affecting the mind, have the effect of highlighting your awareness and appreciation of your surroundings.

At this point, Quarriers sits across on your left in the Gryfe Valley, which stretches beyond, drawing up into the high ground away to the south, and then into the trees and conifers of the Torr Hill plantation.

There are one or two sculptures and such like along the path, which provide elaborate mileage signs. The most striking and noticeable is one of a centurion addressing his men, which has been welded out of a number of old lampposts and other materials diverted from the Irn Bru factory, and should boost your morale no end. Beyond this, the view rises greenly up towards the shapely tops of the Muirshiel Hills, with the cattle grazing in the fields nearby, before it gets very enclosed as the old terminal of Kilmacolm is approached. This does so in very dynamic fashion, as the path becomes bolt straight, hemmed in tightly by sheer solid rock on either side.

This is rock that must have taken a determined effort of graft and gelignite to dislodge and force a way through, making a most dramatic manmade channel which now looks and feels very atmospheric. Darkly and dankly you approach the classic rail bridge, on the other side of which stood the station – now a restaurant, the Pullman Inn. This is you now in the centre of our local millionaires' row, although you don't see much of it from the cycle path. You do see a fairly newish street of large houses in mock-Tudor style (very nice), that you must pass through and which sits on the other side of the old station, before re-joining the track. This will at first be quite different from what has gone before, with the broad straight path now becoming narrow as it meanders through some fairly sparse woodland, giving the impression that a purpose-built path was constructed here to enable the cycle route to continue on its journey.

Beyond this, however, the style of a disused rail line is once again picked up, but there is such a gap between the two sections of obvious rail line that I actually wondered if they had ever even met. They most certainly did, for the line before and beyond Kilmacolm was once all part of the Saint Enoch to Greenock's Princes Pier line.

The section of rail after Kilmacolm saw its last train in the November of '65, though the through trains had actually ceased stopping at stations some six years earlier. The stretch of track between Kilmacolm and Greenock was lifted a year after it closed in 1966, which was approximately 17 years before the rest of it closed in 1983. With such a long gap between the closing of the two stretches, it's easy to see why there appears to have been no connection.

This is where the cycle track can be seriously good in places as it slowly traverses the hillside diagonally down into the Inverclyde towns. This allows much more time to fully appreciate the views, time that you don't get when using either of the two main road options the Clune Brae or the Auchmountain Rd. This shot was taken right above Port Glasgow town centre and gives a good idea of just how much the broad blue blast of the firth can hit you when you see it for the first time that day.

Despite the fact that the Kilmacolm line closed at the same time as Paisley Canal, it was actually older, having opened in 1869 and previously run through Gilmour street. So it was 114 years old when it finally ceased being in use. That's quite an innings and quite a line, especially for the countryside it passes through. As you leave Kilmacolm, you will notice a definite gradient taking you up to the highest point which the railway went to and into some beautiful semi-rugged scenes, with your eyes drawn up to the shapely top of Cairncurran Hill in the

Muirshiels. Even when the line is quite enclosed here, it is still very dramatic by the sheer bare rock which makes up the embankments. It is pretty obvious that it must have taken a monumental effort to force a way through.

The ferns and brambles have reclaimed a lot of their territory back from British Rail. It never ceases to amaze me how Mother Nature can be held at bay by man for decades on end, but the moment that the maintenance stops the recolonisation starts. Shortly you will pass under another classic rail bridge, this one the very last and very noticeable by the fact that it has been partly filled in underneath, making you duck a little as you go under (just to be on the safe side). After a lot of great but enclosed riding, it feels such a release to burst out into the openness of the fields and rolling hills.

The height of the ground is apparent in places by its sparseness, which is part of the reason this area is so special. You know in your mind that you are above Port Glasgow, and that means that stunning views of the Clyde and a long meandering descent into Greenock are now within easy reach.

A view of Cardwell Bay and the Argyll hills. Kempock Point juts out very prominently into the water. It is a breathtaking scene and one I could stand at for hours. In fact you will often meet other people up there doing the same thing. One guy I met on one occasion assured me he came up every single day, I can honestly see why.

This is the added ingredient which makes this area extra special, one you really feel as first you break left and climb up close to Mid Auchinleck Farm, whilst still on the cycle track. The farm gives its name to the grey concrete housing scheme you are just about to enter, and which was built on top of the rail line that you are following. The farm itself still retains a look of remote quaintness, as it sits slightly above and away from the houses, which themselves form a line in the shape of Montrose Avenue.

This is where you enter Port Glasgow proper, and follow Montrose round left and then dive down and over the Dubbs Road. It was here that Upper Port Glasgow station was situated (freight only), though you wouldn't know now, for everything is covered over in sixties' concrete garb. At this point the cycle route cheekily jumps over into Barscube Avenue, then back into the swing of things by re-entering the path and running beside and below the Port's industrial estate – the Devol.

The large factory that you run close to has been closed for some time and was the former Amps place, I've been informed. At first no-one I asked could remember what the hell it did, but I finally got lucky when one of my hires from the airport told me. With windows smashed or boarded up, it's a real eyesore, but that's not too much of a problem because you're looking north now. Glimpses of the Clyde's north bank will be evident above the roof tops of the Mid Auchinleck homes, from the moment you hit the path again. You will shortly pass a funny-looking newsagent's store on your right, sitting in Stane Road, which is housed in what looks like an old railway building or carriage; hence the funny look. It's just about all that's left of the railway here.

As you pad along west, it all opens up instantly because the housing that once stood here has been knocked down, so it's a panorama par excellence – for the time being anyway. The road that slams into and stops dead at the side of the path is Selkirk Road, where just beyond, there are views right down into Port Glasgow's centre, along with its iconic black and white chequered lighthouse, sitting just offshore. There is a road to cross shortly – the brutal Barrs Brae – but before you reach it, the first of two metal bridges also has to be crossed. I urge you to exercise caution when crossing any metal bridge, as they can be extremely slippery when wet (bitter experience talking here). It's best to disengage at least one foot and pad over gingerly.

Once these two interruptions are negotiated, the path straightens and descends down at a fairly easy angle through the Devol area of the town. The woods are fairly dense here and can obstruct the view of the firth; however this is made up for by the tumbling burns that numerously cascade down the steep hillside, all fern-clad and bonnie. In fact, so dense are the woods at times here that all the houses are completely hidden from view, and you can't help but feel you're in a very pleasant remote setting. On occasion I have spied the high chimney pots

This shot is also from Lyle Hill and shows the Argyll ferry berthed at Gourock pier and also what remains of the old wooden pier of yesteryear.

of a cottage sitting just off the path in the woods down to the right, and although I could be wrong here, I think that they may have been former railway houses.

Just after this comes the nemesis of the whole cycle track and that is the approach to the Devol Glen bridge. At this point the track drops steeply and, I would say, quite dangerously down, and again it's much safer to get off and walk, especially if it's wet or if leaves cover the path. The green bridge over the thickly wooded glen is also best crossed cautiously, and the pull up on the other side is almost as steep and awkward. The remnants of the old rail bridge are very apparent on the other side and it must have been quite a dramatic spanning of this deep gorge. What a sight it must have been, with the bridge containing nine arches in its construction. It's a real pity they pulled it down.

On clearing the glen, the path levels and allows the old ticker to settle down, and you now flow downward and onwards into Greenock itself. It starts to open on both sides a bit, as the hills fall back on your left, and there's not the tight hemmed-in feeling of the Port section. Knocknairs Hill is the hill you are riding below, as at the same time you now glide above the Lilybank then Gibshill estates, where there are constant glimpses of the water and docklands through the trees.

The three large cranes of the dry dock (which is still in use), act as a marker, as does the jutting Ardmore peninsula sitting far across on the Clyde's north shore. Open parkland is now entered just as you regain the road, which is slightly tricky to reach due to some daft feature on the path. You are now right beside the Lady Octavia sports centre.

This is Bridgend Road you are joining, which is a great glide downhill; double-bending beautifully underneath two low-lying rail bridges, whereafter it is simply a case of following the blue cycle path signs round the quiet streets of this part of town. This includes the wonderfully named Barwhirley Road, which curves gracefully down towards the James Watt Dock, where the prominent former warehouse building gives a real feeling of old Greenock.

After one or two more twists and turns, you find yourself on Belville Street. Now we are going to dive down right on Lawrence Street to continue on the cycle track officially, but if we went straight on at this junction, we would shortly come to the bottom of the Kilmacolm Road. This would mean we have linked up with the back road we took on our way to Wemyss Bay and Rothesay. So it is possible to get to Rothesay by this route, and this would be the way you would go.

However, we're turning right as stated, and diving down the splendid slope and dodgy road surface of Lawrence Street. This takes us beside the large railway wall and track, before passing under it, and giving a brief taste of gritty old Greenock. We soon encounter the mega busy A-8, which we simply cross at the pedestrian lights, to take us safely round East India Harbour and onto the Clyde in front of the magnificent Custom House building, now sitting beside the not-so-magnificent new theatre building. The Custom House was once open as a museum, but unfortunately closed its doors in 2010.

Now, from the moment the cycle track hits the A-8 til it gets to the start of the Greenock Esplanade at least, it does become a bit meandering and time-consuming. It is still safe for the kids, scenic and interesting. However if you are aiming for a certain Argyll ferry and time is tight – assuming you have no little ones to protect – then the road will be a more direct and quicker option. I often miss out the section round the waterfront here; I like some of it, though a lot is quite tedious, but I rarely miss out the Esplanade. The glorious Greenock Esplanade. It must be about the grandest road on the whole Clyde. An unforgettable stretch of riding that is airy and open, fresh and refreshing, easily accessed by turning first right down Campbell Street, after going under the old rail bridge on the A-770 (Brougham Street).

From the array of stunning dwellings to the light glinting on the Clyde that lights up Kilcreggan across the firth, this street is something magical. This will be felt as you ride along. You will be in no doubt as to the delights of this mile or so of stunning setting, which will require

Here is the former pier which is unreachable now from the land as that portion has collapsed. Much of it is still intact however but I don't think there are any plans to restore it to its former glory, not any day soon at any rate.

the Cal-Mac headquarters. Since June 2011, the ferry service from here has been provided not by Cal-Mac but by their subsidiary company, Argyll Ferries. Two small but nippy craft have replaced the former larger vehicle ferry that used to make the run over from here to Dunoon Pier. These normally take about 25 minutes to cross, weather permitting. I say that because, being smaller, they are often unable to sail in adverse conditions; conditions which are fairly commonplace on the lower Clyde.

However, the Western Ferries can usually run during these periods, and provide a good back-up in such circumstances. Remember, they are only two miles apart, a distance that can be covered in about seven minutes on a bike. There are no outlets on the mainland side that sell Argyll tickets; only on the Dunoon side can you get a 10 ticket card. One can be bought on board. It makes sense to buy a card if you plan to ride a lot across that side of the water, but if only going over occasionally, then a single or return bought on board will suffice. Summer fares are slightly dearer than winter, with kids getting it half price and bikes going free.

There is a half hourly service up until midday, when it then becomes hourly leaving Gourock at twenty past

many more visits to fully appreciate the full extent of all that's around you. Its bright blue painted bannister separates you from the bright blue of the firth, as it curves round and leads to the end of the Esplanade, where stands the modern-looking coastguard station.

When you turn right, back onto the A-770 at the end, the cycle path stays on the pavement before it enters Battery Park. Here the openness and the sight and sweep of Cardwell Bay tells you you're almost there.

The uniformly green and flat playing fields blend into the uniform blue and flatness of the Clyde to the right, contrasting with the creamy white dwellings of Gourock, as they rise up into the hillside ahead and to the left. Soon the Cove Road is reached, where you are quaintly hemmed in between sandstone and shore. This is touching the water's edge now. Waders and gulls search the mud close by, oyster catchers and the beautiful curved bill curlew go about their business. The raucous call of the herring gull heralds your arrival at the coast proper. This is always a calm sheltered spot, still and salty, quiet and peaceful. It's a very gentle way to arrive, as you make your way towards the dead end and through a chink in the end wall to take you onto Tarbet Street.

Only a short purr down to the ferry now, passing rowing boats beached and stood on end, side by side, awaiting their next sail. The old wooden pier (what's left of it), still holds court in the bay. The bay that contains

Just heading round Kempock Point after leaving Gourock and passing the modern smart rail station as we go. The charge over to Dunoon has started and normally takes about 25 minutes. If you just miss a ferry and have some time to kill then the montage of World War II photos in the station are worth a look.

the hour, before resuming its half hourly service with the 4:50 pm sailing. The very first time I boarded, my eyes lit up when I spied the coffee machine – and it delivers a good brew. There is also a sweets and crisp/sandwiches machine as well, should you require such sustenance. The boost that a nice mocha or cappuccino can give on a long run is worth its weight in gold, to me at least.

So as the wee barra tears out round Kempock Point, you should know there is a deck above to go out on and admire the view, and just as you start to batter across the open blue blanket, the Cloch Lighthouse soon shows on the port side. (Note the maritime jargon here.)

The wee Argyll ferry battering across the Clyde Dunoon bound. Although it is a bit more susceptible to cancellation in bad weather than its Western Ferries counterpart it is still a great service and the on board good quality reasonably priced coffee machine gives it the edge for me.

With its prominent position and Arran as a backdrop, it provides a great photo opportunity, as most lighthouses do. So after the sightseeing, I like to dive below and get my first if not second coffee, or even a cheeky wee hot chocolate, just to be well warmed up for the road ahead. The trip over usually involves at least one more visit up top for viewing purposes, before docking near the old Dunoon pier (no longer used), which is still a grand sight in its cream-walled and red-roofed colours, with grey turrets and clock tower topping the grandeur.

You then disembark, bike in hand and looking forward to what will be another jaunt over the water, and right from the word go you are faced with a choice. That is whether to go via Dunoon's main drag, or stay on the shorefront, rounding Hunter's Quay and into Sandbank that way. The direct line through the town will be as near as dammit a mile shorter and is quite a pleasant ride in itself.

Firstly you go into a very narrow section of road – one way at that – passing that Victorian bastion of opulence, the Argyll Hotel. God alone knows how many Glaswegians passed through, or rather staggered through, its doors over the decades.

The paintwork of the Dunoon buildings – flaking off in more places than not – gives the backwater look that is virtually essential to any Clyde Coast dwelling nowadays. The spire of the magnificent Saint John's Church, already visible, is soon passed and saves the day by taking the focus off the mild dilapidation. But it's not all that bad by any means, for the road opens up a tad and pleasant cottages line the street, along with large food stores, schools, fire station, filling stations, and more. The left hand side of town is a threadbare covering of the wild conifer-clad hinterland that rises above.

A tree-lined trout lake, Loch Loskin – boat hut and all – is passed on the left as you leave town, climbing as you go. And after a field or two of rough stuff, you find yourself perched on the road high above Sandbank. At this point, if you look up left, you will see a rather striking sight in the way that some electric pylons cut through the conifers on Finbracken Hill, which are symmetrically uniform either side, looking rather spectacular. Who would have thought pylons and pines could be such a limelight grabber? Ahead, over the glinting tail end of the Holy Loch, sits the massive bulk of Clach Bheinn, towards which you plummet down through the homes that hug the hill, before passing the A-815 on the right coming in from the shorefront.

If you had chosen the shore road, as opposed to the main drag, this would be where you would join the

Dunoon pier from the Argyll ferry just before it docks and the classic looking old building and river are cloud covered and slightly shrouded in a misty damp. I'd expect to meet rain as I head up to Loch Eck under these conditions and on this occasion that's exactly what I got.

If you choose to go via Dunoon's main road as opposed to the sea front then your reward will be a great scenic drop down to Sandbank and the Holy Loch at the end of it. Here big Clach Bheinn stands grandly behind. Soon the choice of whether to go to Ardentinny clockwise or anti will have to be made.

A-885, having made your way up past the Western ferry and round by the Holy Loch, following its guarding stone wall as you went. To get the best of both, I sometimes go main drag out, Holy Loch home, but obviously the choice is yours. Now as you leave Sandbank, you find yourself purring flatly beside the shoreline, which I always find most dramatic when the tide is out and there is a real feeling of stillness. Apart from the usual homes that you'd expect by now, you also pass some different accommodation in one or two places, it being white and more practical in appearance.

The reason for this is it was built to accommodate the American sailors attached to the 14th Submarine Squadron that were based in the Holy Loch itself, from the early sixties til 1992. The ending of the Cold War meant that the Yanks had no more need for a base here, so they pulled out. Only the housing appears left behind by those gun-totting sons of bitches (only kidding!). So there's nothing much to disturb the peace as you clear the head of this very short stocky loch, and shortly pass

a road breaking off left heading for Colintraive and the Kyles of Bute (more of which later).

There are fields either side of you at this point – rough-shod and fit only for sheep, in what is already a rather narrow strath (Eachaig) that will progressively get narrower the further north you head. From the gentle hills that line the Clyde, the glen running north will lead into much steeper terrain, already apparent even at this early stage.

Ahead, guarding the left flank of Loch Eck, is the already mentioned imposing Clach Bheinn, but even the lower hills either side of the Holy Loch wear a much harsher coat, though with a stunning trim. They are, for the most part, sitka spruce conifer-clad, keeping hill walkers, dog walkers, or any walkers for that matter, effectively off their slopes. You contour round right while staying on the flat of the basin, passing a filling station just as you cross the River Eachaig, where it's make-your-mind-up time again.

If you decide to do the Ardentinny loop clockwise then the great Loch Eck will shortly be on your left flank and drawing you up towards the Whistlefield Inn. This is approximately 11 to 12 miles from the ferry and it's where the sharp right turn to take you over Glen Finart must be made. The Eck is a glorious loch to ride beside whichever direction you are going in.

You have a choice as to whether to go straight ahead first, up Loch Eckside and then over to Ardentinny, before skirting back round the coast. Or the coast first and then over the Glen Finglas road, followed by Loch Eck. Usually it comes down to personal preference when a run can be done in either direction, and this one may come down to that for you personally. However, there is a deciding factor in this one, and that is the very tough climb up and over the fairly brutal road that carries you over and through Glen Finglas.

And just to prove what I said about Loch Eck in the previous photo, here is a great shot of it when going south along its banks which shows off its steep dramatic conifer clad west side as we take a crash barrier bend near the bottom end when Dunoon bound.

As hard as it is either way, it's my opinion – and that of other guys I've spoken to – that going up from the Loch Eck side is the easier of the two, or the lesser evil if you like. And it's that way I take you this time. So ignore the right turn after the river and continue up Glen Eachaig,

progressively being drawn up into the sheer-sided ruggedness of this slender pathway.

At first there is still some flat land which the clansmen of old must have worked hard to eke out a living on, I dare say. The two clans I assume, who would have been the holders of the ground – though not at the same time – would have been the Campbells and the Lamonts.

Now mark my words here! No matter how many times you do it, you will never tire of riding the Loch Eck road. We are talking a top quality stretch of tarmac, full of setting and scenery. Even before you reach it, there is great road to cover, which starts the moment you pass the A-880 cut off for Ardentinny. The flat or gently rising elegant curves of the A-815 appear right in front of you now. The tree-lined and smooth road guides you up into the ever-tightening wildness, which still has a valley floor in its early stages, containing numerous places of commerce, mostly tourism-related. The first place belongs to a bloke who makes wood carvings with a chainsaw. He has a display of his handiwork at the entrance to his gaff;

Going clockwise round the Ardentinny loop means that the tough climb behind the Whistlefield Inn leading up into Glen Finart must be taken. However as hard as it is, it is probably the lesser evil as the climb up from Ardentinny itself is longer and more sustained. This photo is taken from the top of the climb above the Whistlefield and shows the great view of Loch Eck that you get when you do go anticlockwise and are descending this very steep brae.

Nearing the top of the pass taking you over Glen Finart going clockwise and the highest point of the road is the one in the picture right beside the sparse line of conifer trees. After that the descent down to Loch Long begins and it is a steep swerving screamer - not one for the faint hearted I might add.

at the moment, this in the shape of an eagle and dinosaur, which I must say look rather impressive.

The trees and hillside of the Puck Glen sit close on the right, the left side still flat enough to provide space for some rough pastures, one of which contains the old stately-looking Uig Hall. The road makes for a fast and exciting trip up just by the way it is set out, and allows for a high average speed, which gets you motoring well and feeling good. Then some great deciduous woodland is encountered, which contains larger grand conifers, signalling your arrival at Ben More Gardens. Even if you have absolutely no interest in horticulture whatsoever,

Loch long comes into view from the high point on the Glen Finart road and so too does the ferocious switch back bends that will carry you down to that magnificent big sea loch. The next mile or so can prove to be very hairy especially in the wet which it often is.

you cannot fail to be impressed by the avenue of giants that leads into the gardens from the large black iron gates beside the old gatehouse.

These trees are over 150 years old, and are made up, not of Giant Redwoods as I first thought, but giant sequoias and Douglas firs. The place was originally known as Younger's Botanical Garden, after the big brewing family of that name who owned them and who sent renowned plants men to places as far afield as Asia and the American North Pacific coast to bring back specimens. I, for one, am glad that they did.

I admit I often stop and look down this tree-lined avenue in awe at this breath-taking site, and just to put that in perspective, I rarely stop the bike. Breath-taking would also describe the road that follows. For after what is the last section of flat ground, containing a sprawling caravan park – one of many in this neck of the woods – before you know it, a body of water is spied through the trees on the left. Rather discreetly and surprisingly for such a dramatic loch, Loch Eck is upon you from this direction. Once on it however, you know it alright. You have to strain your neck to look up to the tops of the hills that line either side, as they plunge mercilessly down, straight into the deep, dark, cold water. Not so much as a yard of even level respite do they yield.

The road builders must be given credit for the way that they must have had to fight every foot of the way up this lochside to form the road you are now privileged to ride on. It doesn't leave the water's edge for just about the entire 7 miles length, probably because there is nowhere for it to go. Not that you'll be complaining. No matter the weather conditions – from glorious sunshine, to the atmospheric damp and misty, which it often is – this slender, elegant, classic Highland freshwater loch is one that will please and delight every single time you ride its shoreline. Yes, this is despite the fact the topography is set to wet. The high stunning mountains and the proximity to the coast, all make for "persistent precipitation", to quote Giles Brandreth.

But the way that the mist clings to those steep hillsides, sometimes showing them, sometimes obscuring them, makes for an unforgettable steamy sight. Not even the Loch Eck Caravan Park can put you off.

With that spurring you on, there is little climbing but much contouring, beneath and round rock and trees, bays and bends. The freshness of the water is apparent from the salt of the coast, aiding your aerobic system, as swiftly corner after corner is covered, while your eye is drawn forward by the natural line of the loch. All this time you know that you must take the high ground to your right to make it over to Ardentinny, but when you look up and see the unrelenting barriers of Beinn Ruadh leading onto Sligrachan Hill, you wonder where on earth the road over is.

There does not appear to be any break in the terrain to allow any way over, as the right flank shows an imposing uniform steepness of rock and grass. Typical of the mountains here, they possess craggy outcrops from summit to roadside, just as steep also from start to finish, making a tough climb by bike or foot. This gives them such an impregnable appearance, but don't worry, a way over is found right at the Whistlefield Inn. The minute

Approaching the pull up in Glen Finart from the Ardentinny side and although it doesn't look much it is a very arduous climb. Most people are of the opinion the Whistlefield approach is the better of the two as you get up quicker but it's no Sunday stroll either.

you pass this old drovers' rest dating back to 1455, a single track road appears in the nick of time to save the day. If you went straight from the Dunoon ferry, it will be 12 miles to this point; 13 if up round Hunters Quay.

After turning right it starts to climb, but not too bad at first. Passing by the Inn's front door, you are still quite comfortable, before shortly the sign tells you a 1:5, 20% gradient lies ahead. Now slim, grey-covered and white-lined, the road here has no room to zigzag really, save the odd place, so it's brutally forward you go – but thankfully not for long. Within about 0.7 of a mile from turning off the low road, you are over the worst, where snaking now – still upward, though a lot more gently – your unclassified guide takes you up into upper Glen Finart.

After all that effort, the view from up here is, to be honest, a bit disappointing and not what you'd have hoped for.

Although the distant views don't measure up, the ruggedness of the closer hills and terrain makes for a feeling of wilderness that does make it rewarding. The crash barrier slenderly slips beside the road, as you ascend still upward through trees, natural and planted. Just be bloody glad that you're still upright, with the old system returning to normal, making enjoyable what's left of the climb. The whole left side of Glen Finart is the domain of Mr impressive himself, Creachan Mor – 652 metres high and at all times displaying a flank more of slab and rock, rather than grass and heather, indicating the harshness of conditions that exist in the upper reaches.

There's literally no plateau in this glen, for after another slight rise in the road, beside a distinct line of conifers that slope down to the right, you find yourself already descending, with only the slightest of glimpses of Loch Long on the horizon. It's almost a mirror image of the way up, as the downward route starts gently enough. But when a fair bit more of Loch Long shows itself, suddenly you're thrown down the first of a series of brutal, tight, twisting, Alpine-like bends. Brutal in gradient, it is also brutal in appearance by the way the conifers nearby have been felled, giving the place the look of a skinhead just out of a bad barber's.

Had the road builders of old had a bit more savvy and made these bends more sweeping in style, then this would be a most pleasurable ascent up, if coming from the other direction. As it is, it is longer, more sustained, and therefore harder to gain the summit, with the steepest sections getting your heart rate up into the mid-190's. Now admittedly there isn't a lot of room at the bottom of the glen for the road guys to incorporate bends, but there is a bit more scope at the top. I assume it just wasn't the style for our road builders to do that, though compared to the Irish, they weren't too direct. Their boys went as straight as a die even over the steepest brae.

So with brake pads and hands holding hard to stay in control, you go through, then come out of the bends, before plummeting rather dramatically down through large greens and along long glides. Here the lower glen can become very tight on the right hand side, with the slopes of Sligrachan Hill obscuring the sun and making it a cool spot on even the sunniest day. As you pass the farmstead at Sligrachan, there is another of those great old, square, stone, black hand-pointing sign posts, that

Loch Long tranquillity is in abundance here just the way this wee red fishing boat sits still in Finart Bay. The shore of this mighty sea loch has been reached and so too pretty Ardentinny Village. Behind the boat and across the loch can be seen the navy's refuelling depot near Glen Mallon.

tells you it's now only 2½ miles to Ardentinny. The accuracy of these is very good.

The run into Ardentinny is quite a straight affair at first, as you get guided in by trees and telegraph totems (poles, that is). A rough, wedge-shaped field to the left heralds your arrival on the valley floor, which begins to expand quite rapidly as you approach the village and pushes the bulk of Creachan Mor further to your left. A ridge, starting at its striking top, diagonally slants down into Loch Long at the far end of Finart Bay. The road winds pleasantly and gently through deciduous woodland before passing another hideous caravan park, this one with a mock tower to add to the glam.

As you enter the village itself, there is a well-serviced toilet in the right hand car park – always handy to know – before you pass some old forestry workers houses among others, before hitting the lochside. These houses seem to sit in a cold sunless hollow, and you can feel a drop in temperature even as you ride by. I wouldn't be keen on buying a property here, with the cost of today's fuel bills, unless you have more money than sense or are prepared to diddle the meter. Finart Bay itself sits away from you, northwards across rough ground, as out of the trees you pop onto the shoreline at quite a picturesque spot. Part of the attraction is due to the white stone houses that are present here, including Ferry Cottage, which sits right on

Coming down Loch Longside on its picturesque single track road heading for Blairmore. It is out of this world road riding regardless of whether you are doing it in bright sunny weather or atmospheric damp conditions

The woods, ferns, and lapping shore are all intertwined quaintly by the single track road, with its numerous passing places despite the fact that you are officially on an A-class road (the A-880).

It opens up as you approach Gairletter with its, dare I say it, caravan park. However, don't look too closely and you'll be alright, for it's still a wonderful winding way down. Go round every bay as you come to them, where long looks down the Long will see Inverclyde sitting patiently awaiting your return. Across the water, gentle Kilcreggan waits for you another day. Equally gently, you enter Blairmore village by a flat, straight, smooth spin and marvel at both the older Victorian houses and the salt water scene.

It is something special no matter which way you are heading, though travelling north is more rugged and dramatic. This is because the slender, snaking Long Loch has those Arrochar Alps for company, where not even the Gairletter caravans – all bright, white, and neatly

the shore. This is a reminder that a ferry actually did once sail from here across the loch to Coulport, which is now the supply base for our nuclear submarine fleet.

A fire was lit to summon the ferry boat, which would transport amongst others the Campbell Chiefs, the Dukes of Argyll no less. With all things considered, this must be the oldest part of the village, I dare say. Right across the road is the outdoor centre which I visited in my schooldays, though I wished I hadn't. So now that we've toughed out the climb and survived the descent and cold hole of the lower glen (depending on the time of year), it is reward time and payback for all the hard work. This starts the moment you pass the Ferry Cottage and rejoin the shore of the mighty Long one. Its salt air and massive bulk leaves you in no doubt that you're now following a sea loch. And what a loch you're following.

It in many ways resembles the shore road of Loch Eck, as it curves low and long, passing the more modern homes of the village, following stone dyke then metal barriers, all of which keep motorists safe on wet dark nights. The sensational curve of Ardentinny Bay and the downward sweep of the south east ridge of Stronchullin Hill, both meet up ahead on the waterfront and at such a precise point as to keep you focused on it. The road enters a delightful wooded stretch when it leaves Ardentinny.

This is the view you get going up the loch from Blairmore when doing the loop anti-clockwise. The Long is a most slender elegant and dramatic sea loch and pleases every time it is ridden on either bank. Here the unmistakable Creachan Mor is prominent and the white caravans at Gairletter Point are just visible.

lined – can detract from the splendour. The old wooden Blairmore pier from 1855 is a right charmer; the white-painted jetty picture perfect when a still Clyde and quiet Kilcreggan form the backdrop. The red-painted pier house is a perfect partner to the pier, and an equally quaint café sits opposite, should you require one. This is the first of three piers and three seaside villages that you will ride past and through. No serious effort is required here, for everything is now flat and glorious; all to come is broad blue and beautiful; the hard stuff's behind; ahead is the big easy.

Approaching Blairmore pier from Ardentinny in very tranquil conditions with Inverclyde almost unnoticeable way across the firth. Soon the swing round Strone Point and into the Holy Loch will be made making every turn of the road different from what has gone before. There is a great looking wee cafe across from the pier and also behind that runs the track like start to the high road that allows fantastic views right down the Clyde.

That's if you so wish, because at the pier you have a chance to turn right and head up to the high road containing the golf course. If you are coming from the other direction, this will be sign posted where the pull up is steep but on good road; from this end it starts off more like a farm track. The view down and up the Clyde from around Dunselma House does make it a worthwhile effort, but the coastal charms usually keep me lochside. Talking of which, you seamlessly enter Strone from Blairmore, as you swing round the headland opening up more by the minute. The only slight disappointment is that you lose Blairmore's quaint stone seaside wall for Strone's modern concrete job, but so grand is the overall setting that it little affects the mood.

About now you pass the village's ace card – its parish church – so easily seen from the approaching ferry, so splendid and solid its tower. After this you'll find yourself curving into the Holy Loch, passing Strone's pier and

inn, where some, but not all of the houses, do have a real tired backwater look. The store I found to be quite poorly stocked, in fact I think I have more provisions in my fridge. The hillside and woods sit so close to the loch that there is only enough room for a row of houses and the road. The Holy Loch itself is very different in character from its contemporaries, being not long and slender, but only 2 or 3 miles short and a mile wide, though she's still a wee smasher.

It's a glorious view up and across the Holy Loch, hemmed in by the hills on three of its sides, making it feel like a real highland ride as you gently rise and then drop into Kilmun. The road won't leave the lochside now but who's complaining? The loch can be so still and the braes so blade-sharp that you won't want it to stop. Nearing the end and knowing it, you may want to sit up and slow a bit, for the history and scenery comes together in Kilmun. Kilmun pier was built in 1827 by David Napier to provide access to Cowal for the "World Famous Tour" (as it was known). The former large hotel that you are just about to pass was also purpose-built to accommodate the holidaymakers. Napier turned his engineering skills and know-how to different theatres, as the masses discovered leisure time.

Just after the pier is Kilmun Parish Church, which again is striking and solid. It is right beside an old tower house, now leaf-clad and stately ancient, dating back to around 1422 and once a Campbell stronghold and burial ground. Incidentally, it was in Kilmun especially, though not exclusively, that aggrieved displaced Lamonts wreaked revenge on Campbell homesteads, the effect of which was

The view you get when you are taking the early bends into Loch Long at Blairmore. The great old sea wall adds plenty of charm as it accompanies you all the way the length of the Long salt.

to lead to their downfall at the later Dunoon slaughter, which I mentioned in the previous run. Following the church, the houses and gardens on the right continue to please and delight with their quaintness. Soon the head of the Holy Loch is reached and the meandering Eachaig estuary and flood plain takes its place.

The steep tree-clad hillside continues to press in from the right, keeping it all wooded and bonnie. But alas the junction with the A-815 must come, and when it does it can provide almost instant succour in the shape of the filling station, which is pretty well stocked should you need some sustenance. If not, mosey on round the roadside, going through the rough pastures to Sandbank then straighten, with a little sadness, along the west shore of the Holy Loch. The tour is coming to an end at this side of the water again, so you ride in along between the shoreline and houses, where the look out to sea down the broad basin of the loch will hold your gaze and continue

to do so till you near the store on the right, where cheap ferry tickets can be bought.

That earlier decision of which way to go presents itself again here, as you have the choice of main street or shore road if you want the Argyll ferry. It's only a mile if going straight ahead, though it does involve a fair wee climb, which may not appeal to you this late in the day. Turning left to go past Hunter's Quay is 2 miles to the Dunoon pier, but has no climbing and is prettier. The other consideration with the Argyll ferry is timing. Remember that during morning and evening it's a half hour service, which drops to an hour in the quieter afternoon when it leaves at ten to the hour from Dunoon.

The half hour service recommences with the 4.20 pm sailing. If you just happen to miss one, it can be a bit of a pain, because if you're like me, you'll like to keep the momentum going. One advantage of going down the side of the loch is that when you come to the Western ferry

This is a view of the shimmering Clyde from the high road above Strone at Dunselma House the former home of James Coats jnr. Dunselma sits right above the local church which is unmissable as you approach Hunter's Quay from the ferry due to its striking steeple. Although most riders will stick to the coast road most of the time I recommend using the high road from time to time, especially when going clockwise as the views it gives are worth all the effort to get up there.

And again just to prove what I said in the caption for the last photo the Strone Parish Church is clearly seen from the Western ferry as it nears Hunter' Quays with the equally striking Dunselma house sitting right above.

you can judge if you will make the Argyll on time. It's 2 miles away, giving an easy 7 or 8 minutes riding, so if you think you're cutting it fine, just dive on the old red girl. I don't mind which one I get, because the 2 miles I save on the Dunoon side will have to be ridden on the Gourock side. It's no big deal either way, as it's all great riding and even if you are parked near the Argyll Ferries pier, the 2 miles along from McInroy's Point is a good warm down before the drive home.

On this occasion, as we have some time to kill on the ferry over, I want to mention something else that has

The Holy Loch from Strone pier. Strone Point has been ridden and now the journey inland begins which is a pretty as anything just ridden and will also delight as through the likes of Kilmun we gently trundle till the A-815 is reached.

been very beneficial to me on a personal level and you might find helpful if you feel you need some self-awareness. This is a very good thing to have, and is something that most of us lack. Again, some of you reading this might not be interested in personal development, or have the time or inclination for such things. But I urge you to read on and store the information for another time at least, as it could prove useful in later life. I am talking about a technique called morning pages. I came across morning pages when I was advised to get a book called *The Artists Way* by Julia Cameron.

This is first and foremost a book for anyone who wishes to become creative by either, painting, or such like. The author Julia has two main tools that she uses to help you develop creativity and also – possibly more important to some people – to get you to know yourself better. The first is morning pages, where you are asked to get up a bit earlier than usual and write three pages. That's it. Just write down all the things that are whizzing around in your mind. This helps you focus on a lot of things and gets rid of a lot of confusion. It will strip away all the layers of social conditioning and reveal the real you to yourself. Not only that, but it will send out a message to the great power of the Universe should you require anyone or anything in your life.

To get the answers you require, Julia suggests you go on what she calls an artist's date. It simply means you do some activity on your own (very important to do it alone), and it's during this down-time that the answers will come. In my experience the answers came when I was doing mundane things like driving, gardening, in the bathroom, or any other activity I did unconsciously. Julia Cameron claims in the book that morning pages will change you, and it is now a proven technique used by many therapists. I recommend you try them and keep using them, especially when looking for answers. Right,

And once back at Dunoon pier we await the arrival of our craft that will carry us back safe and dry and caffeine high to Gourock. Even if I get a coffee from one of the pier side cafes I still like to get one on board and recommend the chocolate mocha.

with that lifestyle lesson over, it's off the ferry we go and back onto the bike.

On the cycle home, even if I am going to use the cycle track for most of the way, I stick to the road till through Greenock centre. On doing so, I warm up again peddling in on the wonderful A-770, where I pass under the old rail bridge on Brougham Street. This leads into the Ocean Container Terminal, the one with the three big blue cranes at the east end of the Esplanade. This was the old Princes Pier station, the very one which was the terminal for the rail track we are using to get us here and back to Paisley, and a fine-looking station it was too. So under the bridge we go, then over the harum-scarum roundabout onto the A-8.

After passing the police station, it's right turn at the harbour roundabout, following Lawrence Street back up and into the twisting quiet back streets, before rejoining the actual cycle path on Bridgend Road at the Lady Octavia sports ground. (I don't know who she was, but she seemed to like her five-a-side football.) Now using the cycle path is where you win big time on the pull up out of Greenock, because this is a much longer and gentler angled glide up, covering the whole braeside overlooking Inverclyde. This allows for a more relaxed and leisurely ascent out of the shipyard town and up towards the top of the Port.

It therefore allows more time and more scope than its two main road counterparts to enjoy the scenery below and across the Clyde, with the shapely Ben Bowie showing up well in the evening sunlight. The easy climbing vista of the docks and firth, albeit obscured from time to time, can for once be appreciated to the full, whilst not either screaming down or labouring up a 1:10 gradient (or worse). However, when the Devol Glen bridge and dip are approached from this side, there is what appears to be a genuinely placed sign telling you that

A view of the Argyll ferry crossing the Clyde after leaving Dunoon pier. And so it's goodbye to Cowal for another day, with another great ride, day out and memory jaunt under the belt. It won't be the last you always wish.

to give history lesson number umpteen here: this was the very railway track that transported countless American GIs and countless others from Greenock (their first place of call in the U.K.) down to the south coast ports for D-Day. Hard-up Greenock youngsters would stand under the rail bridges and hope some kind Yank troop would throw them some candy or gum, which some did to their credit. If you get a chance, it's worthwhile going into the ultra-modern Gourock station, where they have a wonderful assortment of Second World War photos on the wall to back up my claim.

While following in the rail tracks of that prestigious company we retrace our tyre tracks back home to Paisley, following the outward journey back in for the most part. Nothing too taxing, as we trundle along the either flat or slightly sloping rail line, all the way back to Green Road. Oh, and by the way, did I mention our rail system got us through two World Wars?

the gradient on the track will drop at a rate of 40%. Gulp! To be honest, I think someone got carried away there.

So after the usual huff and puff to get beyond that short unpleasant pitch, you'll shortly take your leave of Inverclyde, through the high streets once more, and start straight motoring for home through the cut glass rock of the old line again. As you do so, I'm about

Below are a number of training runs, and the local testing run that I and many other riders from this area use. If they are handy, you may wish to use them yourself or, if not, you can devise your own. These are useful to build up stamina for the longer runs, and can also be used when time is tight or you are just in the mood for a shorter jaunt.

I describe them, very briefly, in the direction I normally do them in. But as they are all loops, they can be just as easily done in the opposite direction. They all, apart from the test run, have at least one good climb in them, to maximise the benefit. All runs are contained within the O'S Landranger 64 map, unless otherwise stated.

ROWBANK RESERVOIR

16.7 MILES
1.07 HOURS
ASCENT 980 FT
713 CALS

This is a great short and very picturesque training run that packs a fair climb in its armour, and one I like to do often. After gaining Howwood on the Beith Road (the A-737), turn left up the Bowfield Road (the B-776) and, after a fantastic long climb, run past the beautiful Rowbank Reservoir. Continue on up to the crossroads at Hall Farm, where a left turn onto the B-775 will run you back to Paisley along the top of the Gleniffer Braes.

FERENEZE HILLS

10.9 MILES
0.50 MINS
ASCENT 860 FT
574 CALS

This is a great quick but hard wee run I like to do, especially if I'm short for time. It involves heading into Barrhead and along Paisley Road, then turning right before the rail bridge and running up to Gateside. Continue up onto the steep side of the Fereneze Hills, which are similar and therefore good training for Arran's roads. The gradient gets up to about 15%. The height gained actually allows views of Ailsa Craig. Continue right to the end of Fereneze Road, til you meet Shilford Road. Turn right and come back over by Middleton Farm, where you descend to the B-775, where a right turn will return you back down Gleniffer Braes.

LOCHLIBO ROAD

15.2 MILES
1.03 HOUR
ASCENT 840 FT
608 CALS

This run also involves running up Paisley Road, Barrhead, but this time continue on to the end til Allan's Corner roundabout. Turn right onto Kelburn Street and climb out of town onto the great Lochlibo (Irvine) Road, the A-736. The Fereneze Hills look awesome, as does the big white Nielson Mill, which is where the road starts to climb up to Shilford Hamlet. When you reach Uplawmoor, turn right at Caldwell Golf Club onto the B-776, and again climb hard to Hall Farm on the B-775. From there, turn right and return back over the Gleniffer Road and Braes to Paisley.

DUNLOP

21.7 MILES
1.29 HOURS
1320 FT/ASC
929 CALS

The Dunlop run is another good climbing one, which follows the same start as the Lochlibo Road run all the way to the top of Kelburn Street, Barrhead. This time take the left fork for Nielson and not the Irvine Road, and climb long and great up into Nielson Village itself. From there, turn left onto the Kingston Road and undulate wildly and upward into the wild country leading to Dunlop. You can either go right to the end of this road and turn right on the A-735 and enter Dunlop that way, or take the right turn before the end, which will lead to the village centre by a slightly shorter route. Return back through Lugton and then the B-775 over glorious Gleniffer.

STEWARTON

28 MILES

2.11HOURS

ASCENT 1680 FT

1320 CALS

The Stewarton run entails heading up through the Barrhead Dams on the Aurs Road, til you meet with the lights at the bottom of the Stewarton Road (the B-769) and then turning right. This will carry you straight to the Ayrshire village with a real tough climb along the way, but a great descent down to finish. This is another high moor road and, when going clockwise, allows another long distance view of Ailsa Craig. On reaching Stewarton, turn right at the centre crossroads and return back through Dunlop and Lugton on the A-735, before that old stalwart the B-775, carries you back to Paisley via bonnie Gleniffer.

EAGLESHAM MOOR ROAD

29.8 MILES

2.15 HOURS

ASCENT 1380 FT

1231 CALS

Without doubt, this is a superb run. One that's long enough to be a run in its own right and was denied to us for years because of heavy traffic on the A-77, until the new M-77 and A-726 Eaglesham bypass were opened. It is enjoyed by many south side riders and why not? Not only is it A-1, but it just falls in handy for good measure. It entails heading for Eaglesham through Barrhead and then along the Humbie Road, or by using Clarkston Toll. Turn right at the Gilmour Street crossroads in Eaglesham centre and climb initially up Montgomery Street (the B-764), running you up and onto Eaglesham Moor. All's

quiet nowadays, with no more thundering dumper trucks; in fact, there is a cycle lane marked out on the road and you may even enjoy the call of the curlew in summer.

Wonderful rise follows wonderful rise until, at the crest of the road, you can see the sea. When you hit the old A-77 (which has a superb cycle lane, too), turn right and return down to Mearns Cross and back by the Barrhead Dams, if it suits. I personally prefer to turn left earlier than that, using the Malletsheugh Road and then come back in down the Springhill Road, Barrhead.

CLUNE BRAE

29.8 MILES

2.08 HOURS

1120 FT/ASC

1165 CALS

O'S MAPS 64, 63.

This run is probably the most famous training run in the whole area, and used by local groups as well as individual riders. It entails heading for Bishopton and then dropping down onto the busy A-8 which takes you to the big Woodhall roundabout. You can either stay on the A-8 or head through Woodhall to take you to the bottom of the Clune Brae. There is a bit of a shortcut when using the Woodhall route, which entails taking a left turn at Woodhall station and climbing steeply up to the middle of the Clune on Heggies Avenue.

If you don't take the shortcut, expect to meet the Clune at its steepest early doors. From the roundabout at the top of the brae, continue to climb, though much more gently, till you are on the road to Kilmacolm. Continue to run right through millionaire's row on the A-761, which allows you a fantastic flier of a fall towards Bridge of Weir. Personally, I prefer to return from Bridge of Weir by Kilbarchan, which requires another short sharp shock of a climb, but gives a great descent into that old weaving village on the other side as compensation. From Kilbarchan, I return along the Beith Road, Johnstone, before taking the Glenpatrick Road, Elderslie, up to Foxbar Road and into Paisley that way.

LOCHER BRIDGE

27.1 MILES
1.52 HOURS
1300 FT/ASC
1181 CALS

This is about the best way to see rural Renfrewshire wearing its prettiest petticoat. This one involves heading for Kilmacolm on the A-761 and then, at the crossroads in the centre, turn left onto the Lochwinnoch Road, the B-786, and climb very highly on that road. It carries you over the Locher Burn, before the road drops splendidly and dramatically down towards Lochwinnoch. Before you reach the top end of that village, however, turn left onto the Howwood (Bridesmill) Road and, after a double whammy climb, descend like a banshee into the centre of that village. A run back to Johnstone then follows on the Beith Road, before the Abbey Road and then Glenpatrick Road, Elderslie, are used to return to south Paisley.

HOUSTON ROAD: TEST RUN

7.3 MILES
60 FT/ASC

Now this is not a training run per se. Rather, this road, the Houston Road (also known as the Georgetown) is used by many riders as a test run. Principally this is because it is one of the few flat roads in the whole area. It is also used by local clubs as a short time trial route. On occasion you may need a flat stretch of road, several miles long, to let you work out your average heart rate and help you set certain training zones on your computer. If you are not attempting to do this, then you need not bother with the Houston Road.

Some guys will actually trip out a certain distance on this road and leave a marker by the side of the road, such as a traffic cone, to let them know exactly where it is for future reference. Others just use their computer trip distance. The road runs off the Barnsford Road, which is the A-726 behind Glasgow Airport, up the roundabout at Crosslee and back down again. On the whole seven mile stretch, there is really only a dip and rise as you pass Loanhead Cottages.

THE BIKE

As I mentioned in the opening run, it can be difficult to know which bike to go for early on, as you simply don't know what you're about yet. If you already have a machine in the garage or one that you haven't used in a while, then simply dust it down, oil it up, and use it to get you going. The price of bikes has shot up in recent years, and unjustifiably so. There is no need to go high-end, top dollar unless you intend to race. Just remember that the difference between a top machine costing thousands and a level-entry one costing hundreds is two miles an hour on a hilly course, with the difference being reduced to negligible on a flat course.

A level-entry machine is more than adequate for non-racing recreational riders, and a lot of the runs in the book can be easily ridden on the modern, lightweight, slick hybrid bikes, but my preference is for the racer. I actually did the Clyde coast run many times on a GT Talera mountain bike before I bought my first roadie, which was a Greg Lemond Reno. So a level-entry machine is a good way to start. And if you do decide to buy one that is a lot higher spec in the future, the level-entry one will make a good winter training bike, which is a good thing to have, as you will find out in time.

Despite what I have already said, I will finish this brief piece of advice by saying that when doing a long run on a top-end, high spec bike, the difference it can make – even from a mid-range descent machine – is quite noticeable. And although it will come down to personal circumstances, such as justification and cost, I would say that if you do decide to splash out and treat yourself to a really good machine, it will be money well spent, especially in the long run. I thoroughly recommend you do.

My two machines, which were used when writing the book, are pictured below. On the left is the trusted trainer, the Dolan, which is pictured at Wemyss Bay station, just before a jaunt over to the Isle of Bute. It is carbon fibre with a Shimano gruppo made up mostly of an ultegra/105 mix. It sports the essential mudguards, of course.

To the right is the pride of the fleet Eddy Merckx Cima, sporting wall-to-wall dura ace. On this occasion she is on Largs pier.

SADDLE BAGS

The photograph shows the two saddle bags which I use, along with their contents and the pumps that I carry on a ride, the lights, and also the home-based track pump I use. Both my bags are Top Peak, though there are numerous other good brands on the market, mostly about a similar price of between £15 to £20. I just like the internal pockets or attachments that come with the Top Peak for keeping money and keys in, etc. The difference between the one on my training bike and my best bike is size. The training bike one is slightly larger to accommodate a beanie hat and thin pair of gloves during the winter time.

The contents are, for the most part, identical, though the multi-tool and patch kits in the smaller bag are more compact. In fact, the only additional thing I carry in the training bag a lot of the time is a couple of cable ties in case my mudguards start giving me gip. Other than that, they are as near as dammit the same.

I did try out some very lightweight expensive compact tubes from Continental in the small bag at one point (they cost £11 each), but they proved to be far too susceptible to punctures, even when you only rode over a small stone, so I don't use them now and don't recommend you do either. Stick to the standard tubes and you'll be fine. The list that I carry is as follows:

- Spare tube
- Tyre levers
- Multi-tool (with chain splitter)
- Two pre-glued patch kits (winter ones in a more waterproof cover)
- Two cable ties (training bike only)
- House keys
- Money bag (I always carry 7 tenners & 7 fivers)

NB. I only use the pre-glued patches to get me home. If I intend to continue to use a tube that has punctured, I have a more traditional puncture repair kit at home, which I will use on occasion to provide a more dependable, solid, and lasting repair.

PUMPS

Both on-bike pumps are Mt Zefals, which are the big babies on the block. I take them instead of the more lightweight pumps, because when push comes to shove they do the business without the strain and effort required when using a mini-pump; therefore, they are my preference. Park Tool do a similar model to Zefal which, although it has a better frame-fitting set-up, the pump action isn't to my liking and therefore I prefer the Mt Zefal.

I also recommend buying a track pump for the house, as it is good practice to check your tyre inflation before every run, and a bike-mounted pump is not adequate for this regular operation. Buying a good track pump, costing between £30 to £40, will save you a lot of time and elbow grease in the short run, never mind the long run. Get one pronto.

LIGHTS

Nowadays you may see some road riders using a flashing rear light even when they are out for a daytime jaunt. I personally don't use them all the time, but do so when the weather turns bad or if I am riding on a busy road. I will, of course, carry lights on a run that I know will end after dark.

My front light is a re-chargeable Cat Eye Nano Shot + and I have two rear lights. Both are Top Peak, as I tend to find their mounting system safe and secure. The larger of the two lights can either be mounted on the frame or clipped into the rear of the saddle bag, but the smaller one can only be mounted on the frame. It weighs nothing, and is ideal to carry on a long run on a day when you suspect the weather might turn bad and you might want to become more visible in the rain.

On top of that, for the winter I also bought a small flashing light that you fit to the top of your helmet. The idea here is the higher the light sits, the better. However,

just to prove that nothing can guarantee your safety, the only time I have ever been brushed by a car was very recently when I was wearing a yellow hi-vis rain jacket and using a flashing rear light. It happened just as I neared the top of the Rest and Be Thankful. In this instance, though, I have a sneaky suspicion the driver was either stoned or drunk, just by the way he drove (he never stopped) after the incident. So it's better to carry a lot of luck as opposed to anything else.

NB. Also please note the rolled-up hi-vis rain jacket and cotton cap that I carry on many long runs, if there is even a hint of bad weather in the forecast. It's a good insurance policy to do so.

SADDLE HEIGHT

I am of the opinion that the most important thing to get right if you are bike riding for any distance at all is your saddle height. Once you get that right then the rest can follow on. That is how I work it. Not only that, but the type of saddle you have can be the real make-or-break component on your bike; if it is uncomfortable even after quite a distance, then it can put you off riding the bike altogether. Simply put, if your saddle is uncomfortable, it doesn't matter how good the rest of the bike components are as they won't even enter into it. Most serious bike commentators will tell you that the frame is the most important part of the bike, which is true in many respects, but you could also put up an argument for the saddle.

There is a chance that the saddle which comes with your bike may suit you, especially if you ride only fairly short distances. However, there is also a high chance that it will not, especially if riding long distances. That's when you have a problem. You have to find a replacement, and this can be a long expensive search for some.

Seeking advice from fellow riders with a lot of experience can help, as can going online and reading reviews of saddles, and such like. One guy whose advice I like to take is Aussie bike-fitting guru, Steve Hogg, who is a man I will refer to several times with regards to fitting of bikes and components. But for the moment let's deal with getting the saddle height correct first, because without that it won't matter if you do have one that is suitable, as you won't be getting the best out of it.

If you ever have to get on a strange bike at short notice (such as a hired machine), or for any other reason you don't have time to do a proper job of setting your saddle height, then a good quick fix is to sit on the bike and – with your heel on one of the pedals – put the pedal in the furthest positon from you (i.e. not straight down but slightly forward). Adjust the saddle height til your leg is bolt straight, and when you move the ball of your foot onto the pedal, there will be as near as dammit the correct amount of bend at the knee to ensure a reasonable fit. That, as stated, is fine as a quick fix. However we want something much more exact and accurate for our purposes, and for that I use and recommend the Greg Lemond method.

GREG LEMOND SADDLE HEIGHT METHOD

This simple but accurate way of getting the correct saddle height was devised by the great man himself, way back when they still used pedals with straps and clips and people still listened to LP records. I mention this because I will, as far as possible, give you the method he used as he described it then, along with some modern substitutes where necessary for you to get the correct height. So here goes.

Greg says stand with your back to a wall, wearing only socks and your riding shorts. Take an LP (long playing) record and, with the side of it placed right along the back wall, jam it as hard as you can into your crotch just the way the saddle would do if you were sitting on your bike.

Measure the distance from the floor to the top of the LP and record this in millimetres. Now get out the old calculator and multiply this number by 0.883. With the number which the calculator gives you (also in millimetres), measure from the centre of the crank bolt to the top of your saddle in line with the seat post – and this is your saddle height (Photo).

I use a flat blade screwdriver to ensure the ruler is in the centre of the crank bolt. Greg also says to subtract 2 millimetres if you are using clipless pedals. Don't forget that this was back in the days when a lot of guys weren't using clipless, even top pros like Shaun Kelly. As just about everyone uses clipless now, remember to subtract the 2 millimetres before setting the saddle height.

Also back in those days just about every household had a stack of LP records, nowadays I doubt if few households even have one. So we need a replacement for the LP. You can go into a second hand record store and get an old LP to do the job, or you can use a square or rectangular piece of very thin wood measuring 10 x 10 inches or 8 x 10 inches, or the cover of a hard-backed book, or one part of a plastic folder (the type you get in W H Smiths) – any of these will suffice. Also, if you don't have anyone to help with taking your leg measurement, it can be helpful to buy a long metal ruler about 2½ to 3 feet long, which will make the job easier if you're doing it single-handed. I bought one from B&Q just for this alone, and thoroughly recommend it. So that is the way I get my seat height.

I also recommend that before you do anything, you ensure your saddle is sitting straight by using a small

spirit level; if you don't have one, it is worth your while getting one for this job alone. You may find that you will need it quite frequently as you adjust saddle height and fore aft position, which we will deal with shortly. Next I recommend you set your cleat position on your shoes first, and then adjust your saddle's fore and aft position.

CLEAT POSITION

One of the most important things to get correct nowadays is the position of your cleats on the bottom of your cycling shoes. I will give another simple method of getting a good starting position, which – like all the other adjustment techniques in the book – requires no previous experience, special training, or specialised expensive equipment to enable a successful operation.

Once the basic set-up position is achieved, I will also talk about a more advanced position, courtesy of Mr Steve Hogg, that dynamic Digger (Aussie) whose advice is always worth having. This operation is probably made a little bit easier if you have an indoor trainer to sit you and the bike on, but it can just as easily be performed when sitting on the bike and using one hand to lean against a wall. So once again, here goes.

The idea is to position the cleat on the shoe, so that the ball of the foot sits over the pedal axle when riding. For expediency, this position will from now on be referred to as BOFOPA. The easiest way to do this is to first remove your shoes and socks, then locate what is known as your 1st MTP (metatarsophalangeal) joint. This is the big, bony, first knuckle joint that sits between the foot and big toe. Mark a small line across this (photo 1). The ball of your foot is obviously on the bottom of your foot, but the 1st MTP joint sits directly above it on the top, so we use it as our guide to make the job easier.

Now we want to mark the part of the outside of the cycling shoe which has the 1st MTP joint right below it.

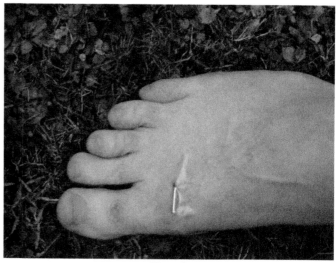
Photo 2

You could just put your shoes back on, without wearing your socks, and try and feel for the joint from the outside then mark the shoe at that point. However to make finding the 1st MTP joint easier, it helps to sticky tape a small metal cable end/nipple (the type you have at the end of your brake and gear cables) to the line you have marked on your foot, then put your shoes back on, again without any socks (Photo 2). You will feel this from the outside of the shoe much easier, and can mark this point with a felt tip pen or a slither of tape or white adhesive paper (Photo 3). If you don't have any cable ends/nipples, then just something small and hard will do.

Once you have marked the shoe, attach the cleats to the bottom of the shoe and tighten them up, but not fully at this point, as there is still some adjusting and manoeuvring to do. Now get back on the bike, click into your pedals and position the cranks horizontally. Then manoeuvre your forward-facing shoe so that the mark on the shoe is in line with the pedal axle. Climb off and tighten the bolts on your cleats, then do the same with the other foot.

It is usually easier to take your foot out of the shoe and leave it in the pedal at this point, as this part of the operation can be a bit higgledy-piggledy, if you are doing it on your own. It is easier if there is someone to help you, but for most of us, it's a one man job.

The final slight adjustment is to ensure that your cleat is facing straight forward. So after you have removed it from the pedal, you may have to loosen the cleat very

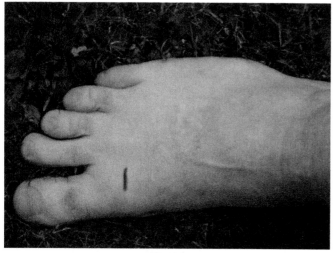
Photo 1

Photo 3

SHOE SIZE	APPROX. POSITION
36-38	7-9mm
39-41	8–10mm
42-43	9-11mm
44-45	10-12mm
46-47	11-14mm
48-50	12-16mm

slightly at this point, ensure it stays more of less where it is, then line it up with the marker lines on the bottom of the shoe. *Voilà*! Job done.

If you have a computer and are online, it may be worth your while to have a look at a website run by an Australian bike-fitter called Steve Hogg. He is a very well-known and respected man in the world of cycling. If you are not online (and many of us aren't), I will give you Steve's thoughts on cleat position. Steve says that the foot in cycling is a lever and not a very efficient one. That's because the piston (which in this case is the leg), is positioned at the end of the lever (foot). Problems can arise when you are cycling hard and applying a lot of force to the cranks, because then the heel can drop more than usual and you lose the BOFOPA position, as the foot tends to slide back.

He therefore advocates actually moving your foot forward of BOFOPA position when setting up your cleats, so as to counteract this movement by the foot under pressure. Steve also goes on to explain that some people are toe-down riders while others are heel-down riders. For each size of shoe he gives a range of adjustments. If you are a heel-down rider, he advises to use the greater length of adjustment. It will, of course, take you a little time to figure out what is your own personal pedalling style, and so BOFOPA is still a good place to start. Steve's recommended adjustments are as follows:

Remember, we are moving the cleat back in the shoe, which in essence means we are moving the shoe forward to make our foot a more efficient lever. I am a size 43 and have moved my cleat back by 10mms. Again, the guidelines on the bottom of your shoe should help you achieve an accurate adjustment. Just get your BOFOPA positon first and take it from there.

SADDLE FORE-AFT POSITION

Getting your saddle in the correct fore-aft position comes next, and it will usually mean with most saddles (with only one exception I know) that the saddle height will need to be checked and most likely adjusted again.

Fore-aft is also easier (just like cleat position) to get right if you have an indoor trainer to put the bike on and then sit on, but it is more than doable with you just sitting on the bike and using one hand to lean against a wall, preferably indoors. The only piece of equipment you need is a plumb line, or as some call it a plump bob. If you don't have the real McCoy, you can make one with a piece of string and some metal washers. It only has to be about 3 feet long to do the job.

So get on the bike and do a few turns of the cranks (if you're on a trainer) just to get your feet settled in the right position. Then position the cranks horizontally. Try and put, then keep, your foot in the position it would be in during a normal pedal stroke. This is where the trainer is handy because you can concentrate and watch how your feet move before stopping to do the adjustment.

Now drop the plumb off the front of your forward protruding kneecap and let it fall to the inside of your shoe. Ideally it should just touch the end of the crank arm. If it doesn't, then adjust the saddle forwards or backwards till it does. That's it. This is a very good starting positon for most riders.

However, don't forget that this is only a *starting* position. Some guys, usually time triallists, will sit further forwards, whereas others may want to sit further back. Once the fore-aft position is set, once again check and re-adjust the saddle height if necessary. This will need to be done with most saddles unless you are using a Selle SMP saddle. I will deal with saddles themselves next.

STEM AND HANDLEBARS

STEM

Once saddle height, cleat position, and saddle fore-aft position have been adjusted, it's time to check the length of your stem. I use a very simple on-bike method to check if my stem length is correct, and so far it has served me well and I've had no back problems or shoulder pain.

First, get on the bike and ride along, either on a turbo trainer or out on the road, and put your hands into the hooks of the handlebars. Now tilt your head down at an angle of about 45 degrees, and try and see the hub in the centre of your front wheel. If your stem is the correct length for you, the hub should be obscured by your handlebars. If the hub can be seen in front of the bars, it means your stem is too short. If the hub can be seen behind the bars, it means the stem is too long. Replace accordingly.

HANDLEBARS

I will only go as far as to say that handlebar style and width are very much a matter of personal preference. I personally prefer a narrower bar, measuring about 40 centimetres from centre to centre. My advice is that if you are thinking of trying a different width and style from the one which came with your bike, buy cheap at first to find out what suits you best before digging deeper for a more expensive one. Carbon bars are really pricey. Aluminium is very cheap by comparison. Just remember, a lot of the pros prefer aluminium.

All I can do on saddles is to give some general advice, mostly based on personal experience. That's because finding the right saddle can be a very unique and personal thing. However, generally speaking, the more padding a saddle has the more comfortable it will be. You may find that some manufacturers do a specific saddle in more than one weight. If you are not racing, don't need to save weight, and are planning to do fairly long runs, then it's a good bet to go for the heavier, more padded one in the range. That said, padding isn't the be-all and end-all of more comfortable riding.

That's because you may suit a narrower or broader saddle, depending on the width of your pelvis. This won't be obvious until you have tried out a few for yourself. Again, you can go online and read horror stories of guys and girls who have spent a small fortune in search of the perfect saddle. I advise you to buy cheap at first til you find out what suits you best, then buy a better quality model in that style when you are sure you know what you are about – and have the funds, of course.

I am of quite stocky build, yet it seems that a narrow saddle suits me best. I found this out by accident when the saddle that came with my Trek mountain bike was narrow and padded. As I used the Trek for a bit of rare cycle touring (the battlefields in France), I soon became aware that even after days of riding, my bum still wasn't sore. About the same time, an expensive, lightly padded and broad Selle Italia saddle which I bought for my Eddy Merckx road bike, started to hurt like hell after about 60 miles. Through that, I learned the narrow job was for me.

Even Steve Hogg in his blog admits that he is wrong about people's pelvic size in about 25% of the cases he deals with. So it will come down to a bit of trial and error, especially when you start riding long. At the moment I am using a Selle SMP saddle on both my bikes. On the Merckx I am using the SMP Evolution, which is about the narrowest in the range. On my training bike I'm using the SMP Stratos, which is just the Evolution with more padding. Without any financial inducements, Steve Hogg recommends the Selle SMP on his website, and he rides one himself.

That said, they are not overly comfortable, as the whole centre section is cut out, and you literally ride on two rails. The nose on the SMP dips down noticeably, and it's one of the few saddles that is designed not to be set up horizontally, but to be tipped slightly nose down, anywhere between 1 and 5 degrees. If you do decide to invest in one, it's worth your while buying a digital spirit level to get the angle of degree of drop correct (this also requires some trial and error).

The SMP also has the advantage of being designed so that you do not need to readjust saddle height if you are adjusting fore-aft position. They are not cheap, costing well over £100 for the top ones, and they do take some getting used to, but at the moment that's my personal choice.

I am about to give some general and also very specific information about using heart rate monitors. But before I do, I want to stress that you do not need to know this or even to use a heart rate monitor if you don't want to. It is not essential or even necessary that you do. Some, however, may be interested in using one as they find they are getting into their bike riding and would like to know more about the benefits of using one. So here it is.

As we are doing a lot of long endurance runs in the book, it helps to pace yourself well, so as not to run out of steam halfway there. It is actually easier to do this on your heavier training bike than your top-end machine (if you have one), as the extra weight keeps you from getting carried away and going too fast too soon. The main device for keeping yourself in check is the heart rate monitor, though power meters are becoming much more common. Now as I mentioned at the start, I know plenty of guys who ride long and never use one; that's fine. It's all a matter of personal choice.

I like to use them, and have invested in a fairly upmarket model – the Polar C.S. 600. This gives me plenty of information, though a lot of it I don't need. A basic model of heart rate monitor/cycle computer will suffice, giving you your current heart rate, distance covered, time ridden, current speed, etc., which will do the job for most people, especially if they are riding for recreation, no matter how long the distance. But even for recreational riding, some of the features on a more advanced model are handy and useful, especially if you are a distance man or woman.

The Polar which I have includes a feature which tells you which heart rate zone you are in. This is very useful for people who are racing and want to know what intensity they are training at, but is also handy when you are on a very long run and are trying to pace yourself. In fact, it is a good idea to take your resting heart rate in the morning, before getting out of bed, to judge just how fit and well rested you are on any given day. The fitter you get, the lower it should become. So if you find you're getting into your riding and want to judge your fitness, simply start taking your resting heart rate in the morning so that you have an idea of your resting rate.

As your fitness improves, the amount of heart beats per minute (bpm) should come down. If you start increasing the riding then this will happen and that is good, because it means you're getting fitter. The lower your resting bpm, then the harder and longer you can ride on any given day. However, after a period of long hard riding, you might find your morning heart rate goes up. Warning!!! Time to back off. Your body is telling you you've done too much and you need more rest. Getting fit has a very simple equation, it goes like this.

STRESS THE BODY-------REST AND RECOVER.

Hard training doesn't do you any good on its own; it simply exhausts you and wrecks your muscles. It is resting that rebuilds you and makes you fitter and stronger for the next doing. To improve, you must have both sides of the equation working in tandem. Too much exercise and you burn out. Too little and you become a couch potato.

As you are not a professional bike rider, don't forget to take in the big picture. Stress is stress. The body doesn't know if it's stress from riding, working, DIY, family quarrels, or whatever. It only knows it's getting stressed. So if your morning rate goes up and you haven't been riding a lot, don't forget to take into consideration everything else that's getting lumped onto your plate.

An easier ride on the old machine in those circumstances should reduce the stress levels most of the time, so a run where you stay in your recovery zone should be the tonic. How do you know what is your recovery zone? Well, that's where the old heart rate monitor comes in. Try not to go for the off button here, for this is a good thing to know, although not essential. I've mentioned Aussie Steve Hogg as the main man on the bike-fitting front, but it's Yankee Joe Friel from Boulder Colorado who is the main man on the training front. I first became aware of him when I bought his excellent book *The Cyclist's Training Bible*, though I was unaware it was a book aimed strictly at people who raced. It was the excellent cover photo of Marco Pantani flying up an Alpine bend that caught my eye.

At one time it was thought that the best way to define training zones was to find your maximum heart rate and then work out the zones from there. However, this required you to sprint up a hill at full pelt and almost bring on a heart attack, at least for some (Joe describes it as a gun to the head). There was also the old theory about subtracting your age from some number like 220 (or thereabouts), but this is wildly inaccurate. So Joe explains it's better to work out your training zones based on your lactate threshold (LT). Here's what's going on. When you are riding at a fairly slow to moderate pace, you are mostly using fat to provide the fuel and oxygen to assist this process, which is called being aerobic.

But once you increase the pace, you start to use more carbohydrate than fat to provide the fuel. When this happens, the muscles produce a by-product called lactic acid. At first the body is still able to flush away the lactic faster than it produces it, so you don't notice this. You are still using oxygen to assist the fuel supply process, and therefore still aerobic at this point. However there comes a point when you further increase your effort and the oxygen supply cannot keep up with demand, and you then cease being aerobic and become anaerobic. This is the point where you produce energy without using oxygen.

This is also the point when you cannot flush away the lactic as fast as you produce it, and it starts to accumulate in the muscles. It's this that gives you the burning sensation in your muscles when you are sprinting hard over a small hill. This is because you are now producing lactic faster than your body can get rid of it. The lactic acid seeps into the bloodstream and becomes lactate, which – being in the bloodstream – is actually measurable. You cannot ride anaerobically for very long as it's too bloody painful. You are riding at your maximum sustainable output just at the point where you are on the threshold of going from being aerobic to anaerobic. This is your lactate threshold (LT). Your heart rate at this point is what we want to find out and then use to determine our heart rate training zones.

Again, no specialised equipment is required here, only an HRM that records average heart rate. The plan is now to do a short time trial and to go as hard as you can and find out what is your average heart rate for that particular exertion[1]. Once we get the average heart rate, we will divide that by a certain number and this will determine our lactate threshold and from that we will determine our training zones. Joe gives several distances with corresponding numbers by which to divide your average heart rate. This also includes whether you did the time trial as part of a race or as an individual time trial.

As most of you won't probably be racing yet, I'll give the two shortest distances he recommends as an individual time trial – one in kilometres and one in miles, depending on what you prefer to use. Either one will do.

1) Ride a 5 kilometre TT and record your average heart rate then divide this by 1.04.

Or

2) Ride an 8 to 10 mile TT and record your average heart rate then divide this by 1.01.

So, for example, if you did a 10 mile time trial and your average heart rate was 177 BPM, divide this by 1.01 and this would give you 175 as your lactate threshold heart rate. So your corresponding zones would look like this:

1 - Recovery	2 - Aerobic	3 - Tempo	4 - Sub-Threshold	5 - Super-Threshold
115-143	144-156	157-163	164-174	175-178

If you have bought Joe's book, *The Cyclist's Training Bible*, it now becomes very easy to find out your training zones with the number the calculator gives you, because on page 27 of the version I have, all the corresponding heart rates and zones are given to you in a very well laid-out table. It may be worth buying the book for this alone. However you can work out the zones yourself, which are as follows, with the corresponding percentage heart rates of your lactate threshold heart rate in brackets.

1) Recovery: (65-81%) This is used for easy days after a previous day's hard ride or when you want to de-stress. It is also the zone to be in when recovering between hard training intervals. It is the ideal zone to be in when working on pedalling technique and such like.

2) Aerobic: (82-88%) This is the zone used for building up the endurance base, and the time spent in it is usually measured in hours. It is the most common zone we use when doing the long endurance runs in the book. It is a very valuable zone.

3) Tempo: (89-93%) A fast form of endurance, but one that is sustainable. It can be handy for building up an endurance base fairly quickly when you haven't got a lot of time to do very long endurance runs.

---

1   Make sure you are well rested on the day you do the TT and choose a flat course on a calm day, if you can manage it.

4) Sub Threshold: (94-100%) This is the fastest you can go and still be aerobic. This zone can be used for several minutes at a time and helps the body deal with lactate build-up and become more efficient at disposing of lactate. This is the highest of the aerobic zones. It is still fairly hard on the body, however, so use this zone wisely. If you are doing training intervals in this zone, it will take at least half to a quarter of the time you spent in the zone to recover before doing the next interval.

5a) Super Threshold: (100-102%)[2] This is you now in the red zone. You are now anaerobic and this is used to help the body deal with lactate build-up. It is very hard on the body, so only short bursts are usual in this zone.

---

2 Please note that zone 5 can actually be broken down into 3 separate zones. The other 2 are zone 5b) Aerobic Capacity: (103-105%) and zone 5c) Anaerobic Capacity: 106%+. These are very, very hard training zones, used by experienced athletes.

Recovery time when doing intervals in the 5a zone are about one to one-and-a-half times the interval time.

Some computers might allow five, three, or one training zone to be pre-programmed. However, even if yours doesn't, as long as you know what your personal numbers are, you can use them for more intelligent and efficient training. This is very useful, especially if training time is limited or you want to take your recreational riding to a higher level and start racing. But remember, none of the above is necessary or compulsory if you only want to ride for fun. That's for sure.

(Main source: *The Cyclist's Training Bible*, by Joe Friel)

UNCOMMON KNOWLEDGE

In route 6, the Toward Lighthouse and Loch Striven run, I mentioned a couple of fine fellows, Mark Tyrrell and Rodger Elliot, who along with their associates, call themselves Uncommon Knowledge or Hypnosis Downloads, if you like. They have built up over 800 very effective downloads and CDs to help anyone not only overcome a problem, but to also grow and expand in their lives. I must own about a dozen at least of their CDs and intend to invest in some more in the near future. I thoroughly recommend you give them a try if you need help in any area of your life, and can assure you that you should see quick results for very little outlay.

Each download costs approximately £12, though I prefer the CDs that come in at about £20. They cover just about everything you could think of and I've had a lot of success on a personal basis with most, though not all, of the ones that I've used. They can help in all areas of your life, with things from losing weight to relationships, from overcoming fears to difficult people. This includes sports performance, personal development, and health issues. They even have one to improve your eyesight. I've got that one and there has definitely been an improvement in my vision, especially in my dominant eye, though not quite to prescription glasses standard.

I've noticed that if you string together two or three really important ones, such as Believe in Yourself, General Anxiety Treatment and Self-Esteem Booster, then you will feel a sure gradual build-up of inner strength the more you use them. They will become the most relaxing and enjoyable part of the day, which is just fine, as constant repetition is the key to success here. Using these hypnosis CDs will make a difference; I can say that from experience, a very good experience at that.

I just want to point out that I am in no way connected to or get any financial support from this company, and am only passing on information that I know to be beneficial. So, as already mentioned, you've got nothing to lose, as the guys do a 90-day money back guarantee. I include their address and telephone number at the bottom. Tell them I sent you…Boom, Boom.

Uncommon Knowledge & Hypnosis Downloads
3rd floor, Boswell House, Argyll Square, Oban.
Argyll, UK
PA34 4BD
01273 776 770
www.hypnosisdownloads.com

INJURIES

Unfortunately, injuries from cycling may occur from time to time, either through a collision or a crash of some sort. Obviously we hope nothing too serious, of course, and it's fair to say the benefits outweigh the drawbacks in the vast majority of runs. Broken collarbones are fairly regular in the ranks of the professionals, but not so much with amateurs, and I've never had one in all the years I've ridden. You are more likely to sustain an injury through over-training than anything else and it's usually the poor old knees that give way, as they take all the pounding.

I usually find that easing up for a few days, or even a week or more till things ease off does the trick, but on occasion I've had to seek some professional help. There are many good physiotherapists out there, of course, but ideally it would be better to get one who knows about cycling as well. If you feel that you require the services of a physio, it might be a good idea to ask at your local bike store if they know of anyone who is a cycling-orientated physiotherapist, or even ask fellow riders.

I do know of one who treated me a few years back and who did a very good job, not only on my knee but also on my cleat position which eradicated any further problems. I contacted this gentleman when I was writing the book and offered him some free advertising along with a glowing reference, but he seemed reluctant for any publicity. So, for that reason alone, I did not include his details in this section.

One bit of advice I would give is if you don't have the money for a specialist and you are letting time alone make the repair, try a balm of some sort. Some guys swear by Tiger Balm, which costs about £7 for a small pot, though I have never used that myself. I have used Wood Lock Balm, which cost about £15 for a larger bottle, and acts like a sort of heat balm and massaging it in helps with easing the pain. Both these balms are used in Chinese medicine. I got mine in the Piazza shopping centre, Paisley, where a very helpful Chinese lady has a small store. You may want to give that a try.

DATA

Below the title of every run will be the information and statistics relating to that run, the details of which have been provided by my Polar C.S. 600 cycling computer. Below this again will be the relevant numbers for the Ordnance Survey Landranger maps that cover the area of the run. The details of the information is as follows:

MILES

The mileage for any given run will be from my front door, in Glenburn, South Paisley, to the destination and then back to my front door, unless stated. Obviously this exact distance is only relevant to me, but it should act as a fairly good indicator as to what is involved for anyone wishing to do the run from their home. In the case of starting from a ferry terminal, the distances will be exactly the same for all. I could have used a more central starting point for the runs, such as Paisley Cross or Paisley Gilmour St station, but most riders wouldn't be starting from there either. The mileage given is only meant as a ballpark figure. So if, for example, you live in Renfrew, you can subtract 6 miles from the Stirling run, but would have to add the same 6 miles for the Turnberry run. Adjust to suit.

HOURS

Hours is simply the time taken to do the run. This will be for a run when no photos were taken and stops were kept to a minimum, i.e. toilet breaks, etc. Despite this, these times are of course approximate, as you may ride at a completely different speed from me. I did consider using an average speed for all the runs, say somewhere around 14 mph, but some of the runs were done partly on single track road, which can slow you down considerably, and other runs involved a lot more climbing than ones of a similar distance, so again the time would differ greatly. Also which bike, training or top machine, traffic, weather, and especially wind strength and direction would also play a part in speed and time, as would how many miles you had done the previous day or two. So remember, the time for each run is merely approximate.

ASCENT IN FEET

This is the amount of climbing involved in any given run or variation of that run. The CS 600 will often give a difference of perhaps 80 to 100 feet of ascent in a run covering anywhere from between 60 to 100 miles, so it is a fairly accurate figure that you are given.

CALORIES/BURNED OR CALS

This again is an approximate figure, as the amount of calories burned per mile can vary greatly from individual to individual. Your age, VO2 Max, the speed you ride at, can all affect how many calories you burn. As a useful guide, if you are trying to lose weight by cycling and using a calorie controlled diet, and you don't have a computer that tells you how many calories you've burned, then 40 calories per mile is a good, fairly accurate figure to use to help you know how much energy you are using and burning off. That should be accurate enough to help in your weight loss.

O/S LANDRANGER MAPS

The numbers for the Ordnance Survey maps that will cover the whole run are given. Although it is handy to have these, they are not totally essential and a good road atlas should suffice for the most part. As each map costs about £8 each, you can save quite a few quid by simply using the road atlas. However, the more detailed maps are both handy and interesting to have, and I consider it worth the expense to get them. They will prove beneficial when you are sitting of an evening and looking to plan out runs in the future or, as stated in the text, you may want to see where you took a wrong turn on some small back road after a run has been completed.

PHOTOGRAPHY

I used two cameras to take all the photographs within the book – both compact digitals, small enough to fit into the rear pocket of my cycling jersey. They were the very small and formidable Panasonic Lumix DMC-FT2 (the T stands for tough) and also the slightly larger Nikon Coolpix P-7000. During the countless runs I made while writing the book, I took countless photographs and none have been enhanced in any way. I wanted it to be quite simply what you see is what you get.

Sometimes I have found that when you, say for example, look at a brochure for an area you wish to visit or perhaps to do a long distance ride or walk like the West Highland Way, the photographs in the brochure will have been taken by a very experienced skilful photographer.

They have waited for the light to be right – usually early morning or late evening, when most people will have ended their days walking or riding. And also they have taken up unusual positions and vantage points, sometimes with the aid of a tripod, often when the weather is at its best. So, of course, when you go and do the ride or walk, the area looks nothing like it did in the photos. Well, I didn't want that. All the photos were taken at the time of day most people would be doing the run and in the very weather that nature threw at me at the time. So again, what you will see is what you can expect to get at the time you come to do the ride yourself.

A word to the wise here, if you do decide to start taking photos yourself when you are out on the bike. It is much more time consuming than you would imagine to continually stop the bike and take photos. I am telling you this in case you wish to buy a camera yourself and record your runs as you go along. You probably won't notice when doing a mainland run, but if you are on an island or aiming for a specific ferry, then it is very prudent to watch the clock continuously or you may miss your ferry and end up being stranded overnight. If your computer has an average speed reading, it will be a good indicator of just how much slower you are going when you are using the camera a lot.

To speed things up, I did invest in a bracket to hold the camera in position on my handlebars and save me from continually stopping to take a shot. Although this did save some time, I don't recommend doing this, as too many of the shots were ruined by camera shake. Certainly this set-up could only be used with a tough camera variant, as the non-tough Nikon proved to be totally inadequate on the bracket, but even the majority of shots with the Panasonic turned out to be well below par. The larger Nikon had the advantage of a viewfinder and more powerful lens, but the Lumix had a better metering system, which coped far better with difficult conditions, such as shimmering sunlight on the Clyde.

The photo shows just some (though admittedly, the bulk) of my cleaning and maintenance tools. But as this is not a book on cycle maintenance, I will not go into any great depth on that subject.

However, learning to do your own repairs is very satisfying, convenient, and cost-effective. So I recommend fairly early on in your cycling life to get a good maintenance manual (the two I have are old but still handy), and start to build up the old tool box as you go along. If the worst comes to the worst and a repair goes badly wrong, you can always take it along to your local bike store and you're no worse off than if you had gone there in the first place.

The cleaning kit does not need to be one of the fancy brush sets that you can buy which are specific to bike cleaning. I find a sponge, a rag, and a small brush, will do most of the jobs better than the purpose-built stuff does, though some small specialised brushes are really handy for getting into awkward nooks and crannies. The basic cleaning kit is as follows:

CLEANING KIT

- Bucket
- Fairy liquid
- Sponge
- Rag
- Stiff, small sweeping brush
- Chain cleaner (a must-have)
- Liquid de-greaser for chain cleaner
- Spray degreaser for other parts
- Specialised small brushes for cogs and mechs (optional)
- Old toothbrush (will do in place of small specialised brushes)

WORKSHOP KIT:

- Workstand (optional, but good to have)
- Wheel truing stand (wheels can be trued in situ, but a proper stand is handy)
- Spare tubes
- Spare tyres
- Rim tape
- Puncture repair kit (old glue style)

- Handlebar cork
- Spare brake pads
- Brake cables
- Gear cables
- Cable ends
- Cable cutters
- Link pin pliers
- Pliers: normal and long-nosed
- Chain checker
- Chain wrench
- Spoke keys
- Assorted combination spanners and shifting spanner
- Assorted screwdrivers
- Lubes: both wet and dry
- Bearing grease
- Multi-tools
- Bottom bracket tools (various)
- Sprocket removal tool
- Allen keys
- Cone spanners
- Small wire brush (for cleaning bolts, etc)
- WD40 (or equivalent)
- Spirit level
- Digital spirit level (if you have a Selle SMP saddle)
- Torq wrenches (good to have)
- Insulating tape
- Oily rags (last but not least, you'll need one or two)

FURTHER READING

The Secret by Rhonda Byrne

The Cyclist's Training Bible by Joe Friel

The Artist's Way by Julia Cameron

The Secret Code of Success by Noah St John

Steve Hogg's online blog

"Just a guy who does a bit".

Liam is an ordinary bloke. When he decided one night that he needed to change his unhealthy lifestyle, he did so in a spectacular way and found a passion for cycling.

He is a taxi driver with an interest in lots of things; bikes, history, photography, psychology and more. If you are lucky enough to share his cab you could find yourself inspired and entertained by his philosophy. Maybe enough to even start a new journey of your own.

Liam's "bit" has taken him on a journey from his home in Paisley around Scotland on his bike. If you'd like to know more please contact him on his Facebook page at

Liam Farrell - The Circle Game

or e-mail him at

liamfarrellthecirclegame123@gmail.com.

Lightning Source UK Ltd.
Milton Keynes UK
UKOW07f1534210716

278934UK00008B/30/P